REFORM AS
LEARNI

REFORM AS LEARNING

School Reform, Organizational Culture, and Community Politics in San Diego

Lea Hubbard, Hugh Mehan, and Mary Kay Stein

Routledge
Taylor & Francis Group
New York   London

Routledge is an imprint of the
Taylor & Francis Group, an informa business

Published in 2006 by
Routledge
Taylor & Francis Group
270 Madison Avenue
New York, NY 10016

Published in Great Britain by
Routledge
Taylor & Francis Group
2 Park Square
Milton Park, Abingdon
Oxon OX14 4RN

© 2006 by Taylor & Francis Group, LLC
Routledge is an imprint of Taylor & Francis Group

Printed in the United States of America on acid-free paper
10 9 8 7 6 5 4 3 2 1

International Standard Book Number-10: 0-415-95377-4 (Softcover)
International Standard Book Number-13: 978-0-415-95377-1 (Softcover)
Library of Congress Card Number 2005027550

Library of Congress Cataloging-in-Publication Data

Hubbard, Lea, 1946-
    Reform as learning : school reform, organizational culture, and community politics in San Diego / Lea Hubbard, Hugh Mehan, and Mary Kay Stein.
        p. cm.
    Includes bibliographical references and index.
    ISBN 0-415-95376-6 (hb : alk. paper) -- ISBN 0-415-95377-4 (pb : alk. paper)
    1. School management and organization--California--San Diego. 2. Educational change--California--San Diego. I. Mehan, Hugh, 1941- II. Stein, Mary Kay. III. Title.

LB2802.S36H83 2006
371.2009794'985--dc22   2005027550

Taylor & Francis Group
is the Academic Division of Informa plc.

Visit the Taylor & Francis Web site at
http://www.taylorandfrancis.com

and the Routledge Web site at
http://www.routledge-ny.com

Contents

To Row, Margaret, and Jack for their support
and understanding through these many years
of data collection and writing.

Figures and Tables

Figures

Tables

Acknowledgments

The work reported herein was supported by a grant from the Office of Educational Research and Improvement, U.S. Department of Education (Grant no. R-305T010076) to Lea Hubbard, principal investigator; a grant from the Spencer Foundation (Grant no. 200100264) to Hugh Mehan, principal investigator, and to Mary Kay Stein. However, any opinions expressed are the authors' own and do not represent the policies or positions of the U.S. Department of Education or the Spencer Foundation. Lauren Young of the Spencer Foundation was particularly helpful in all aspects of this research, for which we are deeply grateful.

We are deeply indebted to the participants in our study who welcomed us into their schools, districts, and offices. Special thanks are extended to Alan Bersin, Anthony Alvarado, and Elaine Fink, who granted us unusual access and gave so freely of their time.

We also wish to thank our colleagues who worked with us on this study: Paula Chapman, Maria Martinez Cosio, Nicole Hildago, Virginia Loh, Melissa Maskin, Sam Patterson, Jeanne Powers, Jim Rodriguez, Judith Toure, Jen Ventura, Irene Villanueva, and Monica Wilson.

Our sincere thanks to Katherine Mooney, whose editorial skills improved the text immensely, and to Teresa Huerta for her help in formatting the figures and tables.

CHAPTER 1

Using Theory to Understand the San Diego Reform

> It's not the politics, it's the quality of the ideas, the quality of the evidence, the quality of the work, the quality of the results that should carry the day.
>
> **—Anthony Alvarado (quoted in Gribble, 2001: 37)**

From 1998 through 2002, the San Diego City Schools (SDCS) engaged in a dramatic, daring, and possibly unprecedented reform. To achieve improved student learning—the reform's principal goal—district leaders set their sights on the heart of the educational enterprise: classroom instruction. As prominent displays throughout the district asserted, "The mission of the San Diego City Schools is to improve student achievement by supporting teaching and learning in the classroom." To reach that commendable goal, the district put in place a content-driven, centralized, comprehensive, and fast-paced reform.

The reform was *content driven* in that the development of literacy skills was at the forefront. Gains in student achievement were viewed as intimately linked to concerted efforts to improve instructional practice through sustained and focused professional development for teachers and educational leaders—from the principal to the superintendent. All educators were to be similarly focused on the teaching and learning of literacy. The reform was *centralized* in that major instructional, operational, and professional-development decisions emanated from the district leadership while instructional leaders, site content administrators, staff developers, and resource teachers provided guidance and direction to teachers. The reform was *comprehensive* in that all schools in the district were expected to implement all dimensions of the reform.[1] Owing in part to leaders' characterization of the reform as a moral imperative (see Chapter 2) and in part to the unique political pressures exerted on the district, the reform was *fast paced* in that its major elements were introduced from the first days that the new district leadership took office. Instead of a preparation period, followed by a pilot phase, followed by full implementation, the district leaders chose to have their educators "learn to fly the plane while flying it."

The impetus for the reform came from the San Diego business community. During the tenure of the previous superintendent, local business leaders had become increasingly vocal about the poor preparation of high school graduates who were joining their firms. They argued that drastic changes in the public school system were needed to maintain the economic well-being of the San Diego region. The business community played a strong role in the selection of Alan Bersin as superintendent and in the election of school board members who would support his reforms. Bersin, a well-known and widely respected attorney, was an appealing choice. He had a solid reputation and state and national connections (he had been a Rhodes scholar at the same time as former president Bill Clinton, he was currently the U.S. attorney for the southern California region, and he was an advisor to California governor Gray Davis).

Bersin compensated for his lack of educational credentials by hiring Anthony Alvarado, widely known as the main architect of New York City's Community School District #2's nationally recognized reforms. The recipient of numerous educational awards (e.g., the American Federation of Teachers' Quality Educational Standards in Teaching Award in 1999; the Council of Great City Schools' Superintendent of the Year award in 1999), Alvarado was a passionate and charismatic spokesperson for underrepresented children and the responsibility public schools have to help these youngsters pursue promising and prosperous lives. Under his leadership, Community School District #2's student achievement ranking rose from near the bottom of thirty-two community school districts in New York City to second from the top. In the process, District #2 became widely heralded as proof that urban districts can succeed.

For both Bersin and Alvarado, winning the favor of local constituencies required overcoming their own histories. Curtailing the flow of illegal immigrants across the U.S.–Mexico border had been one of Bersin's primary responsibilities as U.S. attorney. Now, as superintendent of a school district with a high proportion of low-income Latinos, his motives and values were scrutinized and criticized by some groups, especially those representing low-income Latinos. Some critics were mollified by the appointment of Alvarado. Initial enthusiasm waned, though, when Alvarado's efforts to combine his new responsibilities with his ongoing commitment to assist with a smooth transition for his successor in New York City seriously restricted his time and accessibility. Shuttling back and forth across the country limited Alvarado's ability to make and keep the personal connections to educators and the community that typically are vital to a leader's success. Thus, critics of the reform vilified both Alvarado and Bersin as outsiders with little real interest in the education of San Diego's school children.

At the national level, however, both leaders fared much better. The launch of the reform effort in the SDCS was heavily covered by the national press, with numerous articles appearing in *The Wall Street Journal, The New York Times,* and *The Washington Post.* The district's early developments were widely covered in *Education Week* and other educational periodicals. The reform also captured the attention of private foundations and funding agencies such as the Carnegie Corporation; the Broad, Gates, and Hewlett Foundations; the Atlantic Philanthropies; and a consortium of QUAL-COMM, Applied Microcircuits, and the Wiatt Family Foundation. All made sizable gifts and grants (the most notable was a $22.5 million grant from the Gates and Hewlett Foundations) to the district.

Although the business community's support of the SDCS reform was crucial to the birth and early support of Bersin and Alvarado's plans, it also spawned problems. For example, to maintain the support of their business colleagues, Bersin and Alvarado decided to move the reform forward very quickly—before cultivating teacher buy-in—thereby antagonizing many teachers and certainly the San Diego Education Association, which complained bitterly that the reform was top-down and ignored the voices and expertise of local educators. This perception—that local teachers' knowledge didn't count—was also noted by American Institutes for Research (AIR), the outside evaluator of the district's reform. Of the 1,294 teachers responding to AIR's 2002 survey of district teachers, 88% said that they were not involved in decisions about the reform's implementation, and a minority (39%) reported feeling respected as a teacher by district staff. Other aspects of the reform's design, most notably its comprehensiveness (affecting all schools and classrooms from the start), although daring, also alienated many local educators. By 2001, editorials began to appear in *The San Diego Union Tribune*, an early, staunch supporter of the reform, that the approach to revitalizing the SDCS needed to be rethought.

Throughout these early challenges, Bersin and Alvarado maintained a united front. Their roles, however, were clearly demarcated: Bersin faced outward to the community, defending the reforms and working to maintain a majority of support on the school board. Alvarado's responsibility was to lead the reforms internally. He set the direction of instructional policy and was responsible for the development and supervision of instructional leaders, a group of individuals who had been selected from among district personnel and charged to carry out the reform. Because of his unrelenting insistence on change, his refusal to compromise, and his willingness to make unpopular decisions surrounding the removal of educators, Alvarado became, over time, a lightning rod for criticisms—not only from teachers but also from parents, community members, and, eventually, the local press. Among other things, his mandated Balanced Literacy program came to be seen as a rigid, one-size-fits-all remedy; his insistence on administrative walk-throughs of schools and classrooms (for discussion of the role of walk-throughs—on-site visits involving both evaluation and instruction—see especially Chapters 4, 7, and 8) became widely viewed as an intrusion on teacher autonomy; and his demands that principals relearn their roles and become leaders of instruction at their schools eventually were redefined as misguided. In 2002, Bersin removed Alvarado from his position as chancellor of instruction. From that point on, the reform changed direction dramatically.

Our Contribution to National Understandings of the SDCS Reform

This book chronicles the journey of the SDCS from the arrival of Bersin and Alvarado in 1998, the early enthusiasm and uncertainty that accompanied their efforts to quickly and thoroughly change the way teaching and learning occurred in schools throughout the district, through various midcourse corrections, to the significant redirection of the reform signaled by Alvarado's removal in 2002. Why did a reform that began with so much promise and celebrated leadership not materialize to the degree envisioned either by its architects or by the hopeful public?

The answers are varied and complex, as accounts by a number of researchers and education writers make clear. These commentators' assessments of the SDCS reform offer the following: insight into the early, formative days of Bersin and Alvarado's administration (Cuban & Usdan, 2003; Hightower, 2001, 2002); evaluation of the reform's impact on student achievement (AIR, 2002, 2003; San Diego Achievement Forum, 2002); impressions of the reform's overall accomplishments from the perspective of scholars unfamiliar with local circumstances but informed by knowledge of other reform efforts (Hess, 2005: 6); and treatments of SDCS as an example of a district playing a prominent role in instructional renewal (Hightower, Knapp, Marsh, & McLaughlin, 2002) and in instructional leadership (Darling-Hammond et al., 2005).

Our approach, and thus both our questions and our answers, is different. Our findings sometimes map the painful, familiar territory of school reform, but they also point to new explanations for why reforms take the shape they do and suggest ways we might design and implement reform more intelligently in the future. Thanks to the generosity of the Spencer Foundation and the U.S. Department of Education, we supported a sizable group of field-based researchers (the group was composed of the authors of this book complemented by as many as ten research assistants at different points) over the entire four years of the Bersin–Alvarado reform. We documented (through observations and interviews, many of which were audio- and videotaped) the rollout of the reform at all levels of the SDCS, from Bersin and Alvarado's work with the top layer of leadership in the central office, to those top leaders' work with principals, to principals' work with teachers at individual school sites, and, finally, to the impact of the reform on how teachers worked with students in the classroom.

We use this careful ethnographic work to report on the struggles and push backs along the way, as well as to chronicle instances of smooth enactment. That is, we identify not only how teachers, principals, and other district educators were *shaped by* the Bersin–Alvarado reforms but also the ways in which these educators, in turn, *shaped* the reform and the contexts within which the reform unfolded. Throughout our research, we purposefully sought to identify how actors "lower" in the system—and those outside the system—changed the views of leaders or affected the environment in ways that altered the context of the reform. Because we were able to capture the complex ways in which the San Diego reform unfolded, we can provide an account that engages multiple actors' perspectives on what happened and why.

As with any reform, the real action in San Diego was "on the ground." Teachers, principals, and community members grappled with what these reforms meant and how they could (or could not) be incorporated into what they knew best how to do. Our research reflects a strong belief in the importance of on-the-ground interpretation and action. Thus, we do more than review Bersin and Alvarado's espoused theory of action (Argyris & Schön, 1978). We also spend considerable time (indeed, Chapters 5 through 9) detailing the interpretations of and reactions to the theory as carried out by San Diego's "street-level bureaucrats" and formulated by various political constituencies.

Our study also is unique in that the research team leaders represent an unparalleled confluence of knowledge related to both the SDCS and the reforms in Community School District #2. Mary Kay Stein was the director of research for a study of Community School District #2 from 1994–98. She is the author of numerous papers about the district (Coburn & Stein, in press; Stein & D'Amico, 2002a, 2002b; Stein, D'Amico, & Israel, 1999) as well as a collaborator on the production of a series of videotapes that present the district strategy for reform. When Alvarado was appointed chancellor of instruction in San Diego in 1998, Stein joined with Lea Hubbard and Hugh Mehan—long-time residents and academics who have been closely observing the SDCS for many years (e.g., Datnow, Hubbard, & Mehan, 2002; Mehan & Grimes, 1999; Mehan, Hubbard, Villanueva, & Lintz, 1995)—to study the district's reform efforts. Our team thus benefits from knowledge of Alvarado's previous work in District #2 and deep familiarity with San Diego, as both a city and an educational system.

The research team leaders represent complementary knowledge in other ways as well. Mehan and Hubbard are sociologists who frame their understandings of educational reform in terms of organizations (how decisions are made within organizations and the relationship between formal organizational directives and lived organizational realities) and the power relationships that exist within them. Stein is an educational psychologist who frames her understandings of educational reform in terms of the cognitive underpinnings of what students and teachers are asked to learn and the ways in which their opportunities to learn—as shaped by multiple social contexts—affect the success of the reform. These differences in our theoretical perspectives overlie important shared assumptions and approaches, however. First, both perspectives treat their phenomena of interest as socially constructed. Second, both involve a shift from the mainstream unit of analysis in their respective disciplines. In the case of the psychological learning theory, the shift is from the individual and her or his ideas or representations to the social practice or activities in which members of groups engage. In the case of the sociological study of organizations and policy implementation, the shift is from abstract social structures to concrete social practices (e.g., the work routines members of an organization normally engage in). Thus, although we start from different disciplines, we arrive at a shared commitment to the construct of social practice. We use that convergence as a firm basis on which to then diverge with respect to what aspects of social practice we choose to focus on and what insights we extract from our different analyses of social practice.

Our Approach to Conceptualizing and Making Sense of the SDCS Reform

In the following sections, we briefly review the framework we used to understand and explain the San Diego reform. Our approach blends insights derived from a view of organizations as cultural and practical constructions, a view of policy implementation as a form of learning, and a view of school reform as a process of change along three dimensions—technical, cultural, and political. These perspectives provided the theoretical grounding for how our study frames and accounts for district leaders' actions and on-the-ground actors' responses to those actions.

Organizations as Cultural and Practical Constructions

We treat organizations as cultural and practical constructions. Every school has its own culture that is socially constructed by the members within it (Erickson, 2004; Mehan, 1992; Sarason, 1982, 1997; Tyack & Cuban, 1995; Varenne & McDermott, 1998). One important dimension of organizational culture involves individuals' use of everyday routines to handle the complexity of organizational decision making. A second dimension involves conflicts that arise over differences in individuals' values, beliefs, and taken-for-granted, often unstated, assumptions about the contentious issues that arise in educational reform efforts. A third dimension involves the political forces that shape organizations and influence their attempts at change. We discuss each of these dimensions next.

Practical Action Guides Organizational Life

Practical action within organizations is characterized by the use of routines, conventional practices, and standard operating procedures, all of which permit individuals to operate in semiautomatic, noncalculative ways when making decisions and taking actions. An organization's rules are never sufficient to guide decision making in concrete situations or to plot an appropriate course of action. Rules are often vague or ambiguous; they are very rarely designed to tell the members of an organization how to act in specific situations. As a result, during their moment-to-moment work, personnel in an educational organization such as a school or district invoke their background knowledge of appropriate school norms, funds available, and schedules to fill in meanings and reduce the complexity of the many decisions they must make every day (Hjörne & Säljö, 2004; Mehan, Meihls,

Hertweck, & Crowdes, 1986; Sjöström, 1997). In the language of cognitive science, this is known as searching for a "normal form" (Cicourel, 1973; Schutz, 1964), one that allows the individual to treat the specific situation as a token of a well-known general type. In searching for normal forms that routinize events or circumstances, school and district personnel are able to transcend the uniqueness of situations that might otherwise paralyze their official action. The drawback to using normal forms to reduce the complexity of decision making is that routinized decisions are more likely to gloss over the needs of a particular person or situation.

Practical action is characterized by the use of routines, conventional practices, and standard operating procedures that operate in semiautomatic, noncalculative ways. When social actors in organizations face complex problems, they are known to search for a normal form (Cicourel, 1973; Schutz, 1964) so that the specific situation can be dealt with as a token of a well-known general type. This cognitive strategy reduces the complexity of decision making for any one problem-solving situation but increases the likelihood that any typified decision will gloss over the needs of a particular person or situation.

Other important factors also shape the thoughts and actions of the members of organizations. Norms, cultural beliefs, and various conventions originating within an organization, coupled with political forces emanating from the surrounding environment, create unreflective, routine, taken-for-granted scripts that become part of the worldview of both individuals and the organizations they take part in. These scripts and the "invisible and unacknowledged" rules for behavior they encode "shape choice in some directions rather than others" (Vaughan, 1996: 37). Thus, we characterize the social action that occurs in organizations as resulting from individuals who are acting on the basis of standard operating procedures and routines rather than as the result of individuals making cold and dispassionate cost-and-benefit calculations.

Conflict Rather Than Consensus May Define Stable Organizations

Organizations are messy. Therefore, when change is introduced in any one part of the system, it reverberates throughout the system in ways that cannot be anticipated. As a result of this messy unpredictability, contentious misunderstandings, conflicts, and even power struggles over values, beliefs, and implicit assumptions occur routinely within organizations and between organizations and their surrounding communities.

In educational settings, calls for social justice or for new organizational or curricular arrangements, for example, can challenge traditional conceptions of education. When such ideas diverge too far from educators' common understandings about students' capabilities, the role or function of schooling, and their role as teachers, they can generate conflict. Conflicts also can arise when all members of a school system do not understand or agree with organizational goals and the means to achieve them, when some members down the line conclude that educational leaders' ideas clash with their own interests or beliefs, when educators at school sites intentionally or unintentionally fail to do their leaders' bidding, or when educational leaders in distant offices do not develop sufficient sympathy for the lived experiences and practical circumstances of the people in local sites. The prevalence of such cultural clashes within schools leads us to agree with Binder's (2002: 19) assertion that "seemingly stable organizations ... are more likely to be conflict-ridden entities" than consensual ones (cf. Cuban, 1992; Sarason, 1982, 1997). In these circumstances, "street-level bureaucrats" (Dalton, 1958; Lipsky, 1982) can, and often do, modify, circumvent, or even resist and subvert official organizational goals.

Political Forces Shape Organizations and Organizations Shape Policies

In addition to reacting to internal cultural dynamics, school personnel respond to externally generated directives and mandates. For example, local schools and districts are regularly directed by state and federal governments to enact new policies and procedures. These policies range from directives to expand curriculum to include multicultural themes, drivers' education, or sex education; to accommodate special education students; to limit instruction to English only; to equitably distribute school financing; to reduce class size; and to introduce high-stakes testing. Because schools depend on federal and state funds, district and school site leaders must address these policies, at the very least by shaping their operations to demonstrate compliance.

When new mandates place new demands on local schools, however, educators are apt to maintain previous routines while conforming to the new demands. In the act of trying to balance new demands and established routines, educators transform policies and the innovations that embody them (Berman & McLaughlin, 1978; Binder, 2002; Cuban, 1992; Hall & McGinty, 1997; McLaughlin, 1998: 70). Especially in the later stages of policy implementation, individuals inevitably modify the mandates. They add, subtract, and otherwise transform policy issued by state agencies. In this sense, educational reforms are socially constructed phenomena. In extreme cases, reforms are fully absorbed into the culture of the organization and thoroughly adapted to fit preexisting routines or standard operating procedures. Such adaptations may occur in a variety of settings distributed throughout a school system, and they may have a neutral, positive, or negative effect on the intensity and potential success of the reform.

Our belief in the importance of these aspects of organizational life—the orientation toward practical action, the tendency toward internal conflict, and the influence of external political forces—means that we do not view educational reform as a smooth, rational process best understood by documenting the decisions and actions of top leadership. Although we recognize that the rules of the game are set at the top, we don't take those rules to constitute the reform. Rather, we trace the manner in which educators' day-to-day routines, values, and externally generated political forces shape the way in which the reform is enacted in a particular locale.

Policy Implementation as Learning

Some scholars of educational reform have argued that policy implementation is primarily a problem of learning (Cohen & Barnes, 1993; Cohen & Hill, 2001; Spillane, Reiser, & Reimer, 2002; Stein & D'Amico, 2002a). Mainly on the basis of research on teachers' efforts to implement ambitious subject-area reforms (typically in mathematics and science but also in literacy, English, and history), learning-oriented researchers have described teachers' modifications to reform initiatives as often inadvertent and as a reflection of teachers' limited understanding of the underlying intent of the curricular and instructional intervention. That teachers would have difficulty implementing ambitious subject-matter reforms is not surprising. As the researchers have pointed out, most teachers neither learned nor learned to teach in the ways demanded by today's reforms, and, in addition to this lack of personal experience, school personnel often receive little or no opportunity to learn the basic principles of the reforms they are charged with implementing.

The learning demands for teachers are especially intense for those reforms that view teaching and learning as a highly interdependent activity between the teacher, the student, and the subject matter. Such reforms cannot be entirely scripted in advance. If teachers have impoverished understandings of the subject matter and an incomplete grasp of how students learn the main concepts of the subject, they will necessarily be hampered in their ability to make "in-flight" decisions about how to modify lessons to be responsive to students while, at the same time, getting across the goals of the lesson (Tharp & Gallimore, 1988: 229). The appropriateness of these "in flight" decisions, learning theorists argue, has major implications for the opportunities that students have to learn what is intended.

In addition to stressing the importance of teacher capacity, learning perspectives on instructional reform examine the design of the interventions with an eye toward the extent to which the design anticipates and plans for the teacher learning required to bring about the design's intended impact on student learning (Ball & Cohen, in preparation). Learning perspectives on instructional reform also recognize that contexts of implementation vary and that teachers need to adjust interventions to meet the demands and build on the resources of local situations. All of this, they argue, demands learning.

To date, most research that views the problem of implementation as a problem of learning has focused on teachers as individual learners. Drawing on cognitive learning theory, scholars have argued that teachers come to understand and make meaning of new, often very challenging, forms of instruction through the lens of their preexisting knowledge, beliefs, and experiences (Guthrie, 1990; Spillane, 2000; Spillane & Jennings, 1997). In this view, learning is portrayed as the development of increasingly efficient and powerfully organized mental structures within the mind of the individual. Learners, researchers have argued, "gravitate" toward approaches that are congruent with their prior mental frameworks and practices (Spillane, 2000: 163), focus on surface manifestations (such as discrete activities, materials, or classroom organization) rather than deeper pedagogical principles (Coburn, 2002; Spillane, 2000; Spillane & Zeuli, 1999), and graft new approaches on top of existing practices without altering classroom norms or routines (Coburn, 2002).

Recent work on situated learning (Greenfield, 2004; Rogoff, 1994), as well as earlier contributions from cultural psychologists (Cole, 1996; Scribner & Cole, 1981; Tharp & Gallimore, 1988), activity theorists (Engeström, 1987; Engeström & Middleton, 1994), and community-of-practice theorists (Lave & Wenger, 1991; Wenger, McDermott, & Snyder, 2002), challenge this perspective, pointing out that learning occurs in the *interactions between individuals* and that such interactions often take place within communities that are intact, ongoing, and informal.

In this view, learning happens when individuals bring varying perspectives and levels of expertise to the work before them. As they work together toward shared goals, they create new forms of meaning and understanding. These new meanings and understandings do not exist as abstract structures in the individual participants' minds; rather they derive from and create the situated practice in which individuals are coparticipants. In short, adopting this perspective on learning channels attention away from analysis of the cognitive attributes of individuals and channels it, instead, toward the collaborative interactions that occur as individuals work together toward common goals.

Some learning theorists have begun to apply this socially situated view of learning to teachers' attempts to learn to implement ambitious reforms (Cobb, McClain, Lamberg, & Dean, 2003b; Coburn & Stein, in press; Franke & Kazemi, 2001; Stein, Silver, & Smith, 1998). These authors' recommendations call for the careful design of professional interactions that allow individuals to learn from one another. Similar to organizational theorists' preference for the lived realities of day-to-day work environments, the preference of community-of-practice theorists is the face-to-face, informal groups within which individuals interact on a frequent basis. However, the learning view of policy implementation focuses on asymmetries of expertise and opportunities to learn from more capable others, whereas organizational theorists do not. The learning-oriented view of policy implementation to date, however, has paid less attention to formal organizational structure; the contentiousness stemming from conflicting values, beliefs, and assumptions; and the ways in which political forces shape reform.

The Technical, Cultural, and Political Dimensions of Reform

Oakes (1992) and her colleagues (Jones, Yonezawa, Ballesteros, & Mehan, 2002; Oakes, Quartz, Ryan, & Lipton, 1999; Yonezawa, Jones, & Mehan, 2002) proposed that school change is a multifaceted process with technical, normative (what we will henceforth call *cultural*), and political dimensions. In the final analysis, reform efforts activate actions on all dimensions, but often reformers lead with or emphasize actions on one dimension. When reformers attempt to change or improve schools by leading with technical means, they act in terms of resources. For example, they add labs, equipment, or curriculum; upgrade teachers' skills; or rearrange the manner in which students are organized for instruction. When reformers attempt to change or improve schools by leading with cultural means, they engage educators' values, beliefs, and norms, often on controversial topics such as the placement of teachers and the nature of intelligence and its distribution across race, ethnicity, class, and gender, as well as school sorting or testing practices. When reformers attempt to change or improve schools by leading with political means, they work to build productive professional relationships and galvanize important political constituencies to gain comparative advantage in the distribution of resources, opportunities, and credentials.

Historically, school reform efforts have been guided by a "research–development–dissemination–evaluation" model (Havelock, 1996, cited in Brown, Greeno, Resnick, Mehan, & Lampert, 1999). This perspective posits public policy as a linear process in which policy is formulated by elite decision makers, often taking the form of mandates written by state or federal decision makers, and proceeds through a distinct sequence of stages from formation to implementation (Hall, 1995). Oakes et al. (1999: 19) summarized this position well:

> Ideally, policy makers, acting in the public interest, set ambitious schooling goals and enact policies (including those that provide technical support and resources) to ensure a schooling infrastructure that supports the goals. They also make policies that compel, "incent," and build educators' capacity to change practices so that they can reach the goals, and they work to make the policy seem coherent by bringing prior policies into alignment with new ones. At the local level, school district administrators are expected to implement reform policies by making structural and procedural changes—for example, by adding new course offerings, rearranging school schedules, providing new materials, changing assessment and accountability measures, and by engaging teachers in professional development.

In the research–development–dissemination–evaluation model, the causal arrow of change travels in one direction—from active, thoughtful designers who make plans for passive and compliant implementers who then carry out the plans; that is, complete the predetermined goals and objectives of the design team. The authors of a seminal work on government policy implementation succinctly defined the technical–rational view this way: "Implementation is the ability to forge subsequent links in the causal chain so as to obtain the desired results" (Pressman & Wildavsky, 1973: xv).

A core belief supporting externally devised educational reform is that the external group (state or federal government, district, or design team) is best suited to be the engine driving reform. But instead of facilitating reform, the top-down or outside-in vector of change sometimes clashes with the beliefs and routines of local educators who think they have the knowledge and skill to teach students well and to improve schools. Fullan (1991: 22–23) blamed "hyper-rationalization" for many of the problems that occur when organizational ideas are initiated from outside the school system.

In response to the wide-ranging critiques of the hyper-rationalization that permeates policy-as-implementation, investigators have reformulated public policy as "mutual adaptation" (McLaughlin, 1998), a "conditional process" (Hall, 1995; Hall & McGinty, 1997), or a "co-constructed process"

(Datnow, Hubbard, & Mehan, 2002). From this point of view, social policy is a web of interrelated conditions and consequences, where the consequences of actions in one context may become the conditions for the next (Hall, 1995; Hall & McGinty, 1997). In other words, interactions in one policy context generate "outcomes," such as policy statements and new rules or procedures, which in turn may condition the actions and interactions of other actors elsewhere in the policy chain.

These reformulations eschew treating the participants in the reform process—be they design team members, teachers, or principals—as compliant actors, passively responding to directives mandated from higher levels of bureaucracies. Instead, all of the participants in the reform process are recognized as active agents who make policy in their everyday actions. These actions include attempts by street-level bureaucrats to faithfully carry out directives mandated from the top of a system. They may also include efforts to initiate alternatives or to resist or even actively subvert reform efforts. In all of these cases—passive resistance, active subversion, faithful rendering of top-down mandates—we treat the agency of the participants in the reform process as an act of co-construction. In each case, this co-construction is shaping and is shaped by the technical, cultural, and political features of school and society (Datnow et al., 2002). To capture this sense of the dynamics of reform in our descriptions, we use the expression *enactment* rather than the more conventional *implementation*.

We use Oakes's formulation of the three dimensions of reform to understand the San Diego context. The district's theory of action from 1998 to 2002 (described in Chapter 4) was composed of an intriguing combination of technical, cultural, and political ingredients. We treat all the strategies the San Diego reformers deployed (such as designing "in-the-line" professional development, mandating a single literacy program, and employing walk-throughs as an instructional and evaluative tool) as examples of the technical dimension of change. We treat their attempts to change educators' beliefs, norms, and practices—that is, to "reculture schools" (Hargreaves, 1994)—as examples of the cultural dimensions of change, and we treat their attempts to win and then maintain the loyalty of the business community—including national funding agencies—as examples of the political dimension of change. We contend that the reform process benefits from balanced attention to all three and that when change along one dimension gets too far ahead of the others, the imbalance causes tensions. For example, strong emphasis on the technical dimension (characterized by the introduction of new tools and curricula, lots of professional development, etc.) with less attention to the cultural shifts that type of reform would entail for teachers, principals, and others potentially leads to a backlash from the rank and file. Similarly, failure to anticipate and attend to political forces can sink a reform. We draw on each of these dimensions to help explain what transpired during the four years of the SDCS reform.

Our Framework for Analyzing the San Diego Reforms

The idea that reform entails learning is powerful. The power of this perspective is further enhanced when we explicitly consider learning in the context of social organizations. An organization such as the SDCS district does not reside in its individual members taken separately, even though each individual contributes to it, or exist independently of the actions of the individuals within it. By focusing on the *interrelations* between the activities of individuals, we are able to capture the varied and sometimes contradictory ways in which a complex activity such as school reform plays out on the ground.

We treat learning in organizations as something that happens between people when they engage in common activities because this trains attention simultaneously on individuals and the collective. Only individuals can contribute to an organization's learning; however, an organization's learning is distinct from an individual's learning because it inheres in the interrelated activities of many people, not in the heads of solitary people. Individuals bring varying perspectives and levels of expertise to the work before them. As they work together toward shared goals, people create new forms of meaning and understanding. These new meanings and understandings are emergent—that is, they did not previously exist in the individual participants' minds. Rather, they take shape within the relations among people as they engage in interaction (Hutchins, 1990). Therefore, in the context of the San Diego reform, we will say learning has occurred when communities of individuals gradually transform their practices over time as they engage one another in response to changes in their environment associated with reaching the organization's goal of improved student learning.

To summarize, we view the reforms initiated under Bersin and Alvarado as representing a top-down vector of change that deeply challenged local educators' beliefs about students' capabilities and about their own roles in the education of children, thereby leading to a great deal of organizational conflict. Moreover, similar to educators everywhere, San Diego educators had in place their own routines and standard operating procedures that constituted meaningful, workable solutions to their everyday, lived experiences in the SDCS. The reforms specifically aimed to disrupt these routines and replace them with new ones. Given what we know about complex social organizations and what we know about the learning demands placed on teachers by reforms that require the adoption of new and unfamiliar ways of teaching, we would expect the Bersin–Alvarado plan to face formidable challenges. We reasoned that "intersection encounters"—formal and informal interactions between school personnel at various layers throughout the district—would be fertile places to explore for evidence of disruptions to normal routines and for the pressure associated with increased learning demands.

For analytical purposes, we view the SDCS as a nested set of communities of learners. As we describe more fully in Chapter 4, the district leaders sought to transform the teaching craft from an individual practice into one in which instruction was based on shared ideas, beliefs, and values and communicated in a common language.

Figure 1.1 represents these nested communities and depicts the places where learning is required between the various layers of the organization that we call "intersection encounters."[2] The personnel in the left-hand box of each intersection encounter are viewed as performing teaching functions for the personnel in the right-hand box of the intersection encounter. Starting with the innermost oval, Figure 1.1 depicts teachers working with students to help them to learn subject matter. This activity is viewed as the core of the learning and teaching enterprise, as the touchstone for the learning that needs to occur in intersection encounters further out in the diagram. One layer out we find teachers again, but in this intersection encounter they are depicted as learners, whereas the principal is responsible for teaching; that is, assisting the teachers in learning how to help students learn subject matter. The third layer out shows principals again, but this time as learners, with district and instructional leaders acting as their "teachers." The final layer depicts the district leadership interacting with the many communities that surround the district.

We privilege intersection encounters because they are sites where we were able to observe participants making sense of the reforms as they are being communicated from one community to another. As shown in Figure 1.1, a multitude of distinct communities compose the SDCS. Over time, these communities' shared histories of learning create discontinuities between community members and nonmembers. Often the discontinuities are especially pronounced between communities of learners in different parts of the system because the nature of their work is so distinct (e.g., district leadership communities are concerned with organizing for systemic change whereas teacher communities are concerned with teaching children to read). Because successful districtwide reform depends on messages and activities that span communities at multiple levels of the

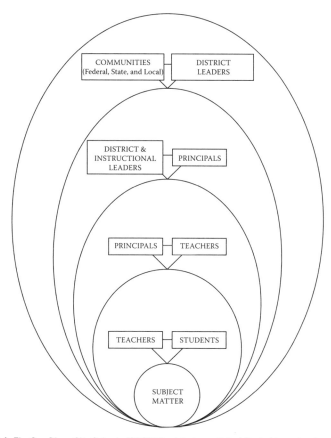

Figure 1.1 The San Diego City Schools (SDCS) Depicted as a Set of Nested Learning Communities.

system, these discontinuities need to be acknowledged and reconciled with one another and with key features of the reform.

Discontinuities between communities, although potentially troublesome, also represent opportunities for learning. We paid special attention to interactions that occurred at these sensitive intersection encounters. We assessed whether participants in any layer of the system were learning from those above, those around, and those below them, and if so, what they were learning. Did the members of the learning community implement the reform as designed? Did they negotiate its meaning? If so, how and when? Did any new learning make its way back up the system? Or, were only those lower in the system learning from those above them?

We looked not only for the ways in which communities may intentionally and unintentionally shift the meanings of district directives to maintain the continuity of their practice but also for the ways in which meanings can be negotiated between layers. For synchronized learning to occur, some direction from district policy is necessary; what we are especially interested in is the extent to which various communities had the opportunity to develop their own meanings and thus assert ownership over the reform directives. For example, what do principals appropriate from their instructional leaders and incorporate into their own communities of practice? Do their particular appropriations, in turn, influence what they pass on to the teacher communities within their schools? And do teachers then appropriate that information in a manner that fits with their shared repertoire or practice?

Note that we situated Figure 1.1 within an outer circle—representing local communities, state and federal government, and granting agencies—because over the years of our investigation, and since, social actors in granting agencies and state and federal settings established policies, and actors in local communities raised issues that affected the reform—often in ways not anticipated by the district leadership at the outset of the reform effort.

Throughout this book, we adopt a critical stance toward the official rhetoric that the district is a community of learners. We did, indeed, uncover many instances of teachers and students learning new practices, clear evidence of learning flowing from district leadership to the classroom. But we also found instances in which miscommunication blocked learning and learners resisted learning opportunities. Two purposes of this book are to trace the extent to which learning flows up as well as down and through the multiple communities of learners that compose the district and to identify the circumstances that enable learning to flow from outside the system to the inside.

The Organization of the Book

The book is arranged in three parts. In the first part (Chapters 1, 2, 3, and 4), we overview our approach to studying the reform, its origins in New York City, and the theory-of-action that undergirded Bersin and Alvarado's work from 1998 to 2002. In Chapter 1, we have presented the theoretical foundations that have guided the manner in which we viewed and made sense of the reform. In Chapter 2, we outline our methodological approach to studying the reform, including our data sources, positionality, and methods of analysis. In Chapter 3, we trace the intellectual origins of the reform back to Community School District #2 in New York City, identifying both similarities and differences between how reforms were carried out in these two cities. Finally, in Chapter 4, we outline the underlying theoretical and moral framing of the reform as seen through the eyes of its leaders.

In the second part (Chapters 5, 6, 7, 8, and 9), we analyze how the reform played out in San Diego from its inception in July 1998 to August 2002, including modifications not originally anticipated by the district leadership that have been influenced by technical constraints, cultural processes, and political forces. We begin with the classroom. In Chapter 5, we provide a close-up examination of the manner in which teachers adopted, changed, or ignored the central tenets of the reform as they worked in the intersection encounter between teacher, student, and subject matter. We then move on to examine professional development between all layers of the system, exposing the challenges involved as a whole organization attempted to learn. In Chapter 6, we focus on the intersection encounter between school leaders (principals and coaches) and teachers as they worked together to enact the reform. In Chapter 7, we move outward one more layer to examine the intersection encounter between district leaders (top district leadership and instructional leaders) and principals, taking up the question of how district leadership provided for the learning of principals. In the third part of the book (Chapter 10), we reflect on the utility of the reform as a learning metaphor and draw the implications of our findings for theories of school reform, public policy, and social organizations.

CHAPTER 2

Using Research to Understand
the San Diego Reform

We seek to help close the gap that currently exists between research and practice in the field of education. The conventional model assumes a linear transfer of research into practice. "Fundamental research leads to applied research which then leads either to the development of products or codified professional practices that can be used by educational systems" (Stein & Coburn, 2003: 4). This dominant linear model divides the labor between researchers and practitioners. Researchers study "basic" educational issues. Findings are transmitted to practitioners through publications and other products such as curricula or instructional materials. Practitioners in districts, schools, and classrooms, in turn, attempt to put research results into practice. A second dichotomy exists routinely between researchers and practitioners. Practitioners are often the objects of study, rather than participants in constructing research and interpreting results. Value orientations, long established in the field, underpin and sustain these dichotomies: the abstract mental work associated with conducting basic research has traditionally been held in higher regard than the concrete practical work of applying research (Labaree, 2003; Lagemann, 2000).

When researchers assume little or no responsibility for making their research useful, and practitioners assume little or no responsibility for evaluating useful practice, then "neither research nor practice benefits" (Brown, Greeno, Resnick, Mehan, & Lampert, 1999: 29). If researchers and practitioners were to share responsibility for research and practice, then alternatives to the current situation would be possible. The National Academy of Education (Brown et al., 1999), the MacArthur Network on Teaching and Learning (Stipek, 2005), and the Strategic Educational Research Partnership (Donovan, Wigdor, & Snow, 2003), among others (Bereiter, 2002: 382–418; Lagemann, 2000; Resnick, Elmore, & Alvarado, 1996), have urged a reconfiguration of the relationship between research and practice.

Emerging Models for Linking Research and Practice

Although the majority of educational research follows the linear research-into-practice model, increasing numbers of researchers have begun to take their laboratories to the field, joining their ethnographically informed colleagues, and forming new, more productive relationships with educational practitioners. These researchers are adamantly determined to make their research useful to the practitioners with whom they work as well as make contributions to theory and research. To do so, they form long-lasting committed relationships with practitioners and take up their problems of practice by codeveloping research agendas, interpretations of data, and, sometimes, even instructional tools and interventions.

Stein and Coburn (2003) identified four ways in which researchers and practitioners interact to improve educational practice and contribute to basic knowledge: designing research, design for scale, provide documentation, and develop systems for sharing and codifying practitioner knowledge. Researchers work collaboratively with practitioners to design a learning environment or innovation and then study the impact of this environment or innovation on student learning, organizational change, or improved practice (Greeno & Goldman, 1998; Newman, Griffin, & Cole, 1989; Pea et al., 1997; Rosebery, Warren, & Conant, 1992). When designing for scale, researchers seek to bring research knowledge to multiple local sites in the form of tools, materials, or processes for the purpose of wide-scale improvement (e.g., Slavin & Madden, 1999; see also Glennan, Bodilly, Galegher, & Kerr, 2004). In documentation studies, researchers learn from observing and analyzing practice that is in the midst of an attempt to improve practice, whereas practitioners learn from ongoing interaction with and feedback from the researchers (Baxter, in preparation; Hubbard, in preparation). The final class of activity identified by Stein and Coburn (development of systems for sharing and codifying practitioner knowledge) places the center of gravity with practitioners (Stokes, 2005). Practitioners engage research knowledge as it is needed to frame or inform the improvement of their own practice and create mechanisms to foster dialogue between clinical and research knowledge (Lewis, 2003; Lieberman & Wood, 2003). All of these approaches seek to reconfigure the relationship between research and educational improvement in a more interactive and productive manner. Although they do so in different ways, all either draw on or contribute to practical understandings of how to improve education as well as more generalized research knowledge.

Our Approach

Our study of the reform of the San Diego City Schools (SDCS) aimed to strike a balance between contributing to research knowledge and improving educational practice. In doing so, we used aspects of design research and documentation studies as discussed by Stein and Coburn. We also drew on some of the major tenets of ethnography, a well-established methodology in the social sciences, but augmented them in ways described next to make our work more useful and usable to educators in San Diego and elsewhere.

In its broadest sense, ethnography has been defined as a description of a culture, community, or society. Regardless of the unit being studied (e.g., a self-contained society, a community, or a cultural setting such as a school), ethnographic investigations have certain methodological features in common. First is the shared belief among ethnographers that a cultural description requires a long period of intimate study and residence among members of the community being studied. A second distinguishing characteristic of ethnography is its comparative or contrastive nature. A cultural system, a community, or a cultural setting such as a school is studied not in isolation but in relation to other known and comparable types of organization. Third, ethnography is vigorously naturalistic; the goal is a richly detailed description of everyday life from the point of view of the natives.

To achieve a "thick description" (Geertz, 1973), ethnographers use a wide range of research techniques, including prolonged face-to-face observations of members of the local group, direct participation in some of that group's activities, and intensive work with a few informants. Ethnographers also take advantage of documentary evidence supplied by official agencies and information gathered in more formal interviews, although those kinds of evidence are not always taken at face value. To ensure validity, ethnographers often triangulate official documents with information gathered from firsthand observations (and the latter increasingly are being augmented by videotaped materials).

From its earliest formulations (e.g., Malinowski, 1922), ethnography has aimed to describe and interpret events, objects, and people from the point of view of members of the society under study, rather than employing names, categories, scripts, or schemas derived either from "objective science" or from the researcher's own culture. The sustained, face-to-face contacts with members of the subject community that ethnographers routinely undertake help ensure that their description of a culture is consistent with the perspective of community participants. Moreover, because ethnographic research is open-ended, it can be self-correcting. Research questions posed at the outset of a study often are changed as an inquiry unfolds, and topics that initially seemed paramount are replaced as new topics emerge. Finally, ethnographers have become increasingly aware of the power dynamics inherent in the relationships between observer and participant (Clifford & Marcus, 1986; Hymes, 1972; Sanday, 1976). Some explicitly recognize that "we [researchers] see the lives of others through the lenses of our own grinding and that they [the study participants] look back on ours through ones of their own" (Geertz, quoted in González, 2004: 19). This critical self-reflection has led to a reformulation of researcher roles, at least in some corners of ethnographically informed educational research, that parallels the reformulation of researcher–practitioner roles in design research and documentation studies:

> Being a so-called participant observer [is giving way] to becoming an especially observant participant. This means paying close attention to not only one's point of view as an observer, but to one's relations with others (who one is studying and working with) and one's relations with oneself. (Erickson, 1996: 7)

Our Research Strategies

In studying the SDCS reform, we followed the tenets of ethnography. We immersed ourselves in the study of day-to-day practice over a four-year period. We compared our analysis of San Diego with a similar reform effort undertaken in New York City a decade earlier (see chapter 3). We adopted a vigorously naturalistic stance toward understanding and describing the reform to produce a richly detailed description. Our commitment to accurately represent the point of view of the participants led us to record and report the competing and conflicting versions of the reform and its enactment in concrete situations, such as classrooms, principals' conferences, and school board meetings.

Our research also followed the emerging tenets of documentation studies for the production of useful and usable knowledge. We were and continue to be committed to formulating general principles and developing useful knowledge. From the beginning, our intention was to solicit San Diegans' input regarding facets of the reform that were most meaningful and important to document. Moreover, we intentionally sought out venues in which to share our emerging understandings with relevant personnel. These included participants' commentary on the analyses we generated along the way and joint presentations at scientific meetings (Hubbard, Beldock, & Osborne, 2003).

Our research began with a six-month planning period—funded by the Spencer Foundation—during which we immersed ourselves in the district to evaluate the feasibility and usefulness of studying it. At the end of that period, we composed an analytic essay (Mehan, Quartz, & Stein, 1997) that described the research questions, aims, methods, and anticipated outcomes. We shared this essay with key participants in the district: the superintendent, the chancellor of instruction and his executive director, the instructional leaders (ILs), the president of the San Diego Education Association (SDEA), and a subset of principals, teachers, and members of the school board. Some participants offered criticism. All offered constructive advice in a spirit of professionalism and commitment to improved education for the children of San Diego. All encouraged us to conduct the research, especially after we made it clear that we perceived our audience to be the entire educational system in San Diego, not one component of it, and that we would not just place our research results in a publication that was aimed at other researchers but share the work with involved practitioners.

Once our study began, we periodically brought together participants from different parts of the system to share what we were learning. We wrote research memos on different topics, sent them to participants to read, and later held meetings with participants to discuss their views of the emerging findings, our ways of conceptualizing those findings, and their desires regarding directions in which the research might productively proceed. In addition to sharing these in-progress memos, we sent copies of our research papers to district leaders and then held follow-up conversations with them.

Finally, we embedded elements of design research in our approach. For example, Hubbard participated in the design of an intervention aimed at improving a single principal's coaching skills. In addition to Hubbard, this miniresearch project involved one IL and one elementary school principal, both of whom were already participating in our larger study.

Hubbard identified the need for the project after participating in a series of walk-throughs at the elementary school. The IL and principal agreed that an intervention aimed at improving the principal's practice and enhancing the learning of the teachers at the school would be beneficial. The collaboration involved videotaping the principal's on-site coaching and staff development efforts and then reviewing, strategizing, and trying new approaches developed through an ongoing dialogue among the three project members. Although the project began late in the life of our study (August 2002), it extended over a period of approximately five months.

Combining ethnography, documentation studies, and design research helped us ensure—but did not guarantee—that the knowledge and understanding gained by sustained and systematic study belongs as much to teachers and other practitioners as it does to the worlds of policy and research. And though—as we describe next—it was no simple feat to assemble groups of busy professionals consumed by the demands of the reform and to facilitate collaboration among them, we remained committed to finding new ways to mediate the local construction of new knowledge about school reform. Moreover, in pursuing our research, we deliberately chose to be "critical friends," willing to write reports and make presentations that revealed what we found, warts and all.

Resolving the Ambiguity of Multiple Roles

Although the tenets of our approach can be clearly stated in theory, the new researcher roles that derive from it are difficult to negotiate in practice. Ongoing, close interaction between practitioners and researchers promises richer and more authentic findings than might emerge from a more traditional audit. In practice, the complexities associated with collaboration are daunting. In our work with the SDCS, we attempted to go beyond writing a description of the setting (the goal of classical ethnography), and we attempted to go beyond assessing the relationship between policy-as-intended with policy-as-enacted (as occurs in traditional evaluation).

Our proximity to the schools and membership in the community both facilitated and complicated our research. Two members (Hubbard and Mehan) of our three-person team live and work in San Diego. Neither is a stranger to the district, either literally or metaphorically, and both had done other work in San Diego that had been received with favor. Thus, compared to strangers from outside the local area, we were more easily able to build the trusting relationships. As locals, Hubbard and Mehan also had access to events as they unfolded daily. This obvious advantage included challenges, however. Ready opportunities for observations and conversations made us feel pressured to be present everywhere, at all times, even though we knew this to be unrealistic and impossible. And personal and professional commitments meant that neither Hubbard nor Mehan could—even if she or he had wanted to—simply write a final report and leave town.

Our research efforts were further complicated by our professional roles and relationships. In addition to carrying out our grant-funded study of the SDCS reform, we occupied many other roles simultaneously. These roles put us into many situations that rendered the research process ambiguous. For example, Mehan serves as director for the Center for Research on Educational Equity, Access, and Teacher Excellence (CREATE) at the University of California, San Diego. CREATE was established in 1997 in response to the University of California's ban on affirmative action. The center's three main functions are to conduct basic and design research on educational equity issues; to work collaboratively with low-performing and underserved local schools to enhance the culture of learning and help students from groups underrepresented in the university be better prepared for and more interested in attending college, thus contributing to greater diversity in the university's student body; and to monitor the Preuss School, an on-campus college prep charter school for underrepresented students.

The partnerships that resulted from these collaborations between the university and the schools placed Mehan in the position of interacting with district leaders, principals, and teachers when CREATE provided assistance in the form of after-school programs, tutors, computers, health programs, parent education, and teacher professional-development programs. The ensuing university–school relationships provided an entrée to schools and other educational situations and also helped build the rapport necessary for effective ethnography and documentation. But Mehan's multiple roles had drawbacks, as well. Many SDCS educators knew him only as a fellow educator, a practitioner who shared their desire to enable disadvantaged students to obtain access to college, not as a member of a research team that was studying the San Diego reforms. As a result, Mehan sometimes found himself privy to information that was significant to the research project but that was not explicitly marked as such. For example, a visit to a school site to introduce to the faculty a professional-development team skilled in literacy might generate a conversation about the status of the district's Balanced Literacy program. Advising the district's director of assessment and accountability about evaluation strategies sometimes granted Mehan access to inside knowledge about the status of district-sponsored evaluation activities. Negotiating with a principal about establishing a CREATE-sponsored tutoring or professional-development program might lead to a spontaneous visit to one or more classrooms.

As director of CREATE, Mehan represents the University of California on the San Diego Chamber of Commerce's Business Roundtable for Education. Although he usually introduced himself at meetings of the group as an educator who was assisting the schools in improving their culture of learning and who was part of a team conducting research on SDCS, and although he made several formal presentations on the research to meetings of business and community members, the people with whom Mehan interacted did not always treat him as a researcher. During the course of normal conversations, they revealed information that had a bearing on the research issues our team was addressing. In addition, as a Roundtable member, he was in the audience when the superintendent or other SDCS personnel addressed the group. In sum, this setting afforded Mehan many interactions with individuals who were participating directly or indirectly in the SDCS reform and provided him with observations of educational practice not conducted under the auspices of a research visit. Therefore, the status of the information he gleaned was ambiguous.

Similarly ambiguous situations developed as a result of Mehan's status as principal investigator of the Carnegie Corporation grant to improve SDCS high schools. This was a separate grant that had no financial bearing on the research reported in this book. Nevertheless, Mehan's Carnegie-based role placed him in regular contact with district personnel, generally in the context of discussions about how to improve the district's reform efforts at the high school level. Also, he was asked by the district to represent the Carnegie-sponsored project before the state legislature and the funding agency. Those events required a more overtly political presentation than the kind of presentation given to a meeting of researchers, such as the American Psychological Association, the American Education Research Association, or the American Anthropological Association's Council on Anthropology and Education.

Hubbard faced similar role ambiguities. Her experiences in the field, working closely with ILs, principals, and other district administrators, illustrate the complexity of being researcher, critical friend, and friend. At the start of the study, some practitioners, although polite, seemed distrustful, anticipating that the team would be critical in its observations and negative in its assessment. Regular interaction with district personnel, including many instances in which Hubbard directly helped practitioners, created a new, positive impression; she frequently heard her district colleagues remark that she "wasn't like other researchers." Her role demanded that she provide a candid and critical perspective, but Hubbard felt that being present and taking notes at weekly walk-throughs and principals' conferences and then withholding constructive criticism until it was time to write a final report was disingenuous, at best.[1] Moreover, as practitioners increasingly began to solicit her advice, she felt compelled to share her observations and to problem solve with her district colleagues. She sometimes felt called on to solve problems out of her area of expertise, yet she was reluctant to reveal her shortcomings for fear of being discredited as a reliable researcher. Other times, she sensed she brought more or different knowledge to a situation but limited or carefully worded her input to avoid being perceived as a "researcher-know it-all." The entire experience of being researcher, critical friend, and friend led to many in-depth discussions designed to identify sources of problems and to construct strategies aimed at addressing them. The process was not always easy. Acting as critical friend sometimes meant offering negative comments that were difficult for practitioners, who, naturally, hoped to have their practice reviewed positively and validated, to hear.

As an out-of-towner, Stein (who resides in Pittsburgh) did not face the same dilemmas as did Mehan and Hubbard. Although she participated in data collection and feedback sessions, her long-term reputation in the city and with the district was not at stake in the same way. For Stein, the chief challenge arose from her long-term acquaintance with Tony Alvarado (and several other former District #2 educators who became part of the San Diego reforms [see Chapter 3]). These existing relationships led some San Diegans who had grown tired of hearing from administrations about how wonderful the New York City reforms were to initially view Stein with suspicion.

As a team, we resolved the ambiguity presented by these multiple roles by deploying a strategy analogous to a journalist's "on the record–off the record" approach. Each of us treated any information we acquired informally or in a situation that was not formally designated as a research encounter as off the record. Because we collaborated with some but not all SDCS educators, in many cases, we had to remind our SDCS colleagues of our research responsibility to report on the dynamics of the reform and explicitly state what had transpired was off the record Only information that was acquired through official channels, such as tape-recorded interviews, public presentations, or published documents, was used as grounds for the interpretations and conclusions that appear in this book. Information we initially received off the record was occasionally put on the record by our conducting a formal interview.

Did our boundary-maintenance efforts always work? No, of course not. Our practitioner colleagues sometimes bristled at the interpretations we made, asserting that we "got it wrong." Or they expressed surprise that certain results were reported in public places. Or, worst of all, they dismissed our observations as obvious. On such occasions, we swallowed our pride and tried to take advantage of the feedback to improve the narrative. We believe the resulting narrative as it unfolds in this book is better for these negotiations. Engaging directly and repeatedly with the reform participants has helped us craft an interpretation that is more consistent with their lived experiences.

Forging Collaborative Relationships

Even as trusting relationships between researchers and practitioners grew, differences between the two remained. Researchers and practitioners come from different backgrounds and in some respects privilege different things. Practitioners want the "What do we do on Monday morning?" question answered. Researchers spend considerable effort developing theory around practice. These are not necessarily mutually exclusive priorities, yet they can impede collaborations because each somewhat differently shapes the way business is done. Thus, collaborative arrangements that lead to real improvement in teaching and learning require conscious effort.

From the outset of our research, we were committed to constructing opportunities for a conversation with our SDCS colleagues. One way of doing so was to report preliminary data and analysis around a particular topic, such as the impact of the reform-mandated high school literacy courses on students' educational achievement. During the course of our study, we drafted three four- to five-page analytic essays outlining information that drew on our fieldwork data, which we then evaluated in terms of the San Diego theory of action (see Chapter 4 for discussion of district leaders' theory of action). The essays focused primarily on (1) points of congruence with the district's theory of action, (2) barriers and points of resistance to the theory of action, and (3) assessments of the overall quality of learning communities at each level. We wanted to stimulate discussions around the mandated features of the reform and draw attention to places where learning seemed to be in place and those where it did not.

A second means of facilitating conversations with our colleagues was provided by school personnel and funding agency representatives. Karen Bachofer, director of accountability and assessment for SDCS, assembled the teams conducting research in the district in January 2001, so that the district could learn about our findings and so that researchers could gain an understanding of each other's work, enhance coordination, and avoid duplication. Marshall Smith, project officer for the Hewlett Foundation, provided funding for research groups to meet with district officials in fall 2001 and a second time in December 2002. In addition to having the research groups share their findings on such topics as districtwide strategies for achieving reform, developing leadership for instructional change, developing strategies for teacher professional development, targeting strategies for all learners, and making data-driven decisions, Smith wanted to push the groups to make their discoveries useful to the district so the leadership could make informed decisions for institutional change. This is a goal we share—and hope this book achieves.

We also fostered collaborative conversations by jointly writing papers. On the basis of the success of their small design-research project, Hubbard, Beldock, and Osborne wrote a paper detailing recommendations for a more broadly applicable intervention, one that could be used to improve principals' practice in other schools across the district (Hubbard et al., 2003). Collaborating to write the paper revealed differences in the project members' educational and experiential backgrounds that led to new knowledge. For Hubbard, co-constructing recommendations based on the project findings meant acquiring a new language and learning a new way to describe the content of instruction that would preserve the integrity of the Balanced Literacy framework (curriculum her practitioner colleagues knew intimately). For the practitioners, the collaboration meant viewing their own practice and the strategies developed from this research in a broader theoretical context, a perspective that would help the IL assist other principals in the district to achieve similar improvements at their schools.

Overall, this design-research project, followed by the joint authorship of a paper, illustrates the advantages of joint participation around a problem of practice. This five-month, intimate collaboration illustrates how the researcher can become an actor who is instrumental in changing practice, and the practitioner can become an actor who guides the research. Our experience with the project also suggests general implications for researcher–practitioner collaborations. The challenge for such collaborations is, on one hand, to respect the local needs of practitioners, whereas, on the other hand, it is to develop more usable and generative knowledge for the field. This methodology demands that research and the development of an end product or innovation occur in cycles of design, enactment, analysis, and redesign, and it demands that researchers and practitioners who hope to develop "sharable theories that will function in authentic settings recognize the importance of context" (Design-Based Research Collective, 2003: 5). School settings and the skills, goals, and knowledge of the participants, as well as the relationships that exist between the actors involved in the work, significantly affect the ability to build and transfer theoretical understandings.

Data Collection

From September 1998 through June 2002, we followed the movement of reform ideas and plans as they traveled from level to level and from group to group in the SDCS system. We concentrated on four of the district's eleven instructional corridors. An "instructional corridor" is a slice of the system running from the district leaders through an IL and then to the schools (and their principals) and the classrooms (and their teachers and students) that compose the community of learners for whom the IL is responsible (see chapter 4 for more discussion of the learning community concept). We solicited the involvement of ILs whose responsibilities included elementary schools and high schools; middle schools were excluded from our study because other research groups were investigating them.

The four instructional corridors we selected are representative of the district. The schools included in the four corridors were diverse in terms of their student bodies' socioeconomic status, ethnicity, and native language; the levels of participation in the reform effort at the individual school sites; and the length of time each learning community's principals and teachers had been at their current assignments.

Within the four corridors, we selected six schools: three elementary schools and three high schools. These schools were selected to be representative of the neediest segments of the SDCS. They were selected based on the ILs' recommendations; the advice of other professionals who were knowledgeable about the system; and the willingness of the principals and teachers to participate in our study.

The three elementary schools in our study were Scripps, Harvey Mudd, and Emmanuel Jackson.[2] Scripps is a K–5 school that in the 2000–2001 school year had a population of 664 students, 96% whom qualified for free or reduced-price lunch. The majority of the students were Hispanic (81.6%); 6.5% were white, 9.6% were African American, and 1.7% were Indochinese, the next largest group. Emmanuel Jackson, a K–4 elementary school, had a population of 775 students. At the time of our study, it had the most mobile student population in the district. It was Hispanic (74.3%), 3.1% white, and 14.3% African American. The next largest other group was Indochinese (5.0%). Harvey Mudd Elementary was the largest elementary school in our study with 1,259 students in 2000–2001. This K–5 school was also predominately Hispanic (64.9%); 4.1% of the students were white and 14.8% were African American. The next largest group was Indochinese (14.9%).

The three high schools in our study were Creeley, Hunter, and Martin Luther King.[3] Creeley, a 9–12 high school, had a population of 1,545 students in 2000–2001. A significant portion of the students (75.2%) were on free or reduced-price lunch. The majority of the students at this school were Hispanic (35.1%); 9.3% were and 23.8% were African American. Indochinese students composed 28.1% of the population. Hunter, also a 9–12 high school, had the largest student population in our study with 2,157 students. In 1999 the school was named a California Distinguished High School. The majority of students were white (55.2%), 26.4% were Hispanic, and 9.7% were African American. Indochinese students composed 3.7% of the school population. Martin Luther King High, a 9–12 school, was developing a curriculum focus on coastal studies and publication technologies. It had a population of 1,604 students and was 40.8% Hispanic, 27.4% white, and 12.7% African American. This school, like all the other schools in our study, drew its next largest group of students from the Indochinese community (12.9%). This information is summarized in Table 2.1.

Of the four ILs who started in our study in September 1998, three remained in June 2001 and none remained when the study ended in December 2002. One IL left the district (citing job stress) during the first year of our study; we added a new IL at that time, thereby enabling us to focus on four instructional corridors.

As noted in Chapter 1, our data collection efforts privileged intersection encounters within these corridors. These interactions were occasions where we were able to observe participants making sense of the reforms in the context of their daily lives and previously established routines. More specifically, we were able to see if participants in a given layer of the system were learning from those above and those below them, what they were learning, and whether the members of the learning community implemented the reform as designed. Did they improvise? Revise? Modify? Did

Table 2.1. Demographic Information about the Schools in Our Study[4]

School	Number of Students	Percentage of Students Eligible for Free or Reduced-Price Lunch	Percentage of URM Students
Scripps Elementary	664	96	91.2
Harvey Mudd Elementary	1,259	Not reported	89.7
Emmanuel Jackson Elementary	775	Not reported	88.6
Creeley High	1,545	75.2	58.9
Hunter High	2,157	Not reported	36.1
Martin Luther King High	1,604	Not reported	52.5

Table 2.2. The Number and Types of Interviews

Interviewees	Number of Interviews	Reported In
Superintendent and chancellor of instruction	3	All chapters
Senior district staff	9	All chapters
Instructional leaders	10	Chapters 6 and 7
Principals	12	Chapters 5, 6, and 7
Teachers	140	Chapter 5
Community members	14	Chapters 8 and 9

any new learning make its way back up the system? Or was the flow of information downward only—that is, were only those lower in the system learning from those above them?

To enrich our understanding of the context surrounding intersection encounters, we interviewed many district personnel who were instrumental in shaping the reform. This list includes the superintendent, the chancellor of instruction, the executive officer to the chancellor, the director of literacy and social studies, two professional consultants, the senior high literacy manager, the biliteracy coordinator, the director of science and educational technology, the director of mathematics, and the executive director, leadership academy (University of San Diego). Each interview was audiotaped and transcribed; the average length of teacher interviews was 90 minutes; other interviews lasted from 30 to 120 minutes. Table 2.2 summarizes the interview sources and numbers and indicates which chapters in the book draw on these data.

In the following sections, we detail the kind of information that we collected for each of the intersection encounters.

Teachers and Students Interacting about Subject Matter

At the core of a learning community, teachers interact with students around the Balanced Literacy framework. Our research was designed to understand how this important component of the reform was enacted in the give-and-take of classroom interaction. In each of the three elementary schools we selected, we observed one teacher at each grade level (grades one through five); at each of the three high schools, we observed teachers in two ninth- and two tenth-grade literacy courses (two-hour block classes initially called Genre Studies). Additional observations were conducted in high school math, science, history, auto shop, and Spanish classes when the ILs visited them during school site walk-throughs (the ILs were looking for signs that the principles of literacy instruction had transferred to these courses). As a group, the teachers we observed taught in bilingual as well as English-only classrooms, and they had a wide range of experience, training, and attitudes toward the reform effort. We conducted a minimum of three rounds of observations each year in each classroom (amounting to approximately 160 days of classroom observations). Observers kept in mind a set of questions to guide them in identifying both the quality of the observed interactions and their congruence with district guidelines. After their visits to classrooms, the researchers wrote summaries of their observations. At the end of each semester, the researchers compiled their field notes into a summary of classroom life.

Each classroom observation focused on an entire literacy lesson. These intensive samples enabled us to investigate deeply the content of literacy instruction and the process and conditions of learning. We complemented our classroom observations with teacher interviews, conducted both before and after the literacy lessons we watched them teach. We looked at how the literacy reform was enacted and evaluated the challenges teachers faced in implementing the reform. Findings from our observations of classroom interaction and interviews with classroom teachers are reported in Chapter 5.

Teachers and Principals Interacting about Instruction

In the second layer of a community of learners are principals and teachers interacting about the instruction that occurs in classrooms. The district provided a wide range of professional-development opportunities to assist principals in supporting teachers in their efforts to improve instruction. At each of our six school sites, we attended the staff development sessions given by the principals for all faculty members, we attended events led by peer coaches and district-hired consultants, and we attended professional-development sessions organized for peer coaches. At the elementary school level, these included faculty meetings, grade-level meetings, and after-school workshops. At the high school level, we attended general faculty meetings as well as department-level meetings and specific training events for genre studies teachers. Observations also included various professional-development days sponsored by the district. These events offered instruction on such topics as literacy minilessons and the units of study for high school teachers. Together, these meetings and events resulted in approximately fifty-five observations.

We also attended district-sponsored summer staff development sessions, offered for both elementary and secondary teachers during the summers of our study. The activities included workshops aimed at strengthening teachers' knowledge of and skill at implementing the Balanced Literacy framework. The sessions covered all grade levels and were designed for teachers of early emergent, emergent, early fluent, and fluent readers.

Being present at these many and varied activities gave us a broader picture of the district's efforts to achieve consistency across schools and gave us more opportunities to learn how district guidelines were being transformed. Observing professional-development events made clear to us what was being taught and how it was being assimilated by teachers, as mediated through their school principals. To triangulate these understandings, we also interviewed the school-based professional developers and district-hired professional-development consultants who worked with teachers. Finally, as noted earlier, we deepened our knowledge of the complexity of the teaching and learning that occurred in the interaction between principals and teachers by launching a collaborative research project with one of the elementary principals and her IL.

Instructional Leaders and Principals Interacting about Leadership and Instruction

In the third layer of a nested community of learners are interactions between ILs and principals regarding leadership and instruction. ILs provided a wide range of professional-development activities for principals, including visits to other similar schools, principal support groups, mentor principals–new principals interaction, principal conferences, and walk-throughs (see Chapters 4, 6, and 7 for details). The most salient of these activities were the monthly principals' conferences and walk-throughs that principals conducted with their ILs.

We attended thirty-three full-day and six half-day principals' conferences and participated in twenty-five site walk-throughs. The principal conferences gave us the opportunity to observe the agenda-setting practices of Superintendent Alan Bersin and Chancellor Anthony Alvarado and provided a better sense of how the district's eleven ILs transferred those ideas to 170 principals. We audiotaped fifteen of the opening speeches Bersin and Alvarado gave at the full-day principals' conferences. Following these often passionate opening addresses, the ILs met with the principals who were part of their learning communities. We attended these breakout sessions and recorded our observations in field notes (we further discuss breakout sessions in Chapter 7).

The general instruction provided by district leaders and ILs to principals during principals' conferences was reinforced and intensified during half-day walk-throughs in which an IL accompanied a principal on visits to the school's classrooms and then met with the principal to discuss needed improvements and strategies for attaining them (see Chapter 7 for details).

We audiotaped these conferences between ILs and principals and took field notes during the walk-throughs.

After we obtained a general understanding of the structure and function of walk-throughs, we selected three for more intense analysis. We limited the in-depth analysis to elementary school walk-throughs to keep the context similar; high schools have unique characteristics that would significantly complicate comparisons. We reviewed and analyzed data from the walk-through field note transcriptions for the three schools. We then selected two to three segments depicting scenarios with a substantive discussion about leadership and instruction—the chief concerns of IL–principal interactions. The six participants in this portion of our study were invited to review the transcription segments before we conducted formal interviews with them. We organized interview questions around the general nature of walk-throughs but also included specific questions that related to the individual scenarios. Interviews with each participant lasted approximately one to two hours and were conducted jointly by Hubbard and Stein.

Because ILs were learning the reform along with the principals they were charged to teach, we attended professional-development events for the ILs. These were conducted by Elaine Fink, executive director of the Executive Leadership Development Academy based at the University of San Diego. SDCS contracted with this academy to teach leadership skills to prospective leaders within the district, using an intensive apprenticeship model. These events included planning sessions to help ILs prepare for the principals' conferences and debriefing sessions after the principals' conferences to critically evaluate the ILs' performance and construct plans for improvement. We attended twelve planning sessions and eight debriefing sessions from January 2002 to June 2002. These events were audiotaped and transcribed verbatim.

In addition to observing this wide range of professional-development events, we conducted an in-depth analysis of videotape from three linked planning sessions, principals' conferences, and debriefing sessions of the professional-development events we had recorded during the 2001–2002 school year. This video footage of interactions between ILs and principals contained information on teaching and learning that enabled us to gauge how learning traversed instructional corridors. Transcripts of the interactions were coded using ATLAS.ti software, a grounded theory program. Members of our research team cross-checked the transcriptions for reliability of codes and themes.

We created another data source by combining observational data from site walk-throughs with responses to questions we posed to ILs and principals in interviews. At least once a year, we conducted interviews with the four ILs and each of the principals responsible for the six schools in our sample. Last, we drew on observations of some ILs and principals who were not part of our sample corridors. Because a trusting relationship grew between us and the ILs who were part of our study, we were invited to observe a wide range of activities involving other ILs and the principals in their learning communities. Most notably, we attended meetings with principals of the lowest performing elementary schools (called "focus schools") and other specially designated professional-development events arranged for various subsets of principals (e.g., cross-site visitations, book clubs, study group sessions, and meetings for mentor principals). In Chapter 7 we report our analysis of the intersection encounters between ILs and principals during principals' conferences and walk-throughs, supplemented with information gleaned when we attended special instruction events with ILs.

District Leaders and Community Members Interacting about the Reform

In the outermost layers of our representation of the SDCS community of learners are interactions between the district leaders and their constituents. Some of these constituents, such as teachers, principals, and ILs, reside within the district. Others, such as the teachers' union (SDEA), parent groups (e.g., English Learners Advisory Committee, and District English Learners Advisory Committee), and the Business Roundtable for Education, reside in the surrounding community. Still others, such as the California state government and granting agencies (e.g., the Gates Foundation and the Carnegie Corporation), reside some distance from the district and yet exert considerable influence over local actions.

We used an eclectic array of data-gathering procedures for this portion of the study. We added an analysis of official documents (school board reports, e-mails, letters) and newspaper articles to our observation and interview protocols. We observed school board meetings (or watched videotapes of them) and community and parent group meetings in low-income and well-to-do neighborhoods. We participated in and observed at meetings of the Business Roundtable of Education, the California state legislature, and gatherings of researchers assembled by the Hewlett Foundation.[5] We interviewed Mark Knapp, SDEA president; the union representatives at our six school sites; the leadership of the Latino Coalition, a citizens' group that advocated on behalf of English language learners; and Superintendent Bersin and Chancellor Alvarado. As we report in Chapter 8, the interactions among district leaders and constituents often involved conflict. Efforts to resolve these conflicts led to significant changes in the scope and

Table 2.3. The Number and Types of Observations[6]

Event	Sites	Participants	Number of Observations	Reported In
Classroom lessons	Six schools	Teachers and students	160	Chapter 5
Staff development sessions	Six schools	Principals and teachers	55	Chapter 6
Collaborative project	One school	Researcher, principal, and IL	2	Chapter 6
Principals' conferences	Throughout the district	District leaders, ILs, and principals	33	Chapter 7
Walk-throughs	Six schools	ILs, principals, teachers, and researchers	25	Chapter 7
Professional development for ILs	District office	All ILs	20	Chapter 7
Community interactions	Schools, district office, state offices, community group, offices	District and community members	45	Chapters 8 and 9

direction of the theory of action guiding reform in San Diego. We report on the subsequent reform changes in Chapter 9.

Table 2.3 summarizes the data types and number of observations and participants and indicates which chapters in the book draw on these data.

Summary

Our data collection efforts worked synergistically to give us an in-depth and comprehensive understanding of the SDCS reform. Consistent with our version of design research we have described in this chapter, we were intimately involved in studying the reform and in recommending revisions to it, challenging its problematic aspects, and contributing to the many efforts to improve the education of all students.

In Chapter 3, we explain that the San Diego reform originated in New York City and describe the contextual features that differed between New York and San Diego.

CHAPTER 3

History of Reform in New York City's Community School District #2

I don't think this is an issue of emulation. Every reform has to be built in the soil of its city.

—Anthony Alvarado (quoted in Magee, 1998)

Rampant speculation accompanied the news that Anthony Alvarado was leaving the superintendency of New York City's Community School District #2 to join the leadership team of the San Diego City Schools (SDCS). San Diego journalists, educators, and business leaders wondered whether Alvarado would try to install in San Diego the same reform strategies that had earned him such success in New York. Alvarado quickly reassured San Diegans (in the statement quoted above) that the reforms under his leadership would be developed with San Diego and its needs in mind.

If for no other reason, differences in demographics and size between the two districts would have dictated a fresh approach in San Diego. With 140,743 students in 1999–2000, San Diego was approximately six times larger than District #2 (which had 23,009 students that same year). Although the percentage of low-income students (measured by number of students eligible for free or reduced-price lunch) was comparable across the two districts, as was the percentage of Caucasian and African American students, San Diego had significantly more Hispanic students (20.3% in District #2, 37.2% in San Diego) whereas District #2 had significantly more Asian American students (34.7% in District #2; 9.1% in San Diego). Furthermore, the overall percentage of students classified as English-language learners in San Diego was twice the percentage in New York (28% in San Diego, 13.9% in District #2).[1] Finally, San Diego was a K–12 district with more than 150 schools, whereas District #2 was a K–8 district composed of 45 schools.[2]

Of course, Alvarado was not unaware of these differences, but his sensibilities about educational reform were deeply informed by his tenure as superintendent of District #2. He came to San Diego with several firm convictions. He believed that *teaching and learning must drive reform*. In our initial interview with him in his new role as chancellor of instruction, Alvarado (2001) noted, "There is no doubt that I've internalized as a human being the idea that teaching and learning must drive the system." He believed that effective teaching *can be learned* by the adults in the system—that it is not a mysterious ability that one either has or does not have. He believed that *teachers' learning must occur on a continuous and public basis, within a community of learners led by the principal*. Finally, Alvarado believed that reform—from the very start—should be expected to *penetrate all schools and classrooms* across the district. Staggered implementation or demonstration schools were counterproductive, he argued, because such reforms often failed to take hold and spread to the remaining schools and classrooms.

These beliefs provided the skeletal frame on which the reforms in San Diego were assembled. Because their efficacy had already been demonstrated by Alvarado's successes in District #2, and because they appeared to be, on the whole, quite reasonable, few observers—at least initially—questioned their applicability to San Diego. This chapter notes the positive role that many of these beliefs did indeed play in the San Diego reform. However, it also identifies ways in which the New York success story was an incomplete and sometimes imperfect guide to reform in San Diego.

The chapter is divided into three sections. First, to help readers envision the end-state Alvarado anticipated for the SDCS, we describe a typical morning in a typical District #2 classroom circa 1998, when Alvarado was just beginning his new position in the SDCS. We also review the typical training and socializing experiences of a hypothetical teacher new to District #2. Then we describe the ways in which Alvarado rolled out the reform in San Diego, including the manner in which he drew on the resources of District #2. In the final section, we highlight differences between the two districts that appeared to contribute to the difficulties of guiding the San Diego reform by the beacon of District #2.

A Picture of the District That Alvarado Left Behind

Shortly after Alvarado became superintendent of District #2 in July 1987, the improvement of literacy instruction became the centerpiece of his reform efforts there. After two years of internal study and consultation with external literacy experts, Alvarado and his staff chose and adopted an instructional model for the entire district, called Balanced Literacy (Fountas & Pinnell, 1995; 2001; New Zealand Ministry of Education, 1996). Balanced Literacy is a theory-driven, literature-based program that assists children who are learning to read by first assessing their current level of comprehension and then providing texts and instructional supports geared to that level (see Chapter 4 for details).

Starting in 1996, Mary Kay Stein joined Lauren Resnick and Richard Elmore in a multiyear study of the organization and practices of district and school leaders, staff developers, and teachers in Community School District #2 (Resnick, Elmore, & Alvarado, 1996). At that point, the Balanced Literacy initiative had been in effect for more than five years; the practices, tools, and ideas that supported it were quite mature, and a shared language centered on the ideas and practices of Balanced Literacy permeated the district (Elmore & Burney, 1999). The array of support and the resultant shared language led to instructional practices across the district that were remarkably consistent with one another and aligned with key features of the Balanced Literacy program; moreover, implementation of the Balanced Literacy program was associated with significant gains in student achievement (D'Amico, Harwell, Stein, & van den Heuvel, 2001; Harwell, D'Amico, Stein, & Gatti, 2000; Stein, D'Amico, & Israel, 1999; Stein, Harwell, & D'Amico, 1999).[3]

When Alvarado departed in 1998, Community School District #2 was a mature, well-functioning organization. Student performance, as measured relative to other community school districts in New York City and by the movement of students out of the bottom quartile on citywide reading and mathematics assessments, was good and improving;[4] experienced principals, most of whom had been hired and coached by Alvarado's team, composed the leadership force; and the teaching force was enthusiastic and competent.

To provide a sense of day-to-day life in District #2, we present two scenarios—one that describes a typical District #2 classroom and one that describes what it was like to be a new teacher in the district. Then we examine two key aspects of District #2's systemic reform: the role played by the Balanced Literacy program as the districtwide intervention and the ongoing preparation of principals.

A Typical Classroom

The room arrangement and furnishings are the first things a visitor to a District #2 classroom notices. In addition to the students' desks, usually arranged in groups of four or five, there is an inviting, homey-looking section of the room demarcated by a bright rug and a rocking chair. The students gather here for instruction and to listen to stories their teacher reads aloud. All over the classroom, student work is prominently displayed—hung not just on the walls but also from clotheslines strung across the room. There are learning centers scattered throughout the room and individual cubbies where the children store their classroom materials.

The classroom's extensive library is housed in bookcases filled with children's literature and organized in a child-friendly, easy-to-access manner. At various points during the day, children head to this section of the classroom to return one book and select another. Each student has his or her own packet of "current reading," containing books selected (by the teacher or—in later grades—by the students) to match his or her reading level and specific interests. Observing a classroom at the very beginning of the morning gives a visitor a strong sense of how important reading is to the students. They are scattered about the room, snuggled into their favorite corners, chairs, or section of the couch, reading silently, deeply engrossed. As the children read, the teacher circulates, clipboard in hand, stopping to engage individual children in discussions about their reading (five to ten minutes per child) and briefly recording assessments of their progress.

When the more active segment of the morning begins, the children gather on the rug to review the day's schedule. Most mornings include shared reading, guided reading, writing, and (sometimes) read alouds—all components of the Balanced Literacy program. For shared reading, the children remain seated on the rug, and they all read in unison from the same "Big Book" (a two-foot-high book with pictures and lettering large enough for all children to see). The teacher guides the lesson toward that morning's particular (preselected) goal (e.g., phrasing, how to read quotations). What is most noticeable is the students' level of engagement: nearly everyone keeps their eyes on the book and all mouths move in unison.

Often, guided reading follows immediately after shared reading. During this segment, the teacher works intensively with one or two small groups of children while the other students either read silently in their seats or work at one of the classroom's learning centers. All students in the guided reading group read from individual copies of the same book—usually a trade book—while the teacher guides them in some aspect of skill development. The children have been purposefully grouped to work on the same reading skill, one that earlier diagnoses have determined they all need help with.

Read alouds, a visitor can see immediately, are eagerly anticipated. The teacher sits in the rocking chair and the students gather on the rug in front of her.[5] Often, she begins by asking questions to remind students where they had left off the previous day. As the teacher begins to read, the students follow her words carefully. They don't seem to mind when, from time to time, she stops to ask them to explain what is going on or to check their understanding of a word. It is clear how much the children value reading, whether they are perusing a book on their own, reading with others, or being read to.

It is not unusual for literacy—which includes writing as well as reading— to take the lion's share of instructional time before the lunch hour. Often, long-term projects, such as a poetry forum, a visit from a well-known children's author, or a publishing party (a celebration attended by parents, school administrators, and other adults during which student-produced books are displayed) are in evidence as well. What is most noticeable, however, is that the students remain engaged and go about their work purposefully.

Nearly as striking is how novel and demanding the instruction in this classroom is of a teacher's skill, creativity, and commitment. Despite the specifications embedded in the Balanced Literacy program, there is a lot of room for teacher interpretation. Selection of texts and plans for the day's teaching points are based on teacher assessments of student needs and thus cannot be easily specified in a programmatic way. The forms of instruction used in District #2 classrooms require teachers not only to continually revisit their plans for meeting students' current learning needs but also to respond dynamically to those needs as they become evident.

Most teachers do not arrive on the district's doorstep ready to practice such a challenging form of instruction. Thus, the Resnick, Elmore, and Stein study of District #2 paid close attention to the supports provided to teachers to help them learn how to implement the Balanced Literacy program. In the next section, we describe some aspects of the learning and development a new teacher in District #2 would experience during her or his first year on the job. The reader is reminded that the following scenario, similar to the classroom description above, is from the late-nineties, after Balanced Literacy had been around for a decade.

A New Teacher Enters the District

Typically, a new teacher finds herself in a school where the Balanced Literacy program is already being enacted with fair to high degrees of fidelity. Her principal, most likely an advocate of the Balanced Literacy approach, has been purposefully selected—primarily because of her or his effective teaching practices or skills in conducting staff development with teachers. Her neighbors—teacher colleagues on either side of her classroom and across the hall—are teachers who have been implementing the Balanced Literacy model for several years.

Before the school year starts, the new teacher's colleagues help her set up her classroom so that it supports the style of teaching she is expected to use. The teachers throughout the building donate books to help her begin to amass a classroom library of children's books appropriate to the needs of her students. Within the first months of her employment, she attends, at her principal's request, several district-sponsored workshops on the Balanced Literacy model. Along with other new teachers in the district, she learns about the theory of how children learn to read that underpins the district's instructional model and, relatedly, she learns why it is important to provide students with reading challenges geared to their level.

Within the first few months of her employment, district leaders observe this teacher during a school walk-through. On the basis of their assessment of her needs, she is provided with the opportunity to visit the classrooms of teachers—outside her building—who are particularly effective implementers of those components of the model she is finding most troublesome. The teachers whose practice she observes are carefully selected to ensure that they are teaching students similar to hers and that they exhibit practices from which she can learn. A staff developer accompanies the new teacher during these visits to help her understand the "thinking behind the practice," not simply the visible aspects of the practice. Finally, within the first few years of her employment, she will be given the opportunity to participate in the Professional-Development Lab, a three-week residency with an expert teacher, which will further enhance her professional growth.

District leaders do not expect new teachers to become proficient in the Balanced Literacy model immediately. They anticipate that novices will struggle at first and are likely to implement the model mechanically. But district leaders also expect that gradually, with assistance geared to the newcomers' level of expertise and with expectations and support from peers and principals, new teachers will become proficient at teaching literacy and that their growing strength will be evident in their practice and in data on student learning in the classroom. (For a detailed discussion of teacher learning in District #2, see Stein and D'Amico, [2002b].)

The Role of the Balanced Literacy Program

The coherence and focus that characterized both classroom lessons and teacher learning opportunities by the mid- to late-nineties in District #2 would have been impossible without districtwide buy-in to a common set of values and beliefs about how children learn to read. In this regard, the Balanced Literacy program can be viewed as the glue that held District #2 together. Adopted districtwide in 1989, Balanced Literacy weathered the comings and goings of many educational trends and fads. Its long life can be attributed to two facts: (1) the dynamic nature of the program—meaning that the program remained open to modifications based on careful observations of its strengths and weaknesses—and (2) its method of implementation—meaning that leaders did not impose Balanced Literacy in a rigid manner but rather used it as a flexible tool for improving and sustaining good literacy instruction. We discuss separately each of these attributes next.

The Dynamic Nature of the Balanced Literacy Program

During the multiyear Resnick et al. (1996; Resnick & Fink, 2001) study of District #2, the Balanced Literacy program went through several iterations and refinements. For example, based on principals', staff developers', and teachers' recognition that some children were not learning to read quickly enough, district leaders augmented the Balanced Literacy program with a daily word study component that focused on letter-sound correspondence (see Stein, D'Amico, & Israel, 1999). Most modifications to the program began just the way the word study addition did—they were initiated by educators in the field. Because teachers, staff developers, and principals spent the most time in close-hand observations of children as they were learning to read, they could pinpoint problems readily and propose solutions. These proposals were discussed at principals' and staff developers' meetings, often a task force was appointed to further investigate the need for the changes, and, if deemed warranted, the changes were made in a shared, public manner. This procedure ensured the instructional constancy the district valued. It also showed the respect that leadership had for practitioners' expertise, the district leaders' awareness that changes might be necessary, and its willingness to approve modifications when conditions called for them. The overriding point is that in District #2, the shape and form of the Balanced Literacy program was negotiated over time, not proclaimed from above.

*Flexibility Surrounding the Implementation of the Balanced
Literacy Program*

"Researchers on the HPLC project" observed district leaders talking comfortably and confidently about schools in which the principal had tailored the Balanced Literacy program to his or her own school's needs (Resnick et al., 1996; Resnick & Fink, 2001) . In these cases, the principals had not altered any of the underlying principles of the Balanced Literacy framework, but they had made other modifications, such as having their teachers use a different combination or pacing of teaching strategies. District leaders' focus appeared to be on whether individual schools and teachers implemented a form of literacy instruction that was coherent with the *underlying goals and purposes* of the Balanced Literacy program, not the overt specifications of the program. This flexibility, in addition to allowing teachers and schools to tailor the program to meet students' specific needs, also permitted experimentation with new and promising strategies.

Managing this degree of flexibility might have proved overwhelming if all teachers had been encouraged to make wide interpretations of the program. Instead, principals encouraged their teachers to experiment with innovative practices based on the extent to which they perceived the teachers and students as capable of effectively teaching and learning literacy using alternate strategies. District #2 leaders worried most about the students and teachers in the schools that were designated "focused literacy" schools. The challenges involved in teaching at-risk students made it difficult for such schools to attract and retain strong teachers. Many of the focused literacy schools also had undergone changes of leadership, and the new principals' endeavors to repair previous poor staffing choices had led to significant numbers of new and inexperienced teachers. These principals faced the formidable task of improving literacy among a challenging group of students with a teaching staff that needed a lot of support. These circumstances led District #2 leadership to strongly encourage principals to insist that their staffs closely follow the specifications of the Balanced Literacy program:

> In those [focused literacy] schools we really expect that the structure is adhered to because ... number one, it's good for the kids. Number two, it supports the learning of the teachers and it really gives them a solid base and foundation in which to know that they are doing a good job until they gain enough experience and enough strategies and enough of a repertoire where they can then flex. Until that occurs, it's very important that those kids get that solid rigorous instruction because they are starting three steps

behind to begin with and you can't afford to let them fall five steps
behind. (Johnstone, 1998)

Thus, the Balanced Literacy program was not viewed as a rigid set of
specifications applied uniformly across all situations. Instead, District #2
administrators used it as a reference point for making decisions about the
forms of instruction best suited to local conditions.

Ongoing Training of Principals

The room for flexibility described previously illustrates the importance of
developing principals as strong instructional leaders. Principals must know
the needs of their student body, along with the strengths and weaknesses
of each and every teacher in their school. In this way, they can make decisions regarding how flexible they can be with respect to implementation of
the Balanced Literacy program.

The socialization of new principals was not left to chance. New
principals were systematically brought into the community of District
#2 principals—a community that valued similar outcomes for children
and believed in a particular set of instructional practices that would
achieve those outcomes. Over time, the new principals were socialized
into this community through monthly principal meetings, a mentoring
program, principal support groups, and, perhaps most important, the
walk-through.

At least twice per year, a representative from district leadership (either
the superintendent or deputy superintendent) and the director of the staff
development together visited each school in the district. The half-day visit
began with a conversation with the principal during which each teacher's
practice, including any changes since the last visit, was discussed. Then
the threesome would visit each classroom, noting the kind and quality of
literacy instruction and student learning. Afterward, they returned to the
principal's office, debriefed the observations, and made plans for actions
to be taken before the next visit. Although the walk-through can easily
be interpreted as a one-way "monitoring" visit (i.e., is Balanced Literacy
being implemented according to district specifications?), our observations
and conversations with teachers, principals, and district leaders convinced
us otherwise. Although unapologetically evaluative in nature (principals and teachers knew they were being held accountable for continuous
improvement), the walk-through also represented an opportunity for
mutual engagement and meaning-making, that is, an occasion during
which learning occurred within and between district leaders, principals,
and teachers.

The official purpose of the walk-throughs was to help principals learn how to assist their teachers' learning of the instructional practices associated with the Balanced Literacy framework (Resnick & Fink, 2001). However, this goal was carried out to meet the specific needs of teachers and children in the particular schools being visited. Efforts were made to understand the context of the particular school (i.e., the developmental level of teachers, the organization of various microcommunities of practice within the school, and the background and needs of the students) and to negotiate the meaning of Balanced Literacy within that context. In this way, district leadership acknowledged that the enactment of district policy must move beyond literal compliance. That is, local communities must, in the end, take responsibility for owning and negotiating the meaning of Balanced Literacy within their school.

These scenarios and descriptions provide insight into the "vision of the possible" that Alvarado brought with him from New York City to San Diego. They—along with the research on which they are based—provide an existence proof that an urban district can effectively educate children to high levels, that principals can design their buildings as continuous learning environments for adults, and that system leaders can provide the facilitating conditions to make this all happen. As an existence proof, District #2 has inspired many districts, not just San Diego. San Diego, however, was arguably in the best position to succeed because the author of the vision—Alvarado—was present to steer the reform in the new setting.

The question to be asked, however, is, How did District #2 get to be that way? Although there can be no doubt that Alvarado, his deputy, and the director of professional development were the visionaries and designers of District #2, details regarding the developmental approach used to *transform* this once low-performing district into a high-performing, continuous learning organization are scant. As noted earlier, the research team arrived on the scene after District #2 was already operating as a mature, well-functioning district. The few details that are known about the early days of the reform in New York City include the fact that, as noted earlier, the Balanced Literacy program was selected after years of internal study and consultation. According to Alvarado and Fink (2000), after Alvarado's top leadership team decided that literacy was the number-one problem confronting the district, they searched for and obtained the services of arguably the best leaders in the field of early reading, including both American leaders and a group of experts from New Zealand and Australia. Months were spent consulting with these experts; selected principals participated in these consultations alongside district leaders.

Read alouds were the first new reading activity that was adopted. Once most teachers and principals were comfortable with the read alouds, other components of the Balanced Literacy program were slowly added. Along the way, modifications were frequently made, based on feedback from principals and teachers. The literacy experts worked side by side with school personnel, helping them to learn the underlying principles of the program, as well as the practicalities of implementation. As such, the rollout of Balanced Literacy in New York was relatively slow paced, it paid attention to the day-to-day needs of teachers and principals, and it benefited greatly from the services of these external experts.

Despite the slow, careful rollout of the program, the expectation was—from the beginning—that all schools and classrooms would leave their basal reading programs behind and implement the Balanced Literacy program. Monthly principal meetings—attended by all principals—covered the theory and the nuts and bolts of the program. Often these meetings were held in schools so that principals could see how the program was being implemented in sites other than their own. New teachers and principals were hired with the explicit expectation that they would get behind the Balanced Literacy program full force. Teachers and principals who resisted the program were urged to learn more about it; resistors were eventually eased out. Although many of these teachers and principals were older and nearing retirement, others were younger but not willing to adopt the district's reform. Overtime, then, District #2 became a Balanced Literacy district. Although district leaders were unrelenting in their expectations that all children should learn to read using the Balanced Literacy model, they were collaborative in their design of that model, slow in the rollout of its implementation, and flexible in the manner in which they held individual schools accountable for its enactment.

In our final interview with Alvarado (2003) as Superintendent of District #2, he stated that his capacity to initiate reform, including new, tougher personnel practices, did not go unchallenged, especially at the beginning of his superintendency. He recalled how, in the early years, he had to learn to deal with school board members who opposed many of his initiatives as well as massive citywide budget cuts. And, although he had a strong relationship with the leadership of the teachers' union, school-level chapter leaders "ruled with an iron fist." Nevertheless, over time, as the power of school boards was curtailed by legislation and as increasing numbers of like-minded teachers and principals were hired, Alvarado's vision prevailed.

How Were the Reforms Rolled Out in San Diego?

Because of the good results that had been obtained with Balanced Literacy in New York City, Alvarado selected Balanced Literacy as the literacy program for the SDCS. As in District #2, all SDCS schools and all classrooms were expected to implement the Balanced Literacy program. Also similar to the District #2 start-up, initially teachers were expected to implement some but not all components of Balanced Literacy. SDCS teachers began with read alouds and independent reading the first year and then added guided reading and shared reading the second year. Unlike in District #2, however, the San Diego reform was not "organically" developed but rather was presented to educators more or less as a finished product to be implemented.

Aware of the importance of principal leadership and of the imperative that top district leadership support principals, San Diego leaders designed an infrastructure for principal training similar to that which existed in District #2. The SDCS district was divided into seven learning communities, each one approximately the size of District #2, and one instructional leader (IL) was selected to lead each learning community. The ILs were to play a role similar to that provided by District #2's deputy superintendent Elaine Fink—namely, training, supporting, and supervising principals.

Among the new chancellor of instruction's first undertakings was to arrange for Balanced Literacy training for the ILs so that they, in turn, could train the principals in their respective learning communities. It would be up to the principals and staff developers to train the teachers at each school site. The manual that accompanied IL training during the first summer of Alvarado's tenure (*Principals' Instructional Conferences: Training Materials;* SDCS, 1998–1999) is one index of the enormity of the task top leadership faced and the time pressures they were under. The manual contains a high degree of specificity and scaffolding for the ILs. In fact, the first three principals' conferences the ILs were responsible for conducting (in August, October, and November 1998) were completely scripted. The ILs' manual included copies of all of the overhead transparencies they would need, instructions of what to say as they displayed each transparency, and copies of all of the handouts they were to distribute. Interestingly, the manual was written by District #2 staff.

In sum, during the early phase of the reform, San Diego leaders set about trying to educate literally thousands of adults (ILs, principals, staff developers, and teachers) in the Balanced Literacy program. As noted earlier, the program is challenging to implement and demands deep, ongoing professional development combined with on-the-job learning that is scaffolded by more experienced colleagues. San Diego's top leadership, under intense time pressure, tried to find a way around this long-term strategy of first developing experts and then having those experts train others. From the very beginning, Alvarado turned to his colleagues in New York for help. Professionals from District #2 provided assistance to San Diego educators in three ways: by hosting visits of principals and ILs in New York, working with these educators in their San Diego schools, and relocating to San Diego to join the SDCS workforce. We describe each form of assistance next.

Visits to District #2

Early in the his tenure at San Diego, Alvarado arranged for the ILs to visit District #2 to view Balanced Literacy classrooms in motion and to meet and talk with principals. On several occasions thereafter, additional educators from San Diego were exposed to District #2 through visits to the district in New York City. A typical itinerary included visits to schools and classrooms, discussions with principals and staff developers, and (sometimes) observations of principals' conferences. One San Diego principal summed up how her visit to District #2 had affected her:

> I really understood then. Up until that time, I think we were getting a picture of it, but it wasn't until I was actually there and going to these schools and taking these pictures [she is displaying photographs that she took of classrooms, hallways, and libraries]. This is what "print-rich" means. And the "libraries." Before, we didn't have any model to really look at. And for me, I have to see it.
>
> These are the things that I came back with. When I did a presentation to the other principals, I stressed the culture of learning, the passions that we saw, the urgency, the engagement of the students and staff, the studying that they did together, all the structures they had in place, all the communication that was very evident—books, books, books and a print rich environment. (Cavanaugh, 2001: 7)

As revealed by this quote, the opportunity to observe classrooms and schools firsthand in New York City was exceedingly important for San Diego professionals. It allowed them to apprehend the end-state toward which they were aiming—and it provided hard evidence that it was indeed possible to achieve this end-state. Others had done it, and so too could San Diegans.

Bringing District #2 Educators to San Diego

In addition to sending San Diego educators to observe in New York, San Diego leaders brought District #2 professionals to San Diego to demonstrate and talk about their practice. For example, three District #2 principals visited San Diego during summer 2001 and led a two-day seminar for San Diego principals. Principals were coached on how to write a work plan (see chapter 6) that would help them take effective action to improve performance at their schools. Principals also learned how to implement a monitoring system for student achievement, understand content using "accountable talk" and meaning-making strategies, and lead and support professional development (see Chapters 5 and 6).

District #2 teachers performed demonstration lessons for San Diego principals as well. For example, in spring 2002 there was a three-day session with a principal, a staff developer, and two teachers, one in literacy and one in mathematics, from District #2. The teachers conducted lessons for area high school students while a group of San Diego principals and teachers observed. After the lessons, the District #2 visitors conferred with the San Diego observers, identifying and discussing the strategies they had used in the lessons to enhance teaching and learning. The teachers also accompanied San Diego principals on walk-throughs of their classrooms, commenting on ways to improve instruction. (See Chapters 6 and 7 for a discussion of SDCS walk-throughs.) In April 2002, District #2 principals and an administrator led the San Diego principals' conference.

For San Diegans, the "visions of the possible" that resulted from the visits they made to New York and the visits District #2 personnel made to San Diego were an important means of reinforcing commitment to the reform in the beginning. Also important were the individuals Alvarado hired from New York to work in San Diego.

District #2 Educators Hired in San Diego

Perhaps the most significant new hire (after Alvarado) was District #2 former deputy superintendent Elaine Fink. Fink, who arrived in 1999, had two roles in San Diego: director of the Educational Leadership Development Academy and primary provider of professional development for the district's ILs (see Chapter 7 for details on Fink's work in San Diego).[6] A second important individual hired from District #2 was Laura Turner, who joined the SDCS district in 2001 as its first nonlocal (i.e., not promoted from within) IL. Turner had been a distinguished teacher, staff developer, and principal in District #2; she was highly respected for her expertise in elementary literacy instruction. In San Diego, Turner was charged with overseeing the reform in the struggling schools.

San Diego also contracted the services of two professional consultants—Albert Jensen and Sarah Thompson—who were extremely influential in District #2. Both spent large amounts of time in San Diego attending to the rollout of the Balanced Literacy program. They worked primarily with staff developers. Finally, there were two individuals who straddled work in the two cities: Carol Fulton, an expert teacher who demonstrated lessons in San Diego and worked with principals and elementary school staffs to improve instruction and build learning communities, and Pamela Zimmerman, a literacy expert who was hired to work in San Diego.

In some ways, the recruits from District #2 acted as San Diego's external experts, meeting many of the same kinds of needs as the literacy experts from New Zealand and Australia had for District #2. In this and other ways, such as the emphasis on districtwide implementation, the principals' training conferences, and the role of the ILs, the San Diego reforms can be viewed as being modeled on District #2—but only to a degree. In San Diego, the timing was quicker, the challenge of training was greater, and the external pressures were different. In the final section, we draw attention to three major differences between the two districts that led to differences in reform practices and, ultimately, to differences in outcomes as well.

Consequential Differences between San Diego and District #2
Size and Pacing

To get ambitious reforms like Balanced Literacy off the ground quickly, high-capacity individuals are needed to model good practice at every layer of the system, to assist the learning of others, and to hold others accountable for learning the new practices. Moreover, these individuals must be present in sufficient numbers to influence the on-the-ground, face-to-face learning of thousands of teachers and hundreds of principals.

San Diego's size—the district is six times larger than District #2—made it especially difficult to find and train sufficient numbers of high-capacity individuals. Consequentially, at the outset of the reform, San Diego had inexperienced principals monitoring instruction, novice staff developers training teachers, and ILs who were only steps ahead of the principals they were instructing.

With complex reforms such as Balanced Literacy, the effects of limited capacity are magnified. The program's underlying theory sees learning as rooted in social interaction. Thus, a shortage of *exemplary* models of leadership and instructional practice is extremely detrimental. The lack of *variation* in expertise is also problematic. In District #2, leaders had an array of models to select from when building a school-visit experience for struggling teachers. Great care was taken in matching individuals, so that the learner was exposed to exactly what was needed at that particular point in his or her development (see Stein & D'Amico, 2002a; 2002b). In San Diego, there were not only fewer but also less varied models to choose from when arranging learning-oriented visits to other schools.

San Diego's limited capacity also meant that communities of reform practice into which teachers—and others—could be socialized were virtually nonexistent. One of the biggest advantages in District #2 was the capacity at the school site to continue supporting teacher learning after teachers had completed the more formal, workshop-based training the district provided (see the previous section "A New Teacher Enters the District"). In San Diego, formal, district-based training was available, but, after returning to their schools, teachers often did not find a community that uniformly valued or reinforced the transfer of their newly learned skills into practice. Missing were the stories of old-timers who had traveled similar paths as they grappled with learning the Balanced Literacy program. Missing were the voices of other teachers who also had felt overwhelmed at first but who had gradually learned, with patience and perseverance, to implement the program. Instead, San Diego teachers were apt to return to a principal and teacher colleagues who were also newly learning the reform. Peers who were capable of supporting their learning were not available, and their principal was likely to reinforce superficial aspects of compliance instead of imparting a deeper understanding of the reform and how it could assist student learning.

These challenges were compounded by the fast pace by which the San Diego reforms were implemented. The training of ILs and principals was hurried and not as deep or theory based as it might otherwise have been. The need for speed also meant that San Diego educators were asked to suspend doubt and to implement the program based solely on assurances that it would work. The hope was that teachers would implement the program, begin to see results, and then become enthusiastic converts to the program. The quick pace, however, does not square with what we know about how individuals learn complex skills. A fast-paced environment that also includes high expectations and accountability pressures is not conducive to deep learning. Without time to internalize the deeper aspects of reform, individuals will quickly adopt its superficial features (e.g., student work hung up around the room, a posted daily agenda) to avoid sanction. This superficiality is particularly likely, and particularly dangerous, in a reform that relies heavily on administrative personnel who combine limited experience and hurried training with full authority to evaluate instructional practice.

Finally, San Diego's large size and the pace of the reform combined to hinder the building of deep relationships. Learning a complex new form of classroom practice requires hard work, risk taking, and trust on the part of all involved. Teachers and others are more willing to suspend doubts and work hard if they know and have faith in the individuals who are leading them. Logic suggests that it is more difficult for district leaders to develop trusting, respecting relationships in a large district. In District #2, the superintendent and his deputy had a personal relationship with each of their forty-five principals; they also knew most of their teachers, if not by name then by their characteristic instructional style. On the basis of these relationships, they developed a sense of shared mission around the teaching of children from high-poverty backgrounds. It is difficult to over-estimate the extent to which the bonds of friendship, interdependence, trust, and respect contributed to the commitment and passion with which they implemented the reform.

Unable to establish personal bonds with all principals in the San Diego system, top district leadership transferred this role to the ILs, each of whom was responsible for a learning community approximately the size of District #2. Much of their training from Fink involved establishing a sense of urgency and a passion for reform; leaders were also expected to get to know their principals well so that they would know how to motivate them. But this kind of relationship building takes time and personal involve-ment—both made very difficult by the size and complexity of the San Diego reforms.

Despite the intentions of Alvarado and other district leaders to listen to and learn from the front lines, the size of the SDCS also made it difficult for good ideas that come from classroom teachers and principals to bubble up to the surface and be noticed by district leaders. Having one's ideas listened to and respected is an important part of trust and relationship building. San Diego teachers' complaints indicate that, especially in the early years of the reform, they felt marginalized, their ideas dismissed, and their feedback ignored (see Chapters 7 and 8).

Organizational Features

The ability of District #2 to act as a guide for the reforms in San Diego was also hindered by organizational differences between the two systems. District #2 was essentially a K–8 district; San Diego schools are K–12, generally organized into K–5, 6–8, and 9–12 units. As superintendent of District #2, Alvarado did not have to confront the challenges of educating high school students. Upon arriving in San Diego, Alvarado did not waver in his conviction that from the beginning, all students must benefit from reform initiatives. Despite the obstacles, he chose not to exercise the option of beginning the San Diego reforms only in the elementary grades and waiting until those better-prepared students arrived in high school before tackling secondary school reform. However, his reform agenda for high school was much less well defined than for grades K–8, in large part because the Balanced Literacy program had not been developed or tested for use with high school students. The centerpiece of the San Diego high school reform was a genre studies block designed to provide intensive remedial assistance to ninth and tenth graders who had fallen behind (see Chapters 4 and 5). Classroom observations revealed, however, that teachers were underprepared to direct long periods of meaningful instruction (see Chapter 5).

The District #2 reforms relied on human resource management in addition to professional development. It was not unusual for District #2 leaders to work with principals to "counsel out" teachers who were not able or unwilling to implement the Balanced Literacy program. This tactic was acceptable in part because these teachers and principals had other options. District #2 was one of thirty-two community school districts in New York City. Disgruntled teachers and principals usually could transfer to another community school district with no penalty in status, salary, or retirement benefits. No similar options were available in San Diego. SDCS educators could either remain in their current position or try to find employment in a completely different district. Thus, teachers and principals who found themselves at odds with district leadership fought longer and harder to stay in their positions than did their District #2 counterparts, and those who stayed often continued to subtly subvert the reforms. Hence, Alvarado and his team could not rely on a human resource strategy as successfully in San Diego as in New York.

Conclusions

Alvarado's success in District #2 should not be minimized. It was real, and there are important lessons to be learned from it, which include making instruction the leading edge of the reform, accompanied by continuously fostering professional development of teachers, principals, and ILs situated as close to the classroom as possible and forming educators into communities of learners. As we have pointed out in this chapter, however, subtle aspects of context enabled the District #2 reforms—aspects that went unnoticed until they were unavailable or different in the new setting of San Diego. These aspects included a district size small enough to allow personal relationships to flourish, an instructional focus limited to grades K–8, and the latitude to implement the reform slowly, over a number of years.

Alvarado was correct: every reform must be built in the soil of its city. San Diego presented a unique set of challenges, many of which became visible only after the work of reform had begun. The key would be to identify these challenges promptly and make midcourse adjustments. The remaining chapters of this book discuss how the district fared in this regard.

CHAPTER 4

Using District Leaders' Theory of Action to Understand the San Diego Reform

In the educational context, a "theory of action" encompasses the beliefs and interconnected explanatory structures that underlie educational leaders' approach to instruction, curriculum, and the organization of schools—especially as these concerns attempt to guide reforms (Argyris & Schön, 1978; Bryk, Sebring, Kerbow, Rollow, & Easton, 1998). A theory of action states educational goals, articulates the relationship among the goals, describes strategies for attaining the goals, and provides justifications (or explanations) for why those strategies should produce the designated goals.

The purpose of this chapter is to explicate the theory of action that guided the educational reform in the San Diego City Schools (SDCS) from 1998–2002. This effort is important, we think, because we can gain a unique perspective on the San Diego reform by interrogating Superintendent Alan Bersin and Chancellor Anthony Alvarado's thinking about what the reform was meant to achieve and how. As leaders of the San Diego system, these men's statements, actions, and plans shaped educational decisions and practices and sparked discussions and debates citywide.

Bersin and Alvarado's theory of action was not universally accepted in San Diego. Indeed, the presence of competing opinions about how the San Diego schools should be organized, instruction should be conducted, and students should be educated contributed in large part to the political free-for-all that characterized the first four years of the SDCS reform effort. We take up those competing views, and how they affected the reform over time, in Chapters 8 and 9.

The district's basic goals and strategies appeared in a variety of documents—most notably, the *Blueprint for Student Success* (SDCS, 1998a), the reform plan approved by the school board on March 14, 1998. But the leaders' underlying beliefs and justifications have seldom been formally recorded—and certainly are not compiled in a single place. They also have not been connected systematically to the goals and basic strategies of the reform. In this chapter, we try to make those implicit beliefs and justifications explicit. We deliberately wrote the chapter using information we had available to us between June 1998 and December 2002. We bound the reform within this period because it was during this time that Bersin and Alvarado worked as a team to reform the SDCS. Late in 2002, Alvarado's leadership responsibilities were curtailed, and his relationship with the district was severed entirely as of September 2003. Thus, our discussion provides a snapshot of the thinking of district leaders at or near the beginning of the reform process.

This chapter is divided into three major sections. In the first section, we describe the primary goals of the San Diego reform and the ways in which those goals are interrelated. In the second section, we examine the basic strategies district leaders deployed to achieve their goals and describe the beliefs underlying the chosen strategies. In the third section, we describe the public justifications or explanations leaders offered for their goals and strategies. That is, we explain why the leaders believed in the efficacy of the reform strategies they chose.

Key Characteristics and Essential Goals of the Reform Plan

Three aspects of the SDCS reform plan made it an unusual undertaking for a large, diverse, urban public school district. The district leadership implemented its reform strategies comprehensively, centrally, and quickly. The reform was *comprehensive* in that all schools in the district were engaged in the reform simultaneously; it was *centralized* in that most of the major decisions about the reform flowed from the top of the system through middle layers of management down to classrooms; it was *fast paced* in that essential features of the reform were introduced into most schools over a single academic year. A final innovative characteristic of the San Diego plan was its single-minded focus on instruction, or "teacher practice."

The comprehensiveness and speed of the San Diego reform effort contrasts with *developmental* or *staggered* reforms—those that start with a pilot program at a few schools and then move on to others in phases or waves, typically over several academic years. Its centralized control contrasts with *decentralized* reforms—those that shift governance or decision making to more dispersed points—whether from federal to state, or state to district, or district to individual school sites. Finally, the focus on instruction and teacher professional development contrasts with *structural* reforms—those that attempt to change the organizational features of schools, such as course scheduling, tracking systems, class size, or school size—but generally do not attempt to modify the teacher–student–subject matter nexus.

Improved Student Learning: Closing the Achievement Gap

The principal goal of the SDCS reform was expressed succinctly and consistently in terms of student learning. All district documents prominently displayed the goal this way:

> The mission of the San Diego City Schools is to improve student achievement by supporting teaching and learning in the classroom.

Improvements in student achievement were viewed as intimately linked to concerted efforts to improve teachers' learning. Teachers' learning, in turn, was linked to improving instructional practice, supported through professional development and strong leadership. Not only teachers but all district members, from the principal to the superintendent, were to be focused on instruction. Restructuring at the district, school, and classroom levels also would be required, but only as needed to support student and teacher learning.

To be consistent with statewide policy enacted at the time Superintendent Bersin assumed office, the reform initially was formulated as a "stop social promotion" measure and a "back to basics" initiative. On occasions that called for a closer specification of the fundamental goals of the San Diego reform, improved student achievement was defined as "closing the achievement gap." The groups on either side of this gap were understood somewhat differently, depending on the audience. Equity-minded educators and parents of students historically poorly served by the area's schools saw the gap as existing between socioeconomic groups (rich and poor students) and ethnic groups (most typically, between Asian and white students on one hand and black and Latino students on the other). Local business leaders seeking workers well prepared for jobs in the global economy saw the critical division as between U.S. students and students from other major industrialized countries.

Over time, more specific goal statements about "rigorous academic instruction for all students" evolved in the context of California's high standards policies, including a call for preparing all students for college (Bersin & Alvarado, 2000a, 2000b). The superintendent and the chancellor contended that SDCS students should be prepared to enroll in the University of California or California State University when they graduate from high school. Such statements led to confusion; often, they were interpreted to mean that *all* students *should* go to college. When pressed, district leaders explained that completing high school courses that satisfy the entrance requirements of California State University or the University of California should be considered proxies for rigorous instruction. That is, students' success in college preparation courses should be taken as a concrete manifestation of high-quality teaching and learning. Not every young adult must or should go to college, but the rigor of a college prep program is good for all because it "exercises the mind" and prepares students for life after high school—whether that involves entering the workforce, joining the military, or enrolling in college.

Improved Instruction: Teacher Learning through Professional Development

A fundamental belief of the SDCS reform was that improving student achievement requires improving the quality of instruction. Because teachers interacting with students around subject matter is the core of education, this nexus is the fulcrum point where the lever of change is inserted to ensure improvement. Consequently, a significant goal of the educational reform in the SDCS was the improvement of teacher quality. Teacher quality, in turn, was to be improved by a particular theory of professional development, one rooted in the concept of a "learning community." Members of a community of learners typically share information, insights, and advice. "They help each other solve problems. They discuss their situations, their aspirations and their needs. They ponder common issues, explore ideas, and act as sounding boards" (Wenger, McDermott, & Snyder, 2002: 4).

District leaders believed teachers' learning should be transformative—that is, based on deep changes in their thinking about teaching and learning and their role in the process. On the basis of his experience in New York City's Community School District #2, Alvarado had concluded such complex learning cannot occur by attending a few workshops or reading an instruction manual. Instead, teachers' learning is better facilitated through long-term engagement with a group of colleagues, some of whom are more expert than others, and all of whom share similar values, goals, and commitments.

The district's commitment to improving teachers' quality was framed in terms of increasing their professional knowledge base and helping them hone their instructional skills in various content areas. District leaders believed that much is known about what constitutes good teaching and that teachers must have access to and use this knowledge base. Their belief in a *community of learners* approach contrasted with the belief that teaching is an individual craft, created anew by each teacher alone in his or her classroom. The district leadership viewed it as their responsibility to arrange opportunities for teachers to become participants in communities of learners.

By attempting to organize the schools to create a community of learners among teachers, the SDCS leadership was trying to do nothing less than "reculture" (Elmore, 1996; Hargreaves, 1994) San Diego's schools. The reculturing had two different sites. One involved teachers as individuals; the other involved teachers as a component of an organization ("the school"). Teachers were being asked to reconsider their role within the institution of the school and to recast their understanding of themselves in their own classrooms—how they interacted with children, how they decorated their classrooms, how they divided up their teaching time, how responsible they were for their students' academic success. Both types of changes were required to occur simultaneously.

Teachers were being asked to recast their practice from that enacted in the privacy of their classrooms to a public practice enacted in all classrooms. They were expected to instruct based on shared ideas, beliefs, and language. The district leadership wanted ideas regarding teachers' skills, practices, and accountability actualized in common because they believed this would contribute to the continuity of students' experience and teachers' instruction—both important considerations in a large urban district with high rates of teacher mobility and student transience.

Restructuring the Organization to Support Student Learning and Instruction

Much as reculturing was the preferred process for changing the norms and practices of the district's teachers, *restructuring* was the preferred process for aligning the district with the goals of the reform. In one of his first public statements as superintendent, Bersin announced there would be two kinds of employees in the district: those who teach and those who support teaching and learning. In this way, Bersin signaled that organizational decisions would be driven by what was needed in classroom learning environments, not by what was convenient for adults.

Proclamations that classroom instruction and student learning drive educational decision making are not new. School boards and superintendents declare the importance of good teachers and ample resources for the classroom with each new budget cycle. In this regard, Chancellor Alvarado worried that although use of the terms *teaching* and *learning* had caught on—become a fetish even, both in the nation and in San Diego—the meaning behind the terms still had not been fully grasped or universally agreed on: "What is happening now is people are using the words [*teaching* and *learning*], but they don't know what the words mean" (Alvarado, 2001: 4). Much of the work in the San Diego schools from 1998–2002 was about reshaping the bureaucracy to support teaching and learning in the context of a districtwide reform so that all educators did understand the language of the reform.

Basic Goal Strategies and the Beliefs Underlying Them

The district leaders deployed basic strategies to achieve the reform's three broad goals of increased student learning, improved teacher practice, and fast-paced organizational change to support learning and practice. These strategies were based on a set of fundamental beliefs about student learning, teacher learning, and organizational restructuring. In this section, we examine both the strategies and the assumptions and convictions underlying them.

Strategies for Increasing Students' Learning

Unlike many educational reform efforts that aim to address the hardships faced by students who attend high-poverty schools, the San Diego leadership made a conscious effort to focus—nearly exclusively—on improving students' *academic* performance. This focus is evident in nearly every move the district made, from decisions to reallocate resources, to determinations on how to organize and deliver professional development. It is perhaps most clear, however, in the unremitting emphasis on instruction.

Focusing Clearly on Instruction

Citing Diane Ravitch's recent book *Left Back* (2002), Superintendent Bersin contended schools have failed because they tried to take on too many responsibilities—providing social service, feeding, clothing, counseling.

These are all honorable commitments, Bersin said, but attending to them all distracts educators from the fundamental purpose of schooling, which is instruction. To be sure, social and support services should not be eliminated from the lives of students and their families. But it should not be the responsibility of the schools and teachers to provide these social services as extra duties, over and above their teaching responsibilities. Instead, other agencies should be enlisted to cooperate with the schools to provide them.

For Chancellor Alvarado, this focus on instruction had very personal roots. When asked directly about his theory of action, he replied,

> I don't pretend to say that *all* one's actions come from a theory of action and then you just march to an internalized theory of action. Some of it is bumbling along the way, and trying to figure it out and testing it. Although there is no question in my mind that I have internalized, as a human being, *this idea of teaching and learning driving it* ... when I look at a problem, I don't ... look at structure, I don't look at personalization [practices designed to personally connect students to educators], not that I don't know that all those things are influences, I look at *what the hell does a teacher do with kids.* (Alvarado, 2001; emphasis added)

Thus, Alvarado, the leader who drove instructional decision making in the district from 1998–2002, believed deeply that the fulcrum for productive districtwide change was the teaching and learning interactions that occur inside the classroom. Therefore, what students need to learn—instructional resources, competent teachers, well-trained principals, and so on—determines how a school or an entire district should be organized. Whenever a decision needs to be made regarding some aspect of system organization or functioning, the question to be asked is, How will this affect teaching and learning in the classroom?

Moreover, in Alvarado's worldview, organizational arrangements (e.g., redesigning large comprehensive high schools into small theme schools, block scheduling, etc.) should emanate from, not dictate, classroom instructional needs. A problem many reform efforts have faced is that organizational arrangements, programs, materials, and procedures become the driving force. Aware of this tendency, San Diego leaders stated that any and all such reform armament should be seen as "tools" only: "If you are doing that [supporting the teaching and learning of children and of teachers], ... the other stuff becomes tools, not ends in themselves. They become tools for accomplishing the things that you want to [get done]" (Alvarado, 2001).

Implementing Content-Based Reform
Educational reform generally falls into one of two broad categories: large-scale, organizationally driven efforts that typically avoid subject matter, or subject-matter-specific initiatives that generally avoid issues of large-scale organizational change. San Diego leaders, by contrast, attempted to combine these two approaches. Their strategy of systemic instructional reform began with the consideration of student-learning needs in a particular subject area and rippled outward to the implications for the professional development and organizational structure necessary to support high-quality instruction in that subject across all the district's schools and classrooms. Referred to as *content-driven reform* (Stein, Hubbard, & Mehan, 2003), this strategy allowed the district to focus on issues at the educational core while simultaneously influencing a large number of schools and classrooms.

On the basis mainly of Alvarado's positive experiences with the Balanced Literacy program in District #2 (see Chapter 3), the SDCS adopted this approach to literacy. The Balanced Literacy approach is informed by the ideas of Russian psychologist Lev Vygotsky (1978) and programs based on his ideas in New Zealand (New Zealand Ministry of Education, 1996), the Early Literacy project at Ohio State University (Fountas & Pinnell, 2001), and Reading Recovery (Clay, 1987; Pinnell, 1989). Vygotsky and scholars in the sociocultural tradition who interpret his work maintain that students who are supported in the learning process by a more experienced person, such as a teacher, will gradually be able to do more than they are able to do on their own.

At the elementary school level, the Balanced Literacy framework provides students with a variety of instructional "scaffolds," practices that support them as they learn to read and write (see Chapter 5 for details). As the students are able to do more and more of the task of reading, support is gradually released and ultimately the learners fully take over the task of reading. To help students move toward becoming proficient and independent readers, some challenging texts that are beyond their current reading capacities are read *to* the students. The teacher demonstrates vocal inflection, teaches strategies for comprehending a text, and promotes a love for reading. Other, much simpler texts are read *by* students independently as they practice the vocabulary and reading strategies they have already learned. Those texts that are just beyond the students' ability to tackle by themselves, the teacher reads *with* them, providing support, guidance, and direct instruction in new reading strategies.

SDCS instructional leaders (ILs) used the terms *to, with,* and *by,* borrowed from Mooney (1990) to describe the important components of reading. *To* reading instruction is an activity conducted almost entirely by the teacher, as exemplified in read alouds. These are opportunities for the teacher to demonstrate proficient reading. Reading aloud introduces students to the joys of reading and the art of listening and provides opportunities to model reading strategies. Students can begin to understand that the language of books is different from spoken language, develop an understanding of the patterns and structures of written language, learn new words and ideas, and learn about and locate models of particular genres or forms of writing. Read alouds are typically conducted as a whole-group activity in which students gather together in close physical proximity to the teacher.

With reading instruction is also a whole-group activity that offers a considerable amount of support but less than in read alouds, where the teacher does all the reading. In *with* reading, students share reading a text with an enlarged print format (such as "Big Books") or a text that everyone can see. This provides a safe environment in which all students, regardless of reading level, have an opportunity to engage in the reading process. Teachers demonstrate the strategies that successful readers use, and students and teacher share the task of reading.

The bridge to independent reading is in *with* and *by* small-group instruction. In guided reading and guided writing, students, grouped on the basis of similarities in their strengths and weaknesses, practice the literacy strategies introduced in shared reading (or writing). They read (or write) together with only limited adult guidance. Teachers listen in as the groups work and make decisions about the instructional needs of each student. Student groups tackle increasingly challenging texts, expanding their level of understanding and fluency, moving them closer to the goal of reading and writing independently. The *with* and *by* component of the Balanced Literacy framework requires sophisticated teaching skills. Guided reading and writing groups are assigned texts that match the students' current needs and abilities, so teachers must be able to identify specific supports and challenges in the available reading material, gauge each student's (changing) abilities and needs, and group all children in the class effectively.

Independent reading is the *by* form of reading instruction. Independent reading gives students opportunities to practice the strategies they have learned in shared reading, guided reading, and read alouds. Teachers provide guidance with book choices, but the goal is to train students to become proficient at independently selecting books that match their interests and reading level. Books from a range of levels are available in each classroom. Teachers also confer with students during independent reading to ascertain if and where problems exist so that they can then tailor instruction to meet student needs. At this point, most support is removed because students can read on their own.

Literacy instruction was structured somewhat differently in SDCS middle and high schools. It was assumed that if *Blueprint* strategies were successfully implemented, the number of students needing additional help in literacy by middle and high school would be greatly reduced over time. However, San Diego, like many other large urban school districts, is the home to many second-language learners and newcomers. This population (along with many other students in the district) was reading below or significantly below grade level. To address their literacy needs, the district launched genre studies classes (see Chapter 5). Secondary students reading below grade level were placed in these classes for two or three periods a day, depending on their need. In genre studies classes, students learned to read and interpret a variety of texts, including journalistic reports, technical writing, textbooks, biography, and history, as well as a variety of types of literature. Students in these classes benefited from a reduced class size (twenty students).

Genre studies classes followed the workshop model of instruction. Workshop classes stretch over long blocks of time; advocate student choice in writing topics or books for independent reading; minimize didactic, teacher-centered activities (such as lectures) in favor of group and independent activities during which the teacher plays a coaching role; feature specific classroom furnishings; and emphasize a sense of community in the classroom (Atwell, 1998; Fletcher & Portalupi, 2001; Ziegler, 1981). A typical genre studies block in the SDCS began with a whole-class, teacher-centered segment known as the minilesson, which ideally occupied about 20% of instructional time and often centered around the read aloud, word study, and shared reading components of Balanced Literacy. Following the minilesson portion came guided practice, which represented about 70% of class time. Teachers coached students as they practiced reading strategies; independent reading time also was included in this segment. The final part of class time (10%) provided an opportunity for students to share their efforts with each other (pair- or table-share) and with the class as a whole (share-out). All activities during a genre studies workshop-style class were supposed to coordinate to serve that day's instructional goal, a technique known as "threading."

Ninth- and tenth-grade literacy block teachers were allocated new, high-quality instructional materials and were expected to participate in enhanced professional development activities. Students who were still not performing at grade level in tenth grade were directed to continue taking a two-hour block genre class.

Setting High Standards for All Students

To close the achievement gap, the San Diego reform focused on student learning. Applying to education the well-worn bromide from economics "a rising tide lifts all boats," a basic strategy for improving student learning is to set high standards for all students. This strategy rests on the assumption that ability grouping, tracking, and other forms of curriculum differentiation are harmful to students—especially low-income students and students of color, who traditionally have been placed in low track classes, with disastrous academic consequences. Instead of setting different goals for students according to their presumed differences in mental ability, the San Diego reform expected all students to meet the same high standards. Chancellor Alvarado (2001) explained the strategy's rationale this way:

> I think there were some people who were concerned [that] if you focus on kids who are struggling, what happens to the kids in the rest of the system? The truth is we increased the number of students in the top quartile—*so the theory [is] that you raise [the number of kids at or near] the ceiling by raising the floor.* (emphasis added)

Providing Support for Students to Meet High Standards

The traditional approach to the education of low-performing students is remediation. When remediation strategies are employed, the curriculum is simplified and students are led through it at a slower pace. Rejecting remediation on the grounds that it segregates and tracks students, the SDCS leadership pursued a strategy that accelerates the pace of learning for struggling students so they can return to the classrooms of their agemates as quickly as possible. For the most part, special accommodations, such as pullout programs, differentiated curriculum, and segregated classrooms, were rejected as solutions for the unique educational challenges that new immigrant students, English-language learners, special education students, and low-income transient students present to teachers. These children's needs were to be accommodated within the boundaries of the teacher–student instructional nexus, not relegated to special programs.

Setting and maintaining the same uniformly high standards for all students is a necessary but not a sufficient condition for improving student learning. High standards must be accompanied by a system of academic supports to achieve this objective. The SDCS leaders devised prevention, intervention, and retention strategies to assist students and teachers to achieve and maintain high standards during the 1998–2002 period.

Prevention strategies were aimed at keeping students on track for academic success and blocking difficulties before they developed. In addition to implementing the Balanced Literacy framework across all elementary classrooms and secondary school English classes, the district offered other resources designed to enhance learning, beginning at first grade (and adding the next higher grade level each subsequent year). These resources were designed to help both teachers and students carry out the *Blueprint* provisions.

Intervention strategies focused on the schools and students who were identified as most at risk of failure. Students who did not meet established performance levels in kindergarten attended a special transition class (called a Junior First-Grade Academy) before they entered first grade. Students who were retained in first grade were placed in intensive classes that focused on literacy and mathematics throughout an extended school year. These students' school day also was extended (by adding classes either before or after regular school hours), and they received scaffolded assistance in the form of personalized tutoring in reading to ensure that they could meet the criteria for promotion. These intensive classes were facilitated by a student–teacher ratio of 15:1.

Retention strategies were designed to give students who were failing, even after receiving support and intervention, extra time at a grade level to attain the knowledge necessary for success in the subsequent grade. San Diego's approach to retention targeted *entry* grades as opposed to *exit* grades. Students who did not meet performance standards in the first, sixth, and seventh grades would not be advanced to the next grade. Instead, they received additional intensive instruction—during intersessions and summer school—with the hope that they would be able to pass relevant exams indicating that they had "caught up" with their classmates. Ninth graders who did not meet performance standards were assigned to a two- or three-hour genre studies block. If these students still did not meet the grade-level criteria by the end of the designated intervention, they were not retained but assigned to two-hour literacy block classes the next year. The literacy blocks were intended to provide an intensive program of support to return underperforming students to classes with their contemporaries.

Strategies for Increasing Teachers' Learning

Just as the San Diego reform incorporated a specific theory about how children learn (embedded in the Balanced Literacy framework) and developed certain goal strategies associated with that theory, so too did the reform include a specific view of how adult professionals learn and promote specific goal strategies linked to that view.

Basic Beliefs about Adult Learning
The reform was predicated on a continuous learning model of professional development for individuals at every layer of the system. Two basic beliefs associated with that model provided much of the foundation for district leaders' strategies for improving learning at all layers of the system.

Effective teaching and leadership can be learned. Underlying San Diego's huge investment in professional development was a conviction that teaching and leadership skills are neither innate nor mysterious. Effective behaviors can be learned, and doing so in groups (learning communities) is preferable. Discussing his views about professional development, Alvarado (2001) explained, "Leadership is no longer some mystic quality and charismatic notion and antidotal stories and a lot of literature. It's actually what the hell you do. ... It's the same thing that you do when you teach. It's not something ethereal, you know? I do something. I look at what I do. I say something about it."

Learning must be continuous and embedded in daily practice. The belief that professional development should occur continuously and on-site contrasts with traditional models in which educators are trained during one-shot or short workshops, college classes or local, regional, or national conferences, during which they listen passively to experts.

Setting High Standards for Teachers and Teaching
The Bersin–Alvarado approach to improving the teaching and learning processes with teachers was much the same as their strategy with students: high standards were established and supports were put in place to help teachers achieve those standards. High standards for teaching practice were communicated along with the basic tenets of the Balanced Literacy program in staff development sessions and through interactions with peer coaches. Teachers were assisted in implementing the program through frequent principal observations, interclassroom visitations, and periodic classroom walk-throughs conducted jointly by ILs and principals.

Providing Support for Teachers to Meet High Standards
To support improved teacher practice, the district provided a range of scaffolds. In addition to receiving guidance from their principal, teachers benefited from on-site help supplied by peer coaches, also called staff developers, who were placed in all schools to help teachers embed the lessons learned from professional development into their daily practice. Peer coaches used strategies such as coteaching, demonstrating, observing, videotaping, and discussing student work to help teachers. The site-based coaching model is especially helpful to new teachers, who can obtain

timely help in the setting in which they need it. The coaches were expected to keep their knowledge and skills current by also participating in coaching. They met weekly with their colleagues to discuss their work and learn new strategies.

District leaders vested peer coaches' and principals' learning support roles with evaluative authority as well. Coupling support for adult learning with accountability implies a commitment to "two-way accountability" (Elmore, 2001), whereby district leadership provides teachers with the support and resources they need to improve instruction in exchange for teachers being held accountable for reaching district goals. As we explain in Chapters 6 and 7, vesting individuals with both support and accountability functions is risky because it can cause confusion, anxiety, and resentment. When sufficient talent was available, the district took a different approach by assigning evaluative functions to a third party. At these high schools, literacy supervisors—individuals from the district who had demonstrable knowledge and skills in literacy development—were assigned to support peer coaches and to assume responsibility for the evaluation of teachers. These literacy specialists were considered to be experts in the field, and their work was intended to relieve some of the instructional responsibility from the principals—who, in many cases, were just learning the instructional role.

Other forms of assistance the district made available to teachers included the following:

- professional-development workshops and seminars conducted during the summer and frequently taught by outside consultants who were considered experts;
- individual coaching by principals and ILs, conducted in teachers' classrooms throughout the school year and at faculty conferences and grade-level meetings;
- opportunities to observe teaching peers who excelled at some component of the teaching and learning processes, both within teachers' own schools and at other sites throughout the district; and
- special workshops during the summer for teachers of at-risk students, as well as professional-development sessions held weekly during extended year sessions.

These supports for teacher learning rest on two important assumptions about classroom practices. First, leaders believed that the research community had reached agreement on a set of effective instructional practices. District leaders insisted that district teachers' practices must rest on this professional knowledge base, rather than being invented (and reinvented) by individual teachers in the privacy of their own classrooms. The district privileged instructional practice that gradually released responsibility from teacher to learner and that based instruction on the needs of individual students. It was not instruction that followed the script of a basal text, as many "teacher proof" approaches, such as Success for All (Slavin, Madden, Dolan, & Wasik, 1996), demand.

Second, district leaders believed that teachers' (mostly) private practice needed to be reconstituted as public practice. The prevailing practice in K–12 education enables teachers to act as nearly autonomous agents. Consistent with the highly prized value of academic freedom, teachers are responsible for the teaching and learning that occurs within their classroom, but seldom are teachers' practices synchronized and calibrated across classrooms at one school, and even less often is there consistency or commonality across schools within a district. Little if any outside evaluation of teachers' practice and accountability for student outcomes occurs when teaching is constituted as private practice (Becker & Riel, 2000; Elmore, 2000).

Strategies for Increasing Leadership Capacity

The SDCS superintendent and chancellor of instruction believed strongly in the importance of school-site leadership to achieve the desired goals of their reform. Therefore, they deployed a set of strategies to support the learning of school principals and ILs.

Assisting Principals to Become Leaders of Instruction

Bersin and Alvarado considered principals the most critical resource in the professional guidance and instructional direction of schools because of their close proximity to the teaching–learning encounter. Accordingly, they changed the principal's role drastically, starting on day one of the reform. Called on to be "leaders of instruction," principals were to spend more time in classrooms, engaging teachers in conversations about instruction, and to spend less time on administrative, logistical, and financial matters. Because district leaders did not establish formal procedures specifying how these essential but noninstructional tasks would be accomplished while principals were concentrating on their new responsibilities, many principals did them after school hours or assigned them to assistant principals or school secretaries.

In part because the district recognized that most principals would have had little preparation for the new dimensions of their role, and in part to develop principals who would provide leadership, direction, and vision for schools as learning communities, the district organized many opportunities for principals to develop the requisite leadership skills. These opportunities included the following:

- Walk-throughs with their IL
- Principals' conferences (where instruction was envisioned as being the *only* topic)
- Mentorship program for principals
- Support groups for principals
- Visits to other schools to observe exemplary practice

The walk-through, conducted by the principals and their ILs, was the heart of the district's professional development for principals. Ideally, the walk-through started with a preconference between the IL and principal, in which they reviewed the goal and objectives of the principal's overall plan for leading the school (called the "work plan") and the expectations that had been laid out following the previous walk-through. Then the principal and IL reviewed each teacher in the school, concentrating on those for whom specific professional development needs had been identified. School achievement data was also reviewed, especially the records of at-risk or low-achieving students. Problems and successes since the previous walk-through were identified and revisited.

After the walk-through of classrooms, which typically took between two hours and two and a half hours, the principal and IL discussed their observations, evaluations of instructional practice, and quality of student work. At this time, plans for specific teachers, including the next steps in professional development, tenure, reassignment within the school, or separation from the school, were considered. Finally, the principal and the IL developed plans for instructional programs and professional development for all educators at the school.

If the walk-through was the heart of the district's professional development for principals, then the monthly principals' conference was its soul. At these conferences, Superintendent Bersin and Chancellor Alvarado shared their key convictions and strategies. For example, at one principals' conference, after explaining his basic beliefs, Bersin provided principals with the words and the encouragement to impart the same message to their teachers:

> Our expectations are that every child will be held accountable and will do well. The *Blueprint* is our best thinking to date. It represents our belief system. You as principals have been providing the support to teachers and now it's up to you to present this *Blueprint*

to the faculty. It is not a statement of a program or direction or mandate. When you present it to your faculty it must be apparent that it is your reflection, your goal, your determination that every child will be taken into account and that every child will be held to high standards. Stand before your faculty with the *Blueprint Phase Two* and make sure they understand that it accompanies your belief system. (Bersin, 2002c)

In addition to being exposed to the district's basic beliefs, conference attendees also learned about reform content and how to become stronger leaders. These topics were addressed in small-group workshops conducted throughout the daylong conferences.

Of primary concern to the district was providing for a constant supply of new principals to lead the reform. As principals retired, transferred to other districts, or, in some cases, were removed from their positions, vacancies threatened districtwide leadership capacity. The Educational Leadership Development Academy (ELDA) was the solution. Formed in 2000 as a district collaborative project with a consortium of local universities and other agencies in San Diego, ELDA prepares aspiring principals for positions in the district. The program also provides course work and pairs novice principals with mentor principals. Each academic year, starting in 2000, an average of twenty-two mentor principals each worked directly with two or three principals. The entire group met monthly to discuss and study the research literature on coaching and to review the issues that concerned them at their school. The course work, mentoring, and hands-on experience are intended to operate synergistically to enhance new principals' professional growth.

Assisting Instructional Leaders to Become True Leaders

The SDCS reform was predicated on the assumption that all educators in the system participate in a community of learners. This notion, implying as it does that *everyone* in the organization is learning to do something new, means that the ILs, just as much as principals and teachers, needed to receive support for their learning.

The previous district practice of grouping schools under area superintendents according to "feeder patterns" was abolished because that practice limited these officials to schools in geographically separate areas of the city. As a result, they were unable to make comparisons of instructional quality across neighborhood boundaries. Bersin and Alvarado reassigned all schools to learning communities led by ILs. Each had a mix of elementary, middle, and high schools located in different neighborhoods—and representing both high-performing and low-performing schools.

ILs were expected to provide instructional support to principals and their schools and hold the principals and teachers within those schools accountable for accomplished practice and improved student-learning outcomes. As of September 2002, nine ILs had responsibility for more than 170 schools. The number of ILs eventually grew to eleven. Two of the original leaders resigned, claiming they were frustrated by the level of responsibility and the top-down manner in which they were expected to lead. Two ILs were hired from outside the district, and other ILs were recruited from principal positions.

In the early days of the reform, ILs received training from the Learning Research and Development Center of the University of Pittsburgh. In 2000, the district hired Elaine Fink to assume this responsibility (see also Chapter 3). Fink, who was executive director of ELDA, helped the ILs accomplish their transformation from area superintendents to ILs (see Chapter 7). Through a series of meetings before the principals' conferences, she taught the ILs to reflect on pedagogy and classroom practice, conduct discussions of current research on instructional strategies and leadership, and impart a message of the vision and urgency of the reform to their principals. Fink (2002a) explained,

> We plan principals' conferences. Principals' conferences in the past, when I got here and I watched one, [I noticed that they] were usually just sharing sessions. Principals would come, and they would talk about something, and they would all just share. There was no goal of what you're trying to accomplish, what you're teaching them, that you're the teacher of your principals. So we had to spend the last nine months working intensely on how to have productive principals' conferences.

Fink also instructed the ILs on how to conduct walk-throughs by accompanying them on some of these events at their schools. On these occasions, she modeled, coached, and guided the ILs as they interacted with their principals to impart knowledge and a sense of urgency.

Strategies for Restructuring the Organization

At the beginning of this chapter, we described the SDCS reform from 1998–2002 as *comprehensive, centralized,* and *fast paced.* The SDCS reform was comprehensive in that it was a systemwide effort. It was not a program. It was not a one-school experiment, not a pilot program to be tried out in a few schools and then, if successful, moved to a few others, eventually affecting the whole district. Instead, the *entire* district was saturated with the reform. Not only did the schools experience the reform *simultaneously* but they also experienced the reform *rapidly*. Finally, the reform was *centralized* insofar as major decisions flowed from the top of the system through middle layers of management into classrooms.

Acknowledging that this centralized approach to reform was a "minority point of view" within the educational community, Alvarado nevertheless advocated for a strong role for district leadership in directing "the system":

> If you walk into a church, the church has some rules. You do certain things that you don't do on the beach because you walk into the church. It's a system. That's what people feel. If you could hold on for awhile, what they may feel is no longer the imposition of the system. They will actually start to feel the benefits of the system, which is actually the opportunity to become professional. (Alvarado, 2001: 8)

Claiming that there was no system in San Diego before their arrival (meaning no culture of professionalism), Bersin and Alvarado concluded that strong centralized leadership was needed to develop a culture of learning. Therefore, they tried to create a system that built the space and felt need for professional knowledge, which in turn, they believed, would foster student learning.

To substantiate their insistence that there would be only two types of employees in the district—those who instruct and those who support instruction—Superintendent Bersin and Chancellor Alvarado unveiled a new organizational chart on the first day of their new administration (see Figure 4.1).

The structure depicted in the new organizational chart was unusual in that it placed students and schools at the top—where CEOs or superintendents usually appear. A new organizational entity—the Institute for Learning—responsible for developing instructional leadership in all layers of the system dominated the center of the chart. The usual operational entities—business, personnel, transportation—appeared off to the sides. The district leaders explained that these operational departments would be reorganized and refocused so that they would support instruction.

And indeed, during the first four years of the reform, the district leaders did restructure the organization so that operational departments treated the support of instruction as their primary mission. Bus schedules were redesigned to get students to schools more quickly. School-level budgets and quarterly rosters detailing individual student achievement were prepared and made available to principals and their school-site decision-making teams. More fundamental, leadership positions—from the superintendent to the classroom teacher—were redefined in instructional and not operational terms. Schedules and practices were rearranged to institutionalize

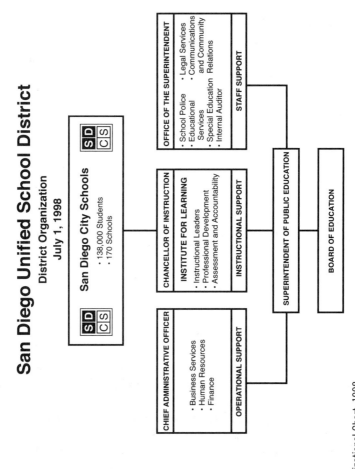

Figure 4.1 SDCS Organizational Chart, 1998.

ongoing professional development "in the line." And the criteria for identifying, recruiting, and promoting leaders became their ability to guide
instruction and communicate this knowledge to the members of their
learning communities. Talented classroom teachers were encouraged to
become peer coaches, and good peer coaches were encouraged to become
leaders of on-site instruction (i.e., principals) through ELDA.

Reallocating Resources
Superintendent Bersin and Chancellor Alvarado issued two rallying cries from
the beginning: "We must close the achievement gap between more privileged
and less privileged students" and "We must improve the overall academic performance of all students." They asserted that achieving these two goals required
an infusion of material, cultural, and political resources. To this end, Bersin,
with significant support from the Business Roundtable for Education of the
Chamber of Commerce ("the business community"), won passage of Proposition MM in 1998, which provided millions in funds to renovate old buildings, upgrade facilities, and build new schools. Bersin also organized a book
drive, "San Diego Reads," which collected thousands of books for distribution
to SDCS classrooms. Both of these efforts were unprecedented in scope, size,
and community support.

The district leadership also recognized that supporters in the business
community, as well as parents from wealthy neighborhoods, were loathe
to back a Robin Hood strategy of taking resources from the wealthy and
reallocating them to the poor. Therefore, the leaders' strategy for increasing resources in underserved schools involved redirecting existing funds
to new tasks. Two notable decisions were to:

- Fire more than ninety employees from the central office in 1998–99
  and use the salary savings to hire peer coaches in all schools, with
  more coaches made available to the lowest performing schools.
- Fire six hundred teachers' aides whose salaries were covered by Title I
  funds and use those salary savings to hire two hundred new teachers.

Because most of the Title I funds came from low-income schools that were
also low performing, these schools received the bulk of the new teacher positions, which made it possible to reduce class size at these sites. The district
leadership also directed significant additional resources to eight elementary
schools that were chronically low performing, as measured by their Academic
Performance Index (API) ranking of 1. (API 1 schools are those performing in
the lowest 10% of elementary schools in the state.) Designated as focus schools,
the district's API 1 schools received more teachers and additional coaches (for
example, a math specialist for grades four, five, and six). Class size was reduced.

Teachers received an additional $3,000 for classroom resources, and students received twenty-four extra instructional days per year. A certificated "Parent Academic Liaison" and "Early Link Preschool" program were assigned to the focus schools as well.

The SDCS estimated that implementing remediation, prevention, and intervention strategies cost about $112 million annually, $68.6 million of which was financed mostly through eliminating the six hundred teaching aide positions. An additional $34 million was generated by converting seventeen district magnet schools into academic academies and redirecting those schools' integration funds. The district was quite successful in securing grants from the Gates Foundation, Hewlett Foundation, and Carnegie Foundation, among others, to help cover the additional costs of the reform.

Sharing Leadership

From the outset, Superintendent Bersin and Chancellor Alvarado introduced a dual or "team" approach to district leadership to more effectively implement their comprehensive, content-based reform. Bersin faced to the outside of the district, assuming responsibility for managing much of the district's massive structure of 170 schools and 138,000 students and huge ($1.4 billion) budget, handling most of the political chores, such as interacting with the school board, the press, the business community, parents, the union, and so forth. Alvarado faced to the inside of the district, assuming responsibility for instruction and student learning. This approach enabled Alvarado to focus on the educational transaction between teachers and students (which Bersin and Alvarado agreed were at the heart of education and the SDCS reform) without having energy absorbed by political wrangles.

Public Justifications for the District's Goals and Strategies

In Chapter 1, we described the unidirectional approach to school reform in which reform ideas are designed by decision makers at the top of the social system and implemented by practitioners down the line. Ideally, in this model, administrative decisions, including reform ideas, are selected for implementation based on solid empirical evidence. Superintendent Bersin frequently cited research on teaching and learning to support reform decisions. The San Diego reform also was justified on moral and political grounds.

*Legitimating the New Structure of Learning and Teaching
on Empirical Grounds*

Vividly demonstrating their unwavering faith in empiricism as a basis for making decisions and as a means of convincing skeptics, the district leadership often claimed that their reform was based on the results of research: "Its not the politics," Chancellor Alvarado insisted, "it's the quality of the ideas, the quality of the evidence, the quality of the work, the quality of the results that should carry the day" (quoted in Gribble, 2001: 37). Research evidence was used in (at least) two ways in the discourse about the SDCS reform: (1) to win public support for improving student learning and (2) to justify investments in instruction and professional development to improve teacher learning.

The Persuasive Power of Test Score Data

Superintendent Bersin and Chancellor Alvarado staked their reputations on improved student achievement. From the first days of their administration, they said that students' performance on the state-mandated test, the *Stanford Achievement Test, Ninth Edition* (SAT9), would improve because their reform invested so heavily in instruction and teacher competence. When the district published studies showing gains in student achievement and improvements in teachers' practices, Bersin and Alvarado predicted, this evidence-based success would convince any skeptical teachers, parents, or members of the public to give the reform their wholehearted support.

The Persuasive Power of Empirical Research

Bersin and Alvarado often said that their administrative decisions to develop certain plans or to implement certain practices were based on the results of research. For example, they often referred to studies (e.g., Haycock & Navarro, 1997) that show investing in improving teacher quality through intensive professional development makes a difference in students' performance. Using a similar logic, their decision in 2000 to replace six hundred teachers' aides with two hundred teachers was legitimated by saying no studies had been conducted that showed that Title I money spent on aides was effective in raising student achievement (Milsap, Moss, & Gamse, 1993).

District leaders asserted that their programs, especially Balanced Literacy, rested on a firm professional knowledge base about how students learn and ways in which teachers can assist that learning (Fountas & Pinnell, 2001; New Zealand Ministry of Education, 1996). Therefore, district leaders contended that teaching strategies should not be invented on the spot by individual teachers but rather be learned as part of becoming a professional.

Calls for teacher professionalism also were used to justify the overriding importance of knowledge and skills rather than seniority or years of service in making promotion and retention decisions regarding teachers and other educators: "What it reduces to is the knowledge and the skill and the performance and the critique of the performance ... it is not about stripes! The new world is not about where you fall in the hierarchy, it is about what you know and what you're able to do" (Alvarado, 2001: 6). More specific, district leaders contended that no one in the system is entitled to a position simply because they've "put in the time." Assistant principals are not owed a principalship because of a certain number of years of service, for example. The system exists to bring about the education of the city's children; it is not an adult employment agency. Thus, the district leadership set the expectation that individuals would be selected for increasingly more responsible positions based on their demonstrated ability to lead instruction.

Legitimating District Restructuring on Moral and Political Grounds

The SDCS leadership legitimated their restructuring of the district comprehensively, simultaneously, and centrally primarily on moral and political grounds.

Moral Reasons

The district's approach to systemic reform was legitimated morally by saying a whole generation of students cannot be asked to wait until an entire system is ready to provide them with the support they need to learn. Reinforcing this moral theme, the district leadership said that public schools perpetuate social injustice when they pass along uneducated students:

> American public education cannot wait for Godot here. So within a very, very short period of time, we are going to be able to show results, but I mean substantive—with [standardized test] scores, certainly within two reporting periods [two semesters]. If thirty-five percent of the children in the eleventh grade read at or above grade level, if we lose three thousand students in our high schools between the ninth and twelfth grade, if seventy-five percent of the kids who hold a high school diploma can't take a college course because they have to take remedial reading, we have to say there's a massive problem. This is institutional failure—if we continue to do what we're doing, we are going to get the results we are getting. (Alvarado, 2001)

Despite never having dealt with high schools on a large scale before, district leaders felt morally compelled to take on the entire SDCS K–12 system from the very beginning, and to do so quickly. Some advisers had urged the district to begin with elementary schools and then reap the benefit of those better-educated children once they reached high school.

Alvarado countered that implementing the strategy piecemeal would take too long and was unethical. And, besides, many of San Diego's high school students enter the system from elsewhere, so the district would not be able to count on new students arriving with good educational training. Alvarado also argued that a system of supports needed to be put in place to assist children *throughout* their public school careers because that is the nature of remediation: "They need support throughout their entire academic life. Not, I give you something, you're cured. Move on." (Alvarado, 2001)

Political Reasons
Political reasons also helped justify the comprehensive, centralized, and fast-paced character of the reform. The district leadership had been elected by a slim (three to two) majority of the school board and had garnered the support of the business community because of the standards-based orientation of the reform effort. District leaders felt they needed to put their changes into effect quickly so that this fragile political support would not be diluted and so that the reform would have a chance to gather momentum before opposition emerged.

The leadership asserted that significant change could not be accomplished piecemeal, because the system has a way of absorbing innovation. "There was no other way to jump start systemic reform," Superintendent Bersin claimed. "You don't announce it. You've got to jolt the system. I understood that. ... If people don't understand you're serious about change ... the bureaucracy will own you" (quoted in Cuban & Usdan, 2003: 81). In the same vein, Chancellor Alvarado (quoted in Cuban & Usdan, 2003: 81) said, "There has to be a boom ... in large scale reform. ... The boom doesn't have to be a political boom, but it has to be an organizational boom ... [and] after you go boom, you need to adjust how you pace and organize ... so there becomes a regularity and that people know what to expect."

Embedded within these statements are four reasons why the reform must be put in place quickly: (1) kids are being cheated out of an education every day; (2) leaders have linked their professional credibility to fast, visible improvement in achievement (jumps in SAT9 scores); (3) political support is fragile and not likely to persist in the face of concerted criticism; and (4) organizations have a tendency to absorb innovation over time. This multiplex of rationales placed particular responsibility on teachers. Teachers were repeatedly reminded that only improvement in their practice could bring about the organization's goals. As we will see in later chapters, not all teachers agreed with this assertion.

Discussing the strategy of getting the *Blueprint* approved by the school board, Alvarado stated, "If you try to piecemeal this [reform] together over time you'd never get there" (Alvarado, 2001). He went on to explicate the challenge of piecemeal reform by comparing it to an arcade game: "When you go to the arcade, there's this little game that you play with the heads that pop up and you have a mallet. You hit it and, boom, it pops up over here. And that's exactly what happens in systems. You try to kill this thing and it pops up over here" (Alvarado, 2001: 3). Not only do aspects of the system that one wishes to extinguish persist but the new aspects that one wishes to install have difficulty persisting: "When you do it piecemeal and with a slow pace, the system has a way of blubbering, sucking in the innovation and looking a lot like it looked before" (Alvarado, 2001: 3).

Summary and Conclusions

"Unrelenting top-down managerial direction at an accelerator-to-the-floor pace" is the way Cuban and Usdan (2003: 82) characterized the theory and action of Bersin and Alvarado as educational reformers. We certainly agree.

As we explained in Chapter 1 and noted again at the beginning of this chapter, Oakes (1992) and her colleagues (Jones, Yonezawa, Ballesteros, & Mehan, 2002; Oakes, Quartz, Ryan, & Lipton, 1999; Yonezawa, Jones, & Mehan, 2002; Yonezawa, Wells, & Serna, 2002) proposed that it is productive to see school change as a multifaceted process with technical, cultural, and political dimensions. Change occurs along a technical dimension when reformers introduce resources such as labs, equipment, curriculum, and more highly skilled teachers into the system. Change is activated along a cultural dimension when reformers challenge participants to, first, transform their values, beliefs, and norms and, then, transform their practices. Change traverses along the political dimension when reformers attack highly charged issues such as class- and race-based advantages by building productive professional relationships and galvanizing political constituencies.

Cast in terms of our modification of Oakes's three-dimensional model of educational change, the SDCS reform can be seen as an intriguing combination of technical, cultural, and political ingredients. The overarching goal of the SDCS from 1998–2002 was to improve student achievement by supporting teaching and learning in the classroom. The unrelenting focus on instruction and teacher professional development prior to considering any structural modifications (such as changing the master calendar, eliminating tracking systems, or reducing class size or school size) exemplifies the technical approach to change. But instructional change was not approached in isolation. By attempting to organize educators into communities of learners, moving teaching from private to public practice, and basing pedagogical and professional development decisions on empirical evidence (defined as improved scores on the state-mandated testing regime), the SDCS leadership attempted to reculture and restructure the schools.

Reculturing involved developing common thoughts and beliefs and a common language about skills, practices, and accountability among educators in every part of the school system to reach the district's goal of improving student achievement by supporting teaching and learning in the classroom. Reculturing also meant changing teachers' practices from actions conducted in the isolated privacy of their own classrooms to a public community of learners in which improved instructional practice was supported through professional development and leadership. Restructuring meant reshaping the organization to support student and teacher learning, notably by redefining roles and responsibilities—from the superintendent down the line to the principals and teachers—away from operational concerns and toward instructional ones.

The reform's political dimension was evident in two sets of actions. One was the leadership's decision to appeal to the business community to support the reform's instructional focus and building plans (Proposition MM). The other was the leaders' attempt to focus additional resources on underachieving schools—which exist almost exclusively in low-income neighborhoods.

The district's "not reckless but fearless" pace (Bersin, 2000, quoted in Cuban & Usdan 2003: 82) and centralized and comprehensive reform was legitimated on moral and political grounds. Comprehensive, simultaneous, and centralized implementation was legitimated morally by saying significant numbers of students cannot be asked to wait until an entire system is ready to provide them with the support they need to learn. The district legitimated politically the theory of action by saying that piecemeal modifications are all too often absorbed by the system and therefore do not lead to paradigmatic shifts. Investments in instruction and professional development were legitimated on empirical grounds. SDCS leaders claimed that their recommendations for changing professional practices rested on a well-established, empirically supported disciplinary knowledge base.

The San Diego reform was laudably innovative and breathtakingly ambitious. However, when the leadership of a school district—and a leadership newly appointed from the outside at that—attempts to completely restructure and reculture the schools, those affected do not respond passively. Tensions and conflicts emerge. Previously enacted and often implicit cultural practices and standard operating procedures clash with the call for new norms, practices, and procedures. We explore in Chapters 5 through 9 the tensions and conflicts that emerged when the content-driven SDCS reform collided with school culture and community politics.

CHAPTER 5

Learning in Classrooms: The Enactment of the Reform between Teachers and Students

KENDRA SISSERSON, CHARLENE BREDDER,
AND TANYA KRAVATZ

This chapter examines the interactions that occurred between teachers and students as they enacted the reform inside the classrooms of the SDCS district. This intersection encounter, which lies at the heart of the overall system (see Figure 1.1 in Chapter 1), is arguably the reform's most fundamental and important site. Meeting the overarching goal of improving student learning rests on the quality and consistency of classroom interactions. The intersection encounter between teachers and students, however, is also the one that is positioned farthest from district leadership. Leaders' reform policy messages reach teachers and their students indirectly; the messages are passed down through all the other layers of the system. In this chapter, we focus on teachers' and students' responses to the reform directives. In Chapters 6 and 7, we take up the responses of the principals and instructional leaders in the layers above them. In Chapter 10, we look across all of these layers of interactions and begin to trace how, when, and why the reform messages may have changed, been diluted, or become distorted as they traveled through the system.

The intersection encounter between teachers and students is represented by the two innermost ovals of Figure 1.1. Those ovals represent teachers working with students to assist their learning of disciplinary subject matter. Because literacy was the first school subject to be addressed by the reform, this chapter focuses on the teaching and learning of literacy, as represented in the interactions between teachers, students, and the discipline of literacy.

Across San Diego, teachers were expected to follow a district-vetted, comprehensive model of K–12 literacy instruction known as the Balanced Literacy framework. As described in Chapters 3 and 4, the framework is intended to help students prepare to tackle increasingly complex text in increasingly independent ways. Although it takes a somewhat different form in elementary and high school, the underlying philosophy of the framework is the same across K–12: tailor instruction to individual student's needs, so that responsibility for learning is gradually released to each student. A Balanced Literacy approach requires teachers to determine each student's capacity to read and understand text, design instructional tasks that will challenge each student to reach the next level of reading, and provide just the right kinds and appropriate amounts of assistance as the student tackles these tasks.

This approach to literacy instruction represented a fairly radical departure from San Diego's teachers' past practices. Although systematic baseline data were not collected on the nature of literacy instruction before the Alan Bersin–Anthony Alvarado reforms, descriptions of earlier practice teachers offered during interviews suggested that instruction was teacher led, with little attempt to fit lessons to students' individual needs. Moreover, instruction did not focus on helping students develop increased independence and responsibility for learning. Finally, most of the instruction focused on tasks that were not cognitively complex. For example, students were more likely to be asked to determine literal meanings from texts rather than to make inferences about what they read. Thus, the framework required San Diego teachers and their students to learn a new way of interacting as they focused on the tasks of learning to read and write. This chapter examines how they responded to that challenge.

The chapter is divided into three main sections. In the first section, we describe how the district intended to implement the model of literacy instruction in classrooms. Then, drawing on our classroom observations, we offer model examples of teachers enacting key components of the framework and discuss what makes each an outstanding implementation of that framework practice. Next, we review observations of teachers' instructional practice to detect patterns of consistency with or deviation from the framework and consider what these patterns in deviations suggest about the reform and its implementation.

Because the district reform effort sought to align all literacy instruction, districtwide, with the tenets of the framework, our analysis is premised on the assumption that patterns of conformity to these tenets imply success on the part of the district leadership in educating teachers and influencing their instruction. The reformers' efforts were, of course, complicated by the fact that each classroom has its own history, capacities, norms, and routines—prisms through which the framework was interpreted, modified, and enacted in each class.

Components of Balanced Literacy

Our discussion of the enactment of the Balanced Literacy framework in classrooms groups the framework components into *structural features* and *enacted features*. We define structural features as those that have formal properties that are measurable in units of space or time. Enacted features are components that reflect reform concepts that are visible only, or almost only, through teachers' practice.

Structural Features

Structural features include components such as the physical environment and the distribution of classroom time. The district subscribed to the view that in a highly functional literacy classroom, the "physical and social structures are created within a print-rich environment to support students' needs and the methodology of the course" (SDCS, 1998b: 2). To ensure such a setting for San Diego's students, the district mandated a particular configuration of furniture, books, reading spaces, and areas devoted to specific pedagogical tasks within all classrooms in which literacy was taught. For instance, teachers were expected to display each day's agenda, the learning standards mandated by the State of California for each grade level, "Word Walls,"[1] charts of reading strategies cocreated by teachers and students, and examples of student work.

Physical Environment

Classroom space was divided into areas devoted to specific components of the framework: whole-class instructional space, group work space, and independent reading and working space. Lessons began with whole-class instruction and minilessons (described later), and each classroom was expected to feature a small area with chairs or floor pillows clustered around a whiteboard or an easel. During large portions of class time, students completed group work, sitting at tables to facilitate collaboration. Classrooms also had spaces filled with couches, throw rugs, and pillows for students to relax during independent reading (described later), and usually they had a few desks for independent study. Teachers organized supplies and journals in easily accessible areas so that students could retrieve them independently.

The class library was a focal point of each classroom. A core objective of the framework was for students to learn to independently select, comprehend, and enjoy books at their individual level of reading comprehension. These were called "Just Right" books, and a considerable amount of time was devoted to teaching students strategies for making a judgment about a book's level of reading difficulty and the degree to which the book might suit their interests. To help students choose Just Right books, teachers prepared classroom libraries organized by level of difficulty or subject, or both. For example, an elementary classroom might include bins of low-level books, books on frogs, and books by specific authors, such as Frank Asch and Lynne Reid Banks; in a high school classroom library, there might be bins of books on teen problems, books on American history, and books by such authors as Sandra Cisneros and Alexandra Day.

Time Distribution

Like the classroom environment, time was a structural feature of the reform. As described in Chapter 4, the daily schedule of literacy instruction in all schools followed a workshop model (for further discussion of workshop structures, see Atwell, 1998; Fletcher & Portalupi, 2001; Fountas & Pinnell, 2001).[2] Although the substance of activities varied across grade levels, the essential workshop structure remained the same (see Table 5.1).

Each workshop lesson began with a whole-class, teacher-centered segment known as the minilesson. This component, which was intended to occupy 20% of the instructional time, included read aloud, word study (vocabulary), and shared reading activities. During minilessons, all student activity remained under the close supervision of the teacher. Workshop continued with guided and independent practice, which represented 70% of the total lesson time. Teachers coached students in groups as they practiced reading strategies and conferred individually with students engaged in independent reading. Finally, the workshop structure provided an opportunity for students to share their efforts with each other and with the class as a whole for the final 10% of class time. The various segments of a daily workshop were "threaded," or conceptually aligned, around a central concept or skill to ensure coherence across that day's activities. Similarly,

Table 5.1. A Workshop Lesson

Segment	Time (%)	Purpose of the Segment	Characteristic Activities	Classroom Example
Minilesson	20	Teacher-led, didactic activities designed to transmit skills, concepts, or content from teachers to students. Expose students to readings that are above their ability level.	Read aloud Shared reading Short lecture Notes Charting	In a first-grade class, students follow along as the teacher conducts a read aloud of a picture book. She asks students to predict what might happen on each upcoming page and charts responses.
Guided practice and independent practice	70	Students choose texts within their interest and ability levels (Just Right books) to read independently. Guided reading and small-group instruction; small-group, pair, or independent work with coaching from the teacher.	Independent reading Conferring Small-group activities Reading journals Working in pairs Guided reading	In a ninth-grade class, students work in pairs to create interview questions for characters in the story. During independent reading, some students select Young Adult literature from the classroom bin as others complete reading journals, writing down questions and reflections that occur to them as they read silently.
Share	10	Students share work with one another and the class. Create charts that can be referred to in further lessons.	Community meetings Share	In a fourth-grade class, students meet in table groups to share their reflections on a short story everyone read independently. Then, each table group selects several reflections to share with the whole class.

teachers would use the central concept of a unit of study to stitch together different workshop sessions across several days.

Enacted Features

Enacted features of the framework are manifest in, and visible almost exclusively through, teachers' *practice*. Much more than the structural features, these components are ones that teachers may interpret, modify, reflect on, demonstrate in varying degrees, and absorb as new learning, with the result that their understandings about their subject matter and teaching changes and grows. Analytically, the notion of enacted features captures the ways in which teachers interpret and teach pedagogical elements of the framework. The workshop structure includes activities designed for the minilesson, such as read alouds and shared reading; activities designed for guided practice, including guided reading and small-group instruction; and activities designed for independent practice, primarily independent reading and conferring.

Enacted features also demonstrate how well teachers' instruction embodies a central tenet of the framework: that the responsibility for learning should be gradually released from teacher to student. The workshop structure is aligned conceptually with this belief. Colloquially, this correspondence is referred to as "*to, with,* and *by*" because in the first segment of the workshop, the teacher introduces a concept or skill *to* the students; during the next segment, students practice the concept *with* the teacher's help; and finally the students practice the concept independently, with the teacher's supervision As students move from minilesson to guided practice to share, they progress toward greater independence in their work, and the teacher's role changes concurrently. Minilesson activities are teacher directed. Through the guided practice activities (which include independent work), the teacher gradually transfers control over subject matter and skill acquisition to students. As the students work in groups or independently, the teacher mediates supervision so that, ideally, by the end of the session students can execute new skills and demonstrate mastery of new concepts on their own.

Six reading strategies form the core of the framework's approach to literacy instruction: making connections, inferring, predicting, summarizing, synthesizing, and visualizing. Although implemented somewhat differently for a first-grade classroom than for a tenth-grade one, these strategies were visible in most workshop lessons. For example, in a ninth-grade workshop focused on visualizing, the teacher's minilesson might feature a shared reading of a descriptive poem, during which she would point out the words that helped her visualize images as she read. During guided practice, she might model discovering descriptive words, and then students would work in groups on a visualizing activity, selecting poems from anthologies and drawing pictures of the images particular poems brought to mind. During independent reading, she might ask students to pay attention to vivid descriptions in their books and to copy particularly descriptive phrases into their reading journals. Finally, during share, students might record their favorite descriptive words and phrases on chart paper, discuss the visualizations these words evoked, and hang the charts on a classroom wall. In a third-grade workshop focused on visualizing, the teacher's mini lesson might feature a read aloud of a paragraph describing a county fair in a chapter book. He and the students together might name and list words that helped them imagine the sights, smells, and sounds of the fair as he read. During guided practice, students might read descriptive paragraphs to one another, emphasizing the descriptive words. During independent reading, students might select particularly descriptive passages from their independent reading books to record on charts and share with the class in the final portion of the workshop.

Examples of Balanced Literacy in Teachers' Practice

In this section, we offer examples of teachers' real-life enactment of components of the framework and discuss variations from the model. We first examine implementation of the structural features of the reform, specifically, the teachers' use of classroom space and of time. Next, we discuss the enacted features, including read aloud, shared reading, guided reading, independent reading, and conferring.

Structural Features

An Exemplary Demonstration of Structural Features
This section describes the classroom of Ms. Grey, a ninth-grade English teacher in her third year of teaching. All of Ms. Grey's professional experience, including student teaching, has taken place in the SDCS. The classroom environment she created reflects an exemplary implementation of the reform's structural components (time and space use). The twelve girls and seven boys in class the day we observed represented a range of ethnicities: African American, Hispanic, Asian, and Somali. As in most SDCS high school classes, there is no classroom aide.

Ms. Grey's classroom was welcoming, warm, and bright. She had divided her classroom space into three distinct work areas organized for minilessons, guided practice, and independent reading (see Figure 5.1). She had arranged chairs in a semicircle near the front of

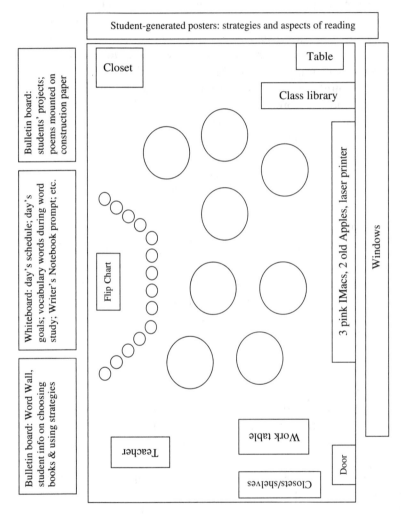

Figure 5.1 Sketch of Ms. Grey's Classroom.

Table 5.2. Ms. Grey's Workshop Schedule, March 8, 2001

Duration	Activity
27 minutes	Minilesson: Synthesis. Shared reading of "There Was an Old Woman Who Had So Many Children She Didn't Know What to Do" by Sandra Cisneros. Chart ideas.
46 minutes	Guided practice: Small-group work on "There Was an Old Woman…" *Synthesize* strategies used to make meaning of this short story, first in pairs and then in table groups.
24 minutes	Guided practice: Share responses to "There Was an Old Woman…"
33 minutes	Guided practice: Independent reading (note strategies used in independent reading journals).
15 minutes	Share reflections from journals with the class: What strategies most help us while we read independently?

the room for minilessons and community meetings. For independent and collaborative work, Ms. Grey had placed large tables around the room. A worktable held supplies (e.g., scissors, staplers, marking pens). A table in the back of the room provided a space for her to meet with small groups.

Ms. Grey had divided the classroom library into separate locations around the room. She had marked the reading level on the spines of most of her books and sorted them into plastic bins with labels such as "Teen Troubles," "Mystery," "Friendship," "Sports," "Nonfiction—Bravery and Courage," and popular authors. Rugs and pillows filled a corner near a bookshelf. She had covered the class walls with student work and charts the students had created that referenced reading strategies, elements of genres, the writing process, and highlights of class discussions of books, poetry, and nonfiction. Ms. Grey posted each day's schedule on the room's whiteboard. Ms. Grey's schedule for March 8, 2001, offers an example of a typical day's activities (see Table 5.2).

Why This Is a Good Example of a Workshop Environment
Ms. Grey's classroom represented an exemplary implementation of the spatial components of the Balanced Literacy framework. All areas of the room, as well as students' supplies, books, and journals, were accessible to students and organized such that her ninth-grade students could move through their daily tasks independently. Separate areas were set up for different activities, and her students understood the behaviors appropriate for each area and its activity. Reading levels marked on the spines of her library books helped students search for Just Right

books efficiently. Charts on the walls answered many questions that might arise during a typical day, several computers were available for students' use, and Ms. Grey kept her student records organized so that she could easily access them and discuss a student's progress with him or her.

Ms. Grey's use of time also closely reflected that in the model. During the workshop session outlined in Table 5.2, the lesson began with a shared reading of "There Was an Old Woman Who Had So Many Children She Didn't Know What to Do," from Sandra Cisneros's collection of short stories, *The House on Mango Street*. Ms. Grey used a cooking timer to help keep activities on schedule, and the percentage of time spent on minilesson (19%), guided practice (71%), and share (10%) represented a nearly ideal division of workshop time.

Enacted Features

This section examines enacted features—those components that are visible primarily through teachers' practice as they implement minilesson, guided practice, and independent reading. The most common minilesson activities are read alouds and shared reading; the most common guided practice activities are guided reading and conferring.[3]

An Exemplary Enactment of a Read Aloud
The read aloud represents one end of the framework's gradual release of responsibility continuum; the teacher assumes essentially all of the responsibility for classroom activity and student learning. Students have no access to the text except through listening to the teacher's reading. This isolates students' thinking skills; by eliminating the step of decoding, students concentrate on making meaning of what they hear. The ideal text for a read aloud meets several criteria: it is above the independent reading level of most of the students in the class; illustrates the skill that will be threaded throughout the lesson; lends itself to a rich, expressive oral reading; and is engaging for students to hear.

In this example of a read aloud, Ms. Atwood instructed her class of fifteen mostly Latino first-grade students. The students gathered on a small rug in front of her to focus on "the problem in the story" in the picture book *The Great White Man-Eating Shark*. Ms. Atwood, a fifteen-year veteran, pointed to a chart of story titles, reminded students of recent stories they had read, and asked them to recall those stories' central conflicts. After the students shared a few, Ms. Atwood reminded them of several others. Then she began reading about Norman, who was having difficulty swimming across a crowded swimming area.

Ms. Atwood [reading from the storybook]: *"This made him cross and resentful."* Look at the character's face. What does [*cross*] mean?

Students: Angry. Mad.

Ms. Atwood: Right. You could say, "Miss [Atwood], I'm cross," instead of saying "angry."

[She asks the class to make cross faces and students make angry faces.]

Ms. Atwood [pointing to pictures in the book]: What about this lady? This man?

[Students agreed that they were in Norman's way.]

Ms. Atwood: Do you sense a conflict now?

Lorena: Norman wants to swim by himself and they are in the way.

Ms. Atwood: This is really great. ... *"Norman thought of a plan."* What do you think his plan will be?

Rafael: He will pretend he is a shark.

Ms. Atwood: He will pretend he is a shark!

[Norman decided to frighten everyone out of the water by strapping on a fake shark fin. Ms. Atwood noted that Norman solved his conflict. People did leave the water, so Norman had the swimming area to himself.]

The exchange between Ms. Atwood and her first-grade students exemplifies an effective read aloud. Ms. Atwood introduced the focus of her lesson at the beginning of the activity, building on students' prior knowledge. She affirmed students' recollections of conflicts they had read about in other books and helped them draw connections between the stories. This preparatory work and her repetition of the focus gave students support for the cognitive work they would be doing during the read aloud. In addition to this exemplary enactment of the broad characteristics of the read aloud, Ms. Atwood also demonstrated command of the subtle techniques that make this activity particularly effective. As she read out loud to students, she used vivid expression, which engaged her listeners and helped draw them into the story. She demonstrated skillful reading and used visual aids, particularly charts she and the class had previously constructed.

A subtle yet powerful practice was Ms. Atwood's repetition of sentences with unfamiliar words. As she repeated these sentences, she prompted students to use the clues in the pictures to figure out what the words might mean. She drew kinesthetic learners into her lesson by having students make "cross" faces, which reinforced the vocabulary word. She waited patiently as students thought for themselves about unknown words. She supported their thinking skills by pointing out strategies they could use, by asking questions they could ask themselves as they read, and by emphasizing when to use those strategies. Ms. Atwood's read aloud offers an excellent example of encouraging participation from students while staying in control of the activity. She consistently kept students' attention focused on her and the cues she provided to help them make meaning of the story.

An Exemplary Enactment of Shared Reading
Shared reading, another minilesson activity, is situated in the gradual release of responsibility model between the read aloud, during which the teacher takes responsibility for students' learning, and guided practice, during which students take up more responsibility for their own work but have teacher support as needed. During shared reading, both the teacher and the students have access to the text. The teacher reads the text aloud and students read along in their texts, either silently or aloud. Teachers carefully select shared reading texts to meet two goals: the books should illustrate the focus of the day's lesson, and they should be too difficult for the majority of students to read on their own. Shared reading encourages discussions of textual features and meaning, practice with decoding, and relationships between written and spoken text.

In the following example, Mr. Thomas, a ninth-grade teacher in his fifth year of teaching, conducts a shared reading activity, focusing on the reading strategy *synthesis* with his class of eighteen students. This class of twelve girls and six boys included four girls who were recent immigrants from Somalia (each spoke and read English fluently), seven Hispanic students, one Caucasian student, and six African American students. Eight of the students were classified as English-language learners.

Mr. Thomas began the lesson by reminding students to look in their writer's notebooks for the definition of *synthesis*. Students volunteered that *synthesis* means "mixing up all the strategies" and "putting the strategies together."

> Mr. Thomas: How is baking something a possible metaphor for synthesis?
>
> Seta: You mix the eggs and the flour and the sugar, all the other parts together, to make something new. A cake.
>
> [Mr. Thomas wrote on the board: "Like baking a cake, taking parts, and combining them to make something new."]
>
> [Mr. Thomas passed out copies of the short story "Geraldo No Last Name" by Sandra Cisneros, and highlighters. On chart paper, he

made four columns: (1) "Thoughts," (2) "Where Is the Evidence?" (3) "Strategy," and (4) "Responses." He drew students' attention to a poster on the wall that featured the various strategies students had studied and would synthesize for this lesson: asking questions, predicting, inferring, visualizing, and making connections between the text and their own lives, other texts they had read, and what they knew of the world.]

Mr. Thomas: I'll read this story out loud and model my thinking on the chart. We will think about this together. You have to be a very active reader; you have to be metacognitive. My very first question is, "Why doesn't he have a last name?" I'm going to fill in the chart. ... What strategy did I just use?

Students: Questioning.

[Mr. Thomas drew a question mark in the "Strategy" column of the chart.]

Mr. Thomas [reading from the short story]: *"And how was she to know she'd be the last one to see him alive. An accident, don't you know. Hit-and-run. Marin, she goes to all those dances. Uptown. Logan. Embassy. Palmer. Aragon. Fontana. The Manor. She likes to dance. She knows how to do cumbias and salsas and rancheras even. And he was just someone she danced with. Somebody she met that night. That's right. And how was she to know she'd be the last one to see him alive?"* Any more reading strategies we used to understand that paragraph?

Nicacio: Maybe he died from dancing ... no, that's stupid.

Mr. Thomas: Okay, well, we had a prediction and then Nicacio thought about it and said no. That's being metacognitive. He thought about his thinking and decided not to make that prediction. Alex? What strategy?

Alex: Visualizing.

Mr. Thomas: What do you see?

Alex: I see a hot girl at a dance. Doing the salsa! [general laughter]

Mr. Thomas: Absolutely. And Rico, I heard you say the story is about Marin, she's the girl in the first sentence. How did you know that?

Rico: It says, *"Marin, she goes to all those dances ..."*

Mr. Thomas: Does it say "Marin is the girl who saw Geraldo for the last time"?

Rico: No.

Mr. Thomas: Then how did you know the story was about Marin?

Rico: I inferred it.

This example captures the key aspects of a shared reading. Mr. Thomas retained primary but not exclusive responsibility for student learning. He determined the pacing, controlled all of the activity, and kept students' attention focused on him. He posed questions and led students toward answers when they needed support. Mr. Thomas provided most of the information and closely guided students' comprehension.

An Exemplary Enactment of Guided Reading
In a typical workshop class, shared reading brings the minilesson to a close and the class moves on to guided practice. Guided practice occupies an important position in the scaffolding of literacy. It addresses the *with* in the "*to, with,* and *by*" continuum, providing a link between teacher-led and independent activities. Managing the guided reading aspect of guided practice is challenging. Students must be organized into small groups according to their reading levels and individual needs so that they can work together on the same skill (such as decoding) or concept (such as visualizing). This requires that the teacher first determine and then care-fully monitor students' reading levels and literacy skills. During guided reading, the teacher provides the groups with targeted assistance, as needed. In the following example, a group of third-grade students who were working on decoding skills read *Henry and the Helicopter*. Each of the four students in the group was a native Spanish speaker who had been speaking English for fewer than two years.[4]

Ms. Ahmed, a third-year teacher, first had students "picture walk" their fingers through the book, considering what the story was about without attending to the written words. Then, she read the story while students followed in their text. She had them pick out particular words and frame them with their fingers.

Next, Ms. Ahmed asked students to read out loud. The first page read, "Henry watched the helicopter flying above." Federico read the first page and got stuck on the word *watched*. Ms. Ahmed prompted him to sound out the /W/, and then he asked if the word was *watched*. She said he was correct and asked him if he should now just turn the page, and he said no, he should go back and reread. Ms. Ahmed asked him to find the character in the picture and describe what the man was doing. Federico said, "He's watching the helicopter. It's watched!" Ms. Ahmed had him reread it again, and this time he got all of the words correct. She praised him, saying that the book was difficult but that he got it.

Ms. Ahmed's work with Federico provided an exemplary demonstra-tion of a guided reading session. Carving out time from a busy day to help four students focus on a very specific skill, she used a combination of techniques, including some commonly associated with whole-language approaches and some associated with a phonics approach. Importantly, she reinforced good reading habits; not only did she address strategies, she supported students as they monitored their own reading and increased their reading stamina.

An Exemplary Enactment of Independent Reading and Conferring
The complementary pedagogies of independent reading and conferring, each an aspect of guided practice, are designed to provide an efficient, productive approach to supporting students as they move to the upper ranges of the literacy continuum. While most of the class reinforces reading skills and strategies by reading Just Right books on their own (independent reading), the teacher holds short, purposeful, one-on-one meetings with students (conferring).

The goal of independent reading is for students to practice reading strategies without assistance, thus achieving the final stage of the gradual release of responsibility model. During the typical independent reading period of twenty to forty-five minutes, students were expected to read books of their choice that were within their ability levels and to respond in writing to what they had read. The choice of an independent reading book was important, and a central objective of the workshop was to help students gain the skills necessary to choose Just Right books for themselves. Teachers also generally asked that during independent reading students focus on the goals of that day's workshop lesson (e.g., for a workshop focused on visualizing, students might be asked to look for examples of vivid imagery in their independent reading books).

The goal of conferring is twofold. This activity permits students to ask questions of the teacher in a safe, private environment, and it allows teachers an efficient means to gather rich information about students' current literacy strengths and weaknesses. Conferring also provides teachers with an invaluable tool for timely intervention in students' efforts to master skills. Literacy experts note that when struggling readers encounter a passage they cannot comprehend, they tend to skip over or block that section and continue reading. Thus, teachers often have no way of knowing which passages were problematic for students or why these sections presented problems (Fountas & Pinnell, 2001; Schoenbach, Greenleaf, Cziko, & Hurwitz, 1999). As students continue skipping over difficult text, they can lose the meaning of the text as a whole. When a teacher asks a student to read a passage out loud during a conference, he can intervene as the student's comprehension is faltering, helping the student *in the moment* by guiding her to use specific strategies to reestablish her comprehension.

Teachers were expected to keep detailed conferring records and to use this information to plan both individual learning paths and group activities addressing issues affecting multiple students. Examples of the kind of detailed information teachers could glean and record include knowledge about the student's preferences for or avoidance of particular strategies, improvements or continuing difficulties in grasping certain skills or strategies, favorite genres or authors, level of mastery of literacy goals such as good reading habits, and specific information about a student's interaction with a particular text. Careful record keeping also helps teachers maintain continuity between conferences. Ideally, at the conclusion of each one-on-one conference, teachers leave students with an assignment for their next meeting—a strategy to practice, a character to learn more about, or perhaps a suggestion to reevaluate a book choice. Teachers can follow up on these assignments and chart growth in students' abilities by referring to their conferring records.

In the example of a model enactment of independent reading and conferring provided next, Ms. Martinez, a ninth-grade teacher with five years' experience, begins by helping her class of eighteen students (eleven boys and seven girls; twelve are Hispanic, four are African American, and two are white) transition to independent reading activities before she turns her attention to Cesar, the first of the students she will talk with in individual conferences.

Ms. Martinez set a cooking timer and told students they had five minutes to get ready for independent reading. Students moved around the room, collecting books from bins, gathering reading journals and pencils, and getting comfortable on the couch or floor. Two students settled in front of a bookcase to choose new books. When the timer beeped, Ms. Martinez called for silence and reset it for thirty minutes. She reminded students that because the day's lesson was about figurative language, they were to record in their journals examples of similes and metaphors from their independent reading books. Soon everyone was silent. The only people in motion were Ms. Martinez, preparing for her first conference, and two students who had just finished books and were quietly perusing the bookcase shelves, looking for new choices.

Ms. Martinez met with Cesar, and the two whispered quietly at a round table near her desk. Cesar said he was enjoying his book but was having difficulty making sense of the actions of the central character.

Ms. Martinez: Can you show me the exact part where it starts to get confusing?
Cesar [pointing to a page in his book]: Here.

Ms. Martinez: How is Ben acting?

Cesar: He doesn't go to school. He don't talk to nobody. He hasn't gone to his work in three days.

Ms. Martinez: Do you think that might be normal for someone who has just been through a traumatic event?

Cesar: But it wasn't his fault. He was just riding in the car. He wasn't driving. He hadn't even had beers, because he just got there after his job.

Ms. Martinez: What can you infer? Do you think there's anything he might feel guilty about?

Cesar: No. He wasn't driving.

Ms. Martinez: Is there anything he could have done that he didn't do?

Cesar: Stayed home.

Ms. Martinez: Why shouldn't Alex have been driving?

Cesar: He was drinking the beer all night.

Ms. Martinez: Could Ben have done anything about that?

Cesar: Ben could have drove or not let Alex drive.

Ms. Martinez: What is your background knowledge about drinking and driving?

Cesar: You can have more accidents.

Ms. Martinez: Let me summarize what you've said to me. Ben is acting strangely, acting like the accident was his fault when it wasn't. He wasn't driving the car, and he hadn't had anything to drink. But maybe if Ben had stopped Alex from driving, there wouldn't have been an accident. So, there's a chance Ben feels guilty because he thinks he could have stopped Alex from driving, and maybe stopped an accident, but Ben didn't do anything.

Cesar: Like the kids at [-----] who knew that guy was bringing a gun to the school. They didn't say anything.

Ms. Martinez: Right. Excellent text-to-world connection, Cesar.

At the end of this short conference, Ms. Martinez felt assured that Cesar was no longer confused by Ben's actions. To reinforce this complicated inference, she asked Cesar to write in his journal about reasons a person might feel guilty even though that person did not do anything wrong. She also asked him to continue to make inferences about Ben's behavior as he read. Before moving on to the next student, Ms. Martinez made notes on her conferring records about her work with Cesar.

She completed four conferences in the thirty minutes before the timer beeped. At that point, she asked students to return to their tables, where they shared their examples of similes and metaphors, and each table group selected a few to share with the whole class. After every table had contributed, and in the few moments before workshop ended, Ms. Martinez reviewed the work of the day and what the class had learned about figurative language.

Ms. Martinez's enactment of independent reading and conferring is exemplary for several reasons. Reading researchers argue that uninterrupted reading is a powerful tool for improving both reading skill and stamina (Atwell, 1998; Keene & Zimmerman, 1997). Perhaps the most important action on Ms. Martinez's part was assuring that independent reading occurred every day. In her class, independent reading time was a protected commodity: no matter how else she might need to adapt her daily schedule to accommodate various activities and interruptions, she rarely omitted independent reading. The importance of this commitment can't be overstated. Soon into the semester, the students came to expect—and to respect and enjoy—their daily reading time. Ms. Martinez had quickly and successfully created a classroom culture in which reading was an honored, safe activity, and one in which students had choice.

Ms. Martinez's conference with Cesar demonstrates how much can be accomplished in a short, focused session. When Cesar said he had enjoyed his book until it became "too confusing," she realized she needed to help him regain control of the text. She first focused both her and Cesar's attention on the section of the book where he had lost command of it, then asked specific, concrete questions about that section. Cesar's answers helped her determine that he had not grasped that Ben felt guilty or why he might feel that way. Instead of asking Cesar to analyze the character, Ms. Martinez asked him to describe Ben's actions. Once he understood that, Cesar was able to think more deeply about Ben and the forces shaping his behavior.

Ms. Martinez suggested to Cesar that "there's a chance" Ben felt guilty because he believed the accident could have been avoided if he, the sober one, had driven instead of Alex. Although it would have been ideal for Cesar to articulate this himself, Cesar immediately offered a real-world example of someone who might feel guilty because he did not help stop a crime. This satisfied Ms. Martinez that Cesar had indeed grasped the concept, and she recognized his accomplishment explicitly. Cesar had regained his confidence in his reading. He was no longer confused by Ben's complicated feelings, and he continued reading independently without a breakdown in comprehension.

Ms. Martinez also managed the independent reading activities well. She used a cooking timer to mark transitions, and she created inviting spaces to facilitate comfortable reading. The materials students needed for independent reading were organized and accessible, making it easy to transition quickly into and out of the activity. She threaded the day's lesson into independent reading time, closing with group and whole-class sharing, so students experienced connections both with one another and between the day's lesson and the books they were enjoying. By threading the day's focus concept (figurative language) through to this end-of-class discussion, Ms. Martinez ensured that the workshop successfully gelled into a coherent whole.

Patterns of Deviations: In Structural and Enacted Features of the Reform

As we discuss in Chapter 6, a great deal of professional development in the SDCS was devoted to preparing teachers to assess students and use the information to plan instruction. The framework required that teachers gather evidence of students' strengths and needs (through a variety of means, including reading journals, conferring notes, and using formal evaluations such as the *Diagnostic Reading Assessment* and the *Independent Reading Assessment* mandated by the No Child Left Behind Act) and use their professional knowledge to shape how each component of the framework was implemented in their classrooms.

Teachers were well aware that their task was to develop their expertise in implementing the instructional strategies vetted by the framework; choosing not to follow the framework was not an option. District leaders emphasized that this did not, in their view, detract from teachers' professional judgment or acumen; the framework made room for and encouraged teachers to individualize how they presented components *within the boundaries of the framework*. A teacher did not have the freedom to choose not to conduct minilessons, for example, but was asked to draw on her professional acumen to assemble the groups and to determine texts and strategies to address in a particular lesson.

According to the framework, each teacher might enact a component of the reform slightly differently, but the general attributes of each component must be visible in every literacy classroom in the district. Therefore, the variation in teachers' practices that we found informative was not the minor individualization of framework components but rather the deviations teachers made from the framework, changes that clearly lay *outside* the reform boundaries.

A second point about our analysis of variations in practices relates to teachers' beliefs in the reform and its tenets. Because teachers' degree of allegiance to the reform goals can certainly help explain variation, we separated teachers into those who generally believed in and made an effort to follow the reform and those who voiced objections to the reform. We made these determinations based on data gathered in several ways. In interviews, teachers were asked to express their attitudes toward the reform and the instructional strategies it supported. Teachers were also asked about their preferred methods of teaching various aspects of literacy, and they were prompted to elaborate on the ways in which they integrated these preferences with the reform's demands. We used classroom observations to triangulate our conclusions, noting ways in which teachers' pedagogy appeared to reflect the reform's ideals and describing deviations from those ideals. In postobservation guided interviews, we asked the teachers to discuss the instruction we'd just witnessed to make determinations about the teachers' understandings of their own adherence to or deviation from the reforms tenets.

Some teachers explicitly stated that they did not support the reform, and our observations revealed instruction that did not reflect the framework. Others were vocal supporters whose instruction provided exemplary illustrations of the reform. The largest group expressed support of the reform and desire to learn and implement the framework. Where their instruction did not reflect the reform, these teachers generally offered their own explanations, such as "I haven't attended the in-service on that yet and am reluctant to try it until I do" or "I have been working with my peer coach on how to better implement that aspect with this particular group of students." It is this largest group of teachers we focus on in this section, because our aim is to understand the variations in instruction among teachers whom we have determined to be making sincere efforts to implement the reform's pedagogy in accordance with the reform's stated goals and procedures.

Patterns of Deviations in Structural Features

In general, classrooms varied less in structural features than in enacted features, and they varied more in high school than in elementary school classrooms. We suggest two reasons. First, structural features are easier to put into place, and second, structural features are easier to teach and to evaluate. In other words, it is less complicated to show teachers how to create an agenda and then to check to see that it has been posted, or to arrange furniture in a classroom than it is to teach the concepts of conferring or of threading.

Deviations in structural features involved variation in the use of space or time. The reformers invested extensive resources in tangible items, such as books for classroom libraries and easels for charting; all classrooms we observed had some portion of the reform's material aspects in place.

The most consistent structural deviations from the model involved the use of time, particularly with respect to conferring and minilessons. Many teachers went days or weeks without holding any one-on-one conferences with students, others held conferences of only a very few minutes, and still others conducted single conferences for nearly the entire independent reading session. Deviation from the ideal length of minilessons also was striking. Many minilessons lasted for half the class time or longer. This suggests that teachers privileged the *to* and *by* segments of instruction, bypassing the intermediate *with* step. When minilessons lead directly to independent reading, there is no time for guided practice.

The observed pattern of long minilessons, short (or no) guided practice sessions, and consistent independent reading sessions suggests several possible explanations. Classroom management may have been a factor in how teachers apportioned their time. In both minilessons and independent reading, students sat quietly, each with her or his attention focused either on the teacher or on their own reading material. The enactment pattern also suggests that teachers interpreted reform components through the prism of already existing norms and routines. For teachers and students used to a lecture style of teaching, the teacher-centered structure of the minilesson would be among the more familiar of the framework components. In many observations, we noted that even when teachers had planned to hold, for example, a ten-minute minilesson, if the activity was successful and students were participating, they often continued, allowing the minilesson to usurp the time set aside for guided practice. Finally, the extensive nature and swift implementation of the reform likely influenced its enactment. When difficult new knowledge is presented at a rapid pace across a large district, it is not surprising that the elements requiring the least new knowledge, such as arranging furniture or posting agendas, or those that most resemble familiar, teacher-centered activities would be the ones most consistently realized.

Patterns of Deviations in Enacted Features: Read Alouds and Shared Reading

Among the enacted features of the reform, the mini lesson activities, read aloud and shared reading, showed the least variation. The goals of read alouds and shared readings were similar: to offer students supported exposure to difficult text and to model good reading habits. Most teachers read with expression and clarity and stopped often to model their thinking. Patterns of disparity in read alouds and shared readings occurred in the ways in which teachers chose texts for these activities, questioned students during the activities, and made their goals for the activities.

The reform goals decreed that teachers choose texts for read alouds and shared readings based on three criteria—ability level, interest level, and reinforcement of the goals of the day's lesson. In our observations, teachers rarely employed all three. For example, when Mr. Newman taught a unit on drama for his tenth-grade students, he conducted read alouds and shared readings using plays that reflected elements of drama, but he did not consider the level of difficulty or students' interest in the plays. Shakespeare's *Macbeth,* for instance, was not a very successful choice for a shared reading (in an interview, Mr. Newman explained that he chose this play because he believed that, despite the new reform's lack of commitment to any particular literary canon for high school, all students should be exposed to *Macbeth*). The play was far too hard for students to comprehend as they followed along in the text and listened to his reading. Because the students did not understand what they heard as Mr. Newman read, they soon lost interest.

Patterns of deviation also occurred in the questioning strategies teachers used. The framework encouraged teachers to devise increasingly difficult questions with several possible answers, eventually requiring students to make sophisticated judgments and proffer varying points of view. The majority of questions we heard posed, however, remained at the level of simple comprehension. Similarly, teachers often supplied the answers to questions they asked, rather than waiting for students to answer.

For example, Mr. Tyson, a ninth-grade teacher, conducted a shared reading of a chapter of Chinua Achebe's novel *Things Fall Apart,* during which he posed the following questions:

Mr. Tyson: Umuofia's potent medicine. What is "Umuofia's potent medicine"?

[No answer.]

Mr. Tyson: It's like a winning tradition. They always, or almost always, win wars. So they have a *reputation* as great fighters. And so they can almost always stay out of wars because nobody wants to fight them. ... Who or what decides if the village should go to war? Who knows this?

[No answer.]

Mr. Tyson: Look in the book. It's on page 32.

Student: We have to look in the book?

Mr. Tyson: Hold on. I'll find it. ... It's the council of tribal elders.

Note that Mr. Tyson provided the answers to questions he posed and provided textual evidence instead of insisting that students look it up; he supplied the cognitive effort. We noted this pattern in many read alouds and shared readings. The district's professional development was focused on framework components; the basics of holding question-and-answer sessions were not covered. Mr. Tyson and his students, like many others we observed, appeared to revert to preform patterns with which they were familiar.

In other examples, teachers used read alouds and shared readings as a means of creating a quiet, teacher-focused time in the school day. For example, one teacher read *Harry Potter and the Goblet of Fire* to her ninth-grade students for forty minutes each day for several days in a row. She chose this text for its high interest level among the students; it did not support a pedagogical goal, and its ability level was too low for a read aloud with this group of students. When the class concluded, the teacher said that she planned to do this more in the future: "These read alouds are an oasis in the chaos of managing six tables of students doing group work, or rather *not* doing group work."

Still, the minilesson activities showed the least variation, with most teachers conducting daily read alouds or shared readings and most students being familiar with the procedure of gathering in a specific area to listen to the teacher read and to answer questions on the reading. It is important to note that among the workshop activities, the minilesson activities offer the least overall pedagogical punch, even if perfectly enacted. These activities lie on the far end of the gradual release of responsibility framework; by design, they are teacher centered, and they are intended to occupy only 20% of workshop time. These same characteristics, though, may help explain why read alouds and shared readings were fairly uniformly enacted by teachers across classrooms throughout the district.

Patterns of Deviations in Enacted Features: Guided Reading

Among the elementary school teachers in our sample,[5] the implementation of guided reading showed much more variation than did minilesson activities, and the variation was more pronounced in upper- than in lower-level grades. Most deviations had to do with how and when teachers convened the groups. Many teachers in the upper grades did not meet with guided reading groups each day, whereas others met only with their very low-level students (many teachers viewed guided reading time as an opportunity to help these students "catch up" to the others and devoted little or no guided reading time to other students). Another difficulty was with focus. Successful guided reading sessions offer groups one clear objective that they can grasp in a short, intense instructional period. Some teachers struggled with finding a good focus for a given group, whereas others assigned several objectives per group meeting. A third area of difficulty concerned questioning techniques. A pattern similar to the one we observed in shared readings emerged. Many teachers in our sample posed simple comprehension questions throughout the guided reading sessions, even though the framework asked teachers to scaffold instruction toward probing kinds of questions that required evidence from the reading. Teachers also tended to use questions that were either too specific, and thus did not encourage conversation, or too vague, and thus did not promote students' use of complex comprehension strategies.

We see these two patterns—the difficulty upper-grade teachers experienced trying to focus the small groups effectively and the variability in questioning techniques—as related. Working with emergent reading skills and concepts, such as decoding and basic comprehension, lends itself neatly to highly structured small-group interactions. In upper elementary grade levels, as both reading skills and concepts and the range of difficulties children can experience grow more complex, so too does small-group instruction.

Patterns in Deviations in Enacted Features: Independent Reading and Conferring

Deviations in independent reading followed two patterns: variations in how independent reading time was spent and variations in the ways in which students chose texts for this activity. In the section on deviations in structural features, we noted that the amount of time spent in the conferring and independent reading portion of the workshop varied widely. Our observations included independent reading sessions lasting from a short fifteen minutes to an astounding sixty minutes.

During this time, some teachers allowed students to engage in silent, independent activities other than reading, such as studying vocabulary words or completing homework. This practice seemed particularly prevalent in the high school three-hour literacy blocks. Several teachers began each day with independent reading because it "settles the students down," in effect using a pedagogical technique as classroom management. Other teachers argued that as long as students were doing something "academic," then the goal of this "quiet time" was being met. This could show a misunderstanding of what independent reading was all about, but it was more likely that teachers were allowing personal goals—receiving completed homework, keeping students occupied at the start of class—to supersede the goals of the framework. Once again, preexisting routines, norms, and ways of operating loom large as an influence on how an element of the reform was enacted.

Teachers also varied in the book selection practices they permitted. Selecting a book was intended to be a joint venture between students and teachers, but in several cases teachers selected books for students and in other cases students selected books without the teacher vetting their choices. We observed many interesting relationships between students and their books: some students read the first few pages of many books without ever completing any; some students consistently read books below their ability levels; and high school students showed a predictable preference for Young Adult novels.

The goals of independent reading included urging students to test their independent reading ability levels with increasingly difficult texts, exposing students to a variety of texts, and helping students develop a love of reading. The free-choice aspect of independent reading did indeed seem to attract reluctant readers to books, which was no small feat. For many teachers, independent reading was an oasis in the day. Allowing students to select what they wanted on their own, change books as often as they wished, and read without being required to do any other activities related to the book made it possible for teachers to *essentially* follow the framework without putting the same effort into it as they had to devote to other activities. Thus, the *affective* goals of independent reading seemed more likely to be achieved than the *pedagogical* goals.

Conferring presented the most deviation from the framework. Patterns emerged in both the frequency of sessions and the substance of the conferences. The ideal methodology for conferring was one five- to seven-minute conference per student, at least every other week. We recorded conferences that lasted less than a minute and conferences that lasted more than thirty minutes, and we observed teachers meeting with individual students anywhere from every other day to less than once a month. Many teachers were conscious of these lapses. In interviews, they asserted that when they turned their attention to one student, the rest of the class was unable to stay focused on their tasks. Many felt unable to maintain a conferring schedule; several teachers conferred with each student so irregularly that it undermined the practice.

More striking was the variation in the substance of the conferences. A prime concern, again, was questioning. Many conferences we observed centered not on deep understanding but on affective or low-level comprehension questions. For example, we often heard teachers ask, "Are you enjoying the book?" without following up with requests that students support their answer with evidence. Students were often asked to "retell" the plot of what they were reading but not to discuss the meanings they constructed as they read. In early elementary classrooms, where it is appropriate to work with students on basic skills, teachers often asked students to read passages and then worked with them on pronunciation and decoding skills. The variation was wider at upper elementary grades and widest in high school classrooms.

In high schools, the teachers we observed were particularly prone to using independent reading time to work at their desks or wander the room keeping order. As a whole, these teachers tended to hold fewer conferences than did their elementary school colleagues. Still, as we noted earlier, independent reading appeared to be a success, at least on an affective level. In almost every high school classroom we observed, students read independently, on a regular basis, for at least twenty minutes each day. Many educators would agree that this must have had a positive impact on students' reading lives. Conferring, on the other hand, although equally important, was less successful. A goal of the framework was for students to read well independently. To measure progress toward that goal, we must know if students are reading Just Right books independently, if they're employing reading strategies as they read independently, if they are choosing increasingly more difficult books to read independently, and if they comprehend what they read when they read independently. Under the structure of the framework, without consistent conferring, it is difficult to know if and to what extent students are independently employing these skills and habits.

Conclusions

The patterns of deviation we have discussed suggest two basic trends. First, there was much more variation in enacted than structural features, and within enacted features, variation increased with the progression from read alouds toward independent reading and conferring. Second, we noted more variation in high school than in elementary school classrooms, and within elementary schools, there was more variation in upper grades than in kindergarten through second grade.

The relative consistency in structural features of the reform is fairly simply explained, we believe. Changes of this kind require the least deep knowledge of the framework on the part of the teachers and therefore are less dependent on professional development than are enacted features. Furthermore, these reform features interfere the least with the regular routines of the classroom. Within structural features, teachers' use of space was less variable than their use of time.

Teachers frequently spent more than the suggested 20% of workshop time on mini lessons. There are two factors that seem to reinforce this practice. First, with students gathered close by and the teacher delivering information from the front of the room, mini lessons most closely resemble the didactic teaching models that were already familiar to many teachers and students. Thus, amidst the anxiety that accompanies any change, the mini lesson portion of the day may have been most comfortable for both students and teachers. Second, mini lessons can be used as a classroom management tool. The reformers' position on classroom management was that a solid pedagogical model, such as well-run guided reading groups or well-managed conferring, would necessarily lead to a well-managed classroom; virtually no professional development in San Diego addressed classroom management as an independent topic. Yet, classroom management proved extremely difficult for many teachers, particularly when they tried to manage several different activities and groups of students during one class period. Mini lessons offered a respite from what many felt was a chaotic classroom environment.

To explain variation within the enacted features, we revisit the gradual release of responsibility model to argue that as students take on more responsibility for their own learning, successful implementation of the components requires teachers to have a more nuanced understanding of the core principles of the framework to guide students' own deeper learning. At first glance, it may appear counterintuitive: Why should teachers have to know more if students have more responsibility for their learning? We believe the answer lies in teachers' changing role across this continuum (see Figure 5.2).

Successful enactment of the gradual release of responsibility model requires deep understanding of and commitment to the principles underlying the framework, particularly as students become more independent in their learning. It is much more difficult to manage students' individual application of new knowledge and skills than it is to impart knowledge and skills to groups of students.

Of the workshop elements, guided reading and conferring showed the most variation and seemed to present teachers with the most difficulty in implementation. There is logic to this: guided reading and conferring are similar activities conducted on different scales. Both require close questioning by teachers of individuals or small groups of students. There was considerable evidence that teachers struggled with the types of questions they should ask to support students' comprehension of texts. We speculate that this is due, at least in part, to teachers' lack of thorough understanding of both the rationale and the practices of questioning for deep meaning.

Conferring showed the greatest variation in both elementary and high schools. During this activity, teachers have least direct control over

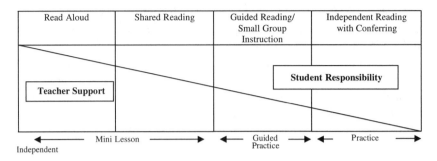

Figure 5.2 The Gradual Release of Responsibility in the Framework.

students' learning and can do the least planning. Although they enter conferences with a goal in mind, conferences are improvisational; teachers must construct them, including questioning strategies, *in the moment,* responding to the information they receive from students as they confer.

According to their interviews, the teachers in our study generally supported the workshop model, as a whole, which suggests that it captured important ideas about teaching and learning literacy. Wide variation in implementation occurred across classrooms, though, including classrooms where teachers were genuinely attempting to teach according to the framework as they had learned it through the district's extensive professional-development activities. This suggests that variation may be due to teachers' uneven understandings of the core tenets of the reform. The variations in guided reading and conferring, in particular, suggest that the work the reformers and teachers undertook was strikingly difficult. In many cases, teachers' knowledge simply was not up to the task. This offers a possible reason why the implementation of ambitious reform, particularly reform that directly targets teaching and learning, is so challenging.

CHAPTER 6

Learning in Teacher Professional Development: The Enactment of Reform between Teachers and School Leaders

In this chapter, we shift our attention to the second oval of San Diego's nested learning communities (see Chapter 1, Figure 1.1), the intersection encounter between school-based leaders (chiefly principals and peer coaches) and teachers. Although one step removed from the core of teaching and learning (the classroom), the interaction between school leaders and teachers is critical. School leaders were expected to work with teachers to assist students to learn subject matter. Because literacy was the first school subject to be addressed by the reform, this chapter, like the previous one, focuses on that subject area in examining the ways in which school leaders assisted teachers.

Professional-Development Opportunities for Teachers

Job-Embedded Professional Development

By design, most professional development for the teachers of the San Diego City Schools (SDCS) occurred on-site, in their own work environments.

Although teachers were offered workshops during intersession and summer, they received most of their training regarding the Balanced Literacy framework and the workshop model *inside* their schools and classrooms during the school year. Professional development, the *Blueprint for Student Success* specified, was to be "job-embedded and focused on improving teachers' knowledge of *what* concepts and skills needed to be taught and their understanding of *how* the concepts and skills should be taught" (SDCS, 1998a: 23). Continuous development around these issues was at the core of the district's instructional improvement effort, which was aimed at increasing student achievement, the reform's ultimate goal.

This emphasis on job-embedded professional development is supported by findings from more than two decades of research on the professional development of teachers. Most of this work questions the usefulness of the "Hello–Good Bye–God Bless You" workshop (Fullan, 1991) and instead endorses professional development that covers all faculty at a school, extends over time, incorporates classroom practice, and includes classroom-based coaching (Desimone, Porter, Garet, Suk Yoon, & Birman, 2002; Fullan, 1991; Hawley & Valli, 1999; Loucks-Horsley, Love, & Stiles, 1998; Wilson & Berne, 1998). Moreover, San Diego's decision to focus professional development on the teaching and learning of Balanced Literacy is backed by research that has demonstrated that successful professional development (as shown in improved student learning) accentuates content over form (Kennedy, 1998). Specifically, programs that focused mainly on teachers' behaviors had smaller influences on student learning than did programs that focused on teachers' knowledge of the curriculum and specific subject they were expected to teach and an understanding of how students learn that subject.

Principals were the linchpin of the SDCS reform effort. They were expected to oversee and deliver continuous professional development to their teachers. Two important vehicles for fulfilling this responsibility were instructionally focused faculty, department and grade-level meetings, and frequent visits to classrooms to model and observe instruction and help teachers individually. This approach to the role of school leadership departs significantly from past practices in San Diego. Dorothy Cavanaugh, principal of Emmanuel Jackson Elementary for twenty years, captured the enormity of the shift from manager to leader of instruction the reform represented: "It's only in the last two years that we [the principals] have become more skilled and knowledgeable about instruction. [In the past] we *said* we were Instructional Leaders, but, number one, I was a plant manager. So, it's a real change, for the better, of course" (Cavanaugh, 2001). Thus, the reform demanded that San Diego principals learn new skills and new ways of interacting with teachers. Just as teachers would no longer be "left alone" in their classrooms to teach as they saw fit, principals would no longer be "left alone" in their offices to attend to paperwork.

Although new for the SDCS, this approach to school leadership was consonant with the historical development of the role of the principal (Andrews & Grogan, 2002). The late 1980s and the 1990s marked a general shift away from the building manager role (Andrews & Grogan, 2002: 2). Principals, as "pioneers in the development and management of new forms of instructional practice in schools," were now expected to "develop a thorough understanding of the rapidly evolving body of research on [student and adult] learning and teaching that motivates new practices" (Rowan, 1995: 116). Consistent with this new model of leadership, the San Diego school district expected principals to make their first priority improving teaching and learning at their sites.

In our six case study schools, the principals remained at their posts throughout the four-year span of our data collection period (1998–2002). Each took seriously the charge placed on him or her to become an on-site leader of instruction. Although all were supporters of the Alan Bersin–Anthony Alvarado reforms, their readiness to tackle a leadership role in instructing faculty varied on a number of dimensions. First, they differed with respect to their level of familiarity with literacy instruction in general and the Balanced Literacy framework in particular. One principal, Cynthia Oliver at Scripps Elementary, was quite knowledgeable about early literacy instruction. As a classroom teacher, she had participated in the Reading Recovery program, an individualized form of literacy instruction with close ties to the Balanced Literacy approach. Dorothy Cavanaugh was from an older generation of teachers and had been a math teacher. She often remarked that the knowledge base for literacy instruction had been so much less well developed at the time of her preservice training: "I was from the era of Basal texts, when publishers supplied teaching scripts, and a kind of 'one-size-fits-all' approach to teaching students reigned" (Cavanaugh, 2002). She did not consider herself skilled in literacy, but she was an eager learner. In the high schools, we found principals who had taught literacy but not one who had specifically taught reading. In general, these secondary school principals felt unprepared to coach their teachers.

Second, the principals we studied differed with regard to job experience. Constance Parker at Harvey Mudd Elementary had been a principal in her building for many years and was well known and respected by her mostly veteran staff. Cavanaugh, although also a long-time principal, was in the process of developing a relationship with her staff at Emmanuel Jackson, all of whom were much younger than she. Oliver was in her first year as principal when the reforms began. Caroline Magionne at Creeley High School had been a middle school principal for many years but was new to the position of high school principal. She followed in the footsteps of a very popular principal (who was promoted to instructional leader [IL]) and was trying to develop relationships with and respect from a staff reluctant to accept a new leader. Hunter High School's principal Mary Bennett had been there for more than fifteen years and was well respected as a kind and caring leader. She was well poised to launch a reform at her school. Terrence Townsend was new to Martin Luther King High, supportive of the reform, and personal friends with his IL.

For all their differences, however, the principals were similar in one respect: all had limited experience working with teachers as learners. Only one (Parker) had any background in staff development; the remainder of the principals had little or no experience assessing teachers' instructional needs and providing assistance to help them develop into better teachers. That lack of experience was a considerable disadvantage, according to Parker, who explicitly acknowledged the value her own background provided:

> I have been a staff developer for the district level, I've been at the Ed Center before, and at different places [in a coaching capacity]. I know how to do it because I went through First Steps [training program for mentor teachers]. [Without that experience] I would probably be overwhelmed like some of these principals right now and not know what to do. (Parker, 2002)

District leadership expected principals to assume much, but not all, responsibility for professional development of their staff, whereas most vice principals assumed operational responsibilities. The principals' primary support for carrying out their new instructional duties was the peer coach. This position represented a major districtwide investment in support of teacher learning at the school site. Working under the direction and supervision of the principal, peer coaches (also called staff developers) were charged with building school capacity. The district's plan called for the neediest schools to be assigned peer coaches and all schools to have peer coaches on staff by the academic year 2000–2001. In addition, literacy administrators (former principals with certified expertise in literacy) were assigned to some high schools in the 2001–2002 school year to provide support to teachers and peer coaches.

In the remainder of the chapter, we explore how three elementary school and three high school leaders, along with their peer coaches, handled their new, reform-initiated responsibilities for helping teachers become familiar with the Balanced Literacy framework and correctly implement its principles and practices in their classrooms. We begin by examining the role of the peer coach. Then we describe and analyze two key activities all school leaders were expected to undertake, namely, planning and executing meetings of all faculty, individual departments, and grade-level teachers and making regular visits to individual classrooms. We conclude by identifying patterns in the conduct of these activities, paying particular attention to the kinds of learning the meetings and visits encouraged.

The Role of Peer Coaches and Literacy Administrators

The peer coach role was designed to be nonevaluative; in fact, peer coaches retained their formal status as teachers (including their union membership). The literacy administrator position was somewhat different. Literacy administrators were former peer coaches or teachers who received their training while in that position and now supported teachers in implementing the Balanced Literacy framework (e.g., by designing professional development that responded to specific teachers' needs).

Under the leadership of the principal, peer coaches and literacy administrators were expected to work to deepen teachers' knowledge of the reform. Their efforts took many forms. They led the substantive portion of grade-level meetings, faculty meetings, and study groups. They also worked side by side with teachers in their classrooms. In fact, peer coaches argued that they were most effective when they were working one-on-one with teachers, analyzing practice, and wrestling with how to change that practice to meet students' needs. This strategy was often criticized, however, because it reduced the time peer coaches had available to provide schoolwide support. In the later years of the reform, schools identified "core" teachers—faculty who showed instructional capabilities beyond those of their peers. Coaches began to work individually with these core teachers, with the expectation that with additional training, these core teachers could address issues of schoolwide capacity.

Although peer coaches typically were appointed at the recommendation of the principal on the basis of their expert teaching ability, they varied in their capacity and effectiveness for several reasons. Their ability to effect change was dependent on their background knowledge and experience. One of the most capable coaches had been an excellent teacher who rose from the ranks of his school's teaching staff. Teachers respected his knowledge and considered him "one of their own." When coaches were brought in from outside the school, however, problems often arose. A teacher from Martin Luther King High School explained it this way:

First of all, I think it's because they bring the people in from other schools. And, so, no one knows them. It's kind of like, the community thing. When you don't know a person, it's really easy to hate them. I don't think schools focus enough on like letting them—people get to know the person first—so they feel very intimidated by them, like they're coming in to say you are doing this wrong or you're doing this wrong. And so it creates like a hostility. (Cline, 2002)

Another limitation on the effectiveness of peer coaches was teachers' perceptions that the coaches' role was evaluative. Even though peer coaches did not possess the formal authority to evaluate, teachers suspected that they shared evaluative information with their principals, who did have the authority to evaluate them. This commonly held belief constrained the coaches' professional-development efforts. For example, one high school coach stated, "We have a lot of new, and a lot of struggling teachers, and so I sort of operate on a theory that I need to be invited in." This coach focused her work mainly on the teachers who were most confident and advanced in their understanding of the workshop model, and although she claimed she was building rapport and gaining trust among the other faculty the fallout was that she was always "putting out fires" (Murphy, 2002) and was working with only a small fraction of the faculty. The knowledge coaches had of the reform varied widely. Many, although considered very good teachers, had limited experience with Balanced Literacy or the workshop model. Now they were expected to lead others toward a deep understanding. The coach quoted previously was not surprised that there was "shallow knowledge among teachers," because most coaches were learners themselves. Some were very frank during interviews, admitting that they didn't really feel prepared for the job and sometimes felt as though they knew little more than the teachers they were coaching. Laura Thompson (2002) at Martin Luther King High, explained, "It wasn't until that second year that we kind of went, okay, so now that we see the whole picture—and I'm a very whole-picture person—now I know what you want me to do—go teach." But, she continued, this new feeling of confidence was short-lived: "It was hard because they would train us in something and then something else would come, and it seemed a little different from what they were asking us to do before." Not only was there a tremendous amount of information to learn, the content of the reform kept growing as one piece, such as guided reading, was rolled out after another piece, such as read alouds.

Coaches received most of their training from the district's literacy staff. However, some training was also provided by outside consultants, mainly from New York City's Community School District #2. These consultants' notions of good practice were not always identical to those of district trainers, which caused even more confusion. One example involved the district's directive to level books (see Chapter 5 for details about leveling). At one training session for high school peer coaches and teachers, a consultant argued against leveling. The consultant maintained that at the high school level, the stigma struggling students would experience when assigned low-level texts and the difficulty teachers would face in trying to locate books pitched at low levels that nevertheless would be of interest to this age group would outweigh the benefits of "Just Right" books for high school students. When the district realized that some consultants' directives were not consistent, the leaders would, according to one peer coach (interviewed on April 12, 2002), "take them [the peer coaches] to lunch and redirect them." Sometimes, however, this was too little too late. As Roberta Vasquez, the Creeley High School literacy administrator, explained, "Initially, we talked about classroom libraries and whether or not to level books. Well, we have … decided that we are *not* going to level books, explicitly." Not surprisingly, district administrators were not happy with this decision, but the high school staff, citing the consultant's advice, stood by their group decision. Another source of confusion occurred when the messages coaches received differed from the information their principals had learned during monthly principals' conferences. ILs and the managers in the district's literacy department often presented slightly different perspectives on the same topic. It became the principals' and peer coaches' job to sort out the conflicts before passing information along to teachers.

The challenges peer coaches faced resulted in a high turnover rate that affected capacity-building efforts at the schools. Emmanuel Jackson Elementary, for instance, experienced a tremendous turnover in peer coaches. Frustrated by the intensity of the work, many peer coaches opted to return to the classroom. In other cases, principals elected to remove them from their positions and hire different teachers, whom they perceived as more competent. Overall, however, principals faced a shortage of competent and qualified peer coaches. Moreover, there was a very real possibility that the best coaches would be recruited away from their schools to fill other key positions within the district (such as principalships). For example, peer coach Carl Lichter left Harvey Mudd Elementary after two years to enter the apprenticeship program for new principals sponsored by ELDA, the Educational Leadership Development Academy run by the University of San Diego in partnership with the SDCS (ELDA is described in more detail later in this chapter). Because the school's other peer coach left at the same time, Principal Constance Parker abruptly had no coaching capacity, despite having sufficient funds to cover the costs of three coaches.

Similarly, San Diego schools were plagued by shortages of literacy administrators. Martin Luther King High School was fortunate to have a strong peer coach but only benefited from having a literacy administrator several years into the reform, after the peer coach was qualified to assume the position. Hunter High School had the same peer coach every year during our study but never had a literacy administrator. After assessing the capabilities of individuals in the district's pool of candidates and evaluating his faculty's receptivity to "outsiders," Hunter's principal strongly urged district leaders to promote someone from the school's teaching staff to this position. The request was denied. Another literacy administrator in the district was asked to step down because, having alienated the entire faculty, she could not be effectual.

Although district leaders were well aware of these kinds of leadership capacity problems, resolutions proved difficult to effect. The size of the district and the speed of the reform forced district leaders to hire inexperienced individuals, who were then given incomplete training for their new positions. Peer coaches' training primarily involved observing videotaped or real-time lessons in which lab teachers taught students reading or writing skills.[1] This approach helped peer coaches identify the actions of one teacher in interaction with his or her students, and it helped acquaint them with the instructional strategies teachers should be using with their students, but it was difficult for coaches to apply this knowledge in their day-to-day interactions with their own teachers. The training the coaches received tended to stay at the level of "this is how good coaching looks" rather than providing theory and practice regarding when and how to apply various coaching techniques in the messy, sometimes chaotic and often rushed environments they found in their own schools.

Not unlike the interactions that characterize the guided reading and conferring components of Balanced Literacy (see Chapter 5), the teaching and learning that occurs between coach and teacher is constructed in the moment, as the two interact. It is complex and demands that the coach be "on the balcony" (Heifetz, 1994), observing and reflecting on the interaction, while at the same time being engaged in it. The process requires that the coach, similar to a teacher conducting a guided reading session, analyze and make meaning of the interaction *as it is occurring* and be able to construct appropriate questions and make teaching points explicit to the teacher. This is difficult work that cannot be scripted and that requires sustained effort over time—time neither the coaches nor the teachers had in the context of this fast-paced reform. Understandably, many coaches tended to adhere to specific language, scripts, and tenets that were repeated in their own training as opposed to addressing the unique problems of the individual teachers with whom they interacted. To be effective when venturing into the unknown territory inherent in spontaneous interpersonal communication requires building knowledge and confidence in advance. It requires adaptive teaching that can arise only out of a deep understanding of content and process. Like the teachers we described in Chapter 5, most peer coaches appeared to have difficulty mastering this interactive, learner-centered approach.

Coaches' efforts to help teachers also were stymied by the incomplete leadership preparation the district provided. High school peer coaches typically assumed responsibility for training all genre studies (literacy) teachers and sometimes were responsible for an entire literacy department faculty. Elementary school coaches led professional development for the whole school. Principals held peer coaches accountable for changing teachers' practice. This meant changing the culture of teaching. It meant carrying the district's ideology to the teaching staff, navigating political tensions (e.g., those between principals and teachers), and building the capacity of teachers who were fearful of losing their jobs and more comfortable adhering to familiar teaching methods. Lacking the benefit of systematic leadership training, each coach dealt with the unanticipated, or at least unplanned for, aspects of his or her role as best he or she could. This led to wide variation across the district in the level and quality of professional development teachers received. As put by one teacher after three years of the reform, "If you've got a good peer coach, she could be absolutely invaluable. … If you don't have a good peer coach, what can I say?"

Interactions in Teacher Professional-Development Events

Faculty, department, and grade-level meetings provided principals and peer coaches with high-visibility opportunities to practice their emerging instructional leadership skills. Likewise, our observations of these meetings offered a unique opportunity to evaluate the ongoing successes, struggles, and challenges experienced by school leaders.

Interactions in Faculty, Department, and Grade-Level Meetings

The content and organization of faculty meetings differed somewhat between high schools and elementary schools. In the high schools, principals most often addressed the operations of the school. Because high school faculties are composed of teachers from multiple disciplines, some only tangentially involved with the literacy reform, principals elected to save discussions of reform practices for professional-development events led by their site literacy administrator(s) and peer coach(es). Thus, the high school faculty meetings we observed generally were not about instruction. During one faculty meeting at Hunter, the principal spent two hours providing budget information, discussing how well the athletic teams had done, and relating other details about operational issues. At Martin Luther King High, one meeting was devoted to the upcoming accreditation visit, committee reports, and the like.

As the reform unfolded, ILs began requiring their high school principals to videotape faculty meetings so that ILs could critique the principals' efforts to teach their staff about Balanced Literacy. Given the operational focus of the high school faculty meetings, this request was problematic. For the most part, the principals did not alter the design of the meetings; they did, however, take a more active role in certain other professional-development events for literacy faculty. This move enabled the principals to meet their ILs' requests for evidence of involvement in educating their faculties about the framework.

At the elementary school level, where the entire faculty was responsible for teaching the Balanced Literacy framework, most principals scheduled either weekly or biweekly meetings of all teachers or grade-level teams of teachers. Although some business items were addressed (e.g., testing dates were announced), coverage of operational items typically was limited to a very brief segment at either the start or the end of the meetings. The majority of time was devoted to the details of implementing the Balanced Literacy framework. The length of meetings varied. Some occurred before or after school for thirty to seventy-five minutes. Although the arrangement of elementary school teaching schedules permitted holding meetings for two to three hours, this practice took regular teachers out of the classroom. At some schools, staff meetings were so frequent that teachers complained they spent entirely too much time away from their classrooms. The faculty and grade-level meetings nearly always followed the same format as the monthly principals' conferences (see Chapter 7 for details). They began with an opening address that explained the purpose of the session's work and the urgency of the reform; this was followed by an interactive work session on some aspect of the reform content. The final part consisted of carefully prepared concluding remarks that restated the purpose of the session and the ideology of the reform.

Meeting topics usually were determined by what principals had been exposed to at their most recent monthly principals' conference. Thus, in any given month, we were likely to observe professional development on the same topic (e.g., how to organize classroom libraries, how to conduct one-on-one conferences with students) across our three case study elementary schools, especially in the early years in the reform. An analysis of the topics of faculty meetings at the three elementary schools during the 2000–2001 and the 2001–2002 school years reveals that the majority dealt with either the guided reading or the conferring components of the Balanced Literacy framework, paralleling what principals were learning in their own professional development. After the first year of implementation, the district realized that teachers' limited understanding of the underlying purpose and rationale of the components of Balanced Literacy undermined their ability to enact the program well. Thus, early in the second year, district leaders began instructing principals to instruct teachers to think more deeply about the framework rather than simply mimicking a set of practices. As we explained in Chapter 5, teachers found the guided reading and conferring aspects of Balanced Literacy the most difficult to implement. By focusing first the principals' conferences and then the faculty and grade-level meetings on these two components, leaders hoped to address the uneven classroom-level implementation of the reform.

The principals (and their peer coaches) in our case study schools made concerted efforts to help faculty reach a deeper understanding of the Balanced Literacy framework. Oliver's experiences at Scripps Elementary are typical. At a K–3 faculty meeting (October 9, 2001), she began by setting the tone. After introducing the topic of the meeting (conferring), Oliver noted that as a group, the teachers had studied how to conduct various components of the workshop (read aloud, shared reading, etc.). Today, however, she stated, they were going to spend their time talking about *why* having an independent, one-on-one conference with each child was so important. Then she described the advantages of conferring—that it allows the teacher to sit down next to a child and adjust instruction to meet the child's needs (see Chapter 5). She continued to talk passionately about what teachers can offer during one-on-one sessions, saying that individualized conferencing constitutes "powerful teaching on the go"—teaching that works well when teachers know their students. Getting back to the purpose of the meeting, she reiterated, "Today, the group will deepen their understanding of what conferring is about."

In this meeting, Oliver and her peer coaches strove to go beyond the superficial. We observed many similar efforts on the part of our case study principals. Sessions typically began with principals framing the purpose for the professional development and discussing the urgency of doing better for the children. Then they turned the main part of the session over to the coaches, who guided the teachers through a planned activity. Often smaller groups were formed to interrogate a text, review materials, or generate a list of ideas related to the meeting theme to pursue in their own classrooms. After members of the small groups shared their experiences, an inspirational message from the principal closed the day's meeting.

We also observed principals adopting many of the same professional development techniques that they experienced when they were in the position of learners in the monthly principals' conferences. For example, one principal appropriated the technique of first exposing workshop participants to a task as adult learners and then asking them to imagine what it might feel like from a student's perspective. She had her faculty read a particularly challenging passage of adult-level text and asked them to reflect on the strategies they had used to make sense of it. Then, she asked the teachers to examine a student text and consider what strategies students might use to make sense of it.

Thus, principals appeared to be carrying out district leaders' messages and even adopting some of their pedagogical techniques. An analysis of our thirty observations of faculty and grade-level meetings across the three schools, shows, however, that despite principals' and coaches' good intentions and hard work, the content and kinds of interactions that typically characterized these meetings were not conducive to deep learning. Although teachers were exposed to the official rhetoric about the underlying purpose and rationale for guided reading and conferring, their attempts to interpret and make sense of these new ways of interacting with their children (by asking questions during sessions or trying to apply new knowledge to their classroom practice) often resulted in frustration. In the next section, we examine some of the reasons for teachers' ongoing problems with implementation of the reform.

Challenges to Achieving Deep Understanding of Balanced Literacy

Three challenges to the district's efforts to implement the Balanced Literacy framework across all schools and classrooms emerged as most significant: the need to accomplish deep learning within the constraints of a limited time frame, principals' and coaches' limited understanding of the concepts that they were trying to teach, and the difficulty of reaching common ground between school leaders and teachers. We address each in turn.

The Need to Accomplish Deep Learning in a Limited Time Frame

Faculty and grade-level meetings were intended as occasions for "moving teachers to the next level" of understanding. Principals and, sometimes, peer coaches devoted considerable time and energy planning these events. At the meetings we observed, however, time management often was a problem. Time would run out before the group reached the culminating activity—the point when the meaningful learning, often involving application to practice, should have crystallized. For example, teachers were asked to read a chapter on conferring by Lucy Calkins in *The Art of Teaching Reading* and then to discuss the reading using a "What? So What? And Now What?" format. Discussion of "What?" revolved around summarizing and checking for understanding of the main ideas of the chapter. Discussion of "So What?" consisted of exchanges about how innovative Calkins's idea was, during which several teachers claimed they had "seen it before." By the time the group had reached "And Now What?"—the part of the event in which they would be most likely to discuss implications for their own practice—they were out of time. Thus, the aspect of the meeting that encouraged application to practice—what arguably could have had the most powerful impact on their teaching—was not enacted.

Even if the meetings' effectiveness had not been hampered by time shortages, though, they might not have attained their goal. Concentrating efforts to communicate the deeper meaning of the framework on meetings alone may have been a pedagogical error. What occurs in between meetings could conceivably be just as, if not more, important. For example, it might have been helpful if Oliver and the peer coaches had supplemented the meeting on conferring by visiting teachers individually and devising plans with them aimed at improving their conferring based on ideas from Calkins's chapter. Follow-up of this type requires capacity that was not always available, however. Many coaches claimed that they *tried* to follow up individually with teachers. In reality, each coach was responsible for helping large numbers of teachers; there were not enough hours in the day to permit individual sessions with even a majority of them, let alone with every teacher. Moreover, coaches were not always sure how to follow up or which topics might require supplemental work. Thus, to our knowledge systematic or sustained follow-up rarely took place.

Occasionally, principals or peer coaches asked teachers to bring something to the next meeting (e.g., notes that they took while conferring with three different students). But our observations of "the next meetings" suggest that the teachers usually did not take these assignments seriously. Some did no meeting-related assignments, whereas others did these assignments halfheartedly. Moreover, we rarely observed or were told about a coach or a principal following up with teachers about meeting assignments in between meetings.

The absence of follow-up activities that could connect theory with practice suggests that both leaders and teachers had more experience and a greater comfort level with the traditional stand-and-deliver approach to professional development. The small-group work during meetings also suggests some familiarity with and valuing of actively involving meeting participants. What was less often tackled, though, was the hard work of identifying what these ideas meant for individual teacher's practice, suggesting that leaders had little past experience with guiding and shaping individual teacher's absorption and translation of ideas from professional-development sessions into the classroom. We suspect that past practices in these schools placed little or no emphasis on changing classroom practice as the result of professional development, leaving both teachers and principals with no clear expectations of change and few ideas about how to make change happen. As a result, what they appeared to do was embed the new professional development into old routines and standard operating procedures: teachers and principals showed up at their respective professional-development sessions, listened respectfully, did the activities required of them during these sessions, and then returned to their sites to continue doing much as they had always done.

The parallels between principals' and teachers' struggles are striking. In Chapter 5, we noted that teachers privileged the *to* (the minilessons) and *by* (students' independent work) aspects of the Balanced Literacy framework. Here we see school leaders' privileging stand-and-deliver-style introductions (i.e., minilessons) to their instructional faculty meetings and planning portions of these meetings to include small-group activities during which the teachers worked without principals' or coaches' explicit direction. If teachers had difficulty with—or even tended to skip—the *with* (working side-by-side with students to assist their individual application of newly learned skills) component of Balanced Literacy, school leaders tended to have difficulty with—or skip—the part of their leadership that involved interacting with teachers as learners: diagnosing their (changing) level of expertise, negotiating goals for further skill acquisition, and planning appropriate types and amounts of assistance to help teachers reach the agreed-on goals.

Another explanation for the limited time school leaders spent working with individuals or small groups on the application of ideas to their practice may have been the principals' and coaches' limited understanding of the Balanced Literacy framework. We discuss the implications of this partial understanding on the leaders' effectiveness next.

Principals' and Peer Coaches' Limited Understanding of the Framework
To perform well, school leaders needed to be deeply familiar with the framework and with the overall structure of the reform (the *Blueprint*) within which it was embedded. They also needed to be able to inspire teachers to follow the reform and be able to assist them in applying it to

their classes. Limitations in leaders' knowledge constrained this process. In our sample schools, during faculty meetings, the principals whose knowledge was most limited (Cavanaugh and Parker) tended to parrot what they had been exposed to in principals' meetings. For example, in a faculty meeting in early spring 2001, Cavanaugh's goal was to inform her teachers about the next iteration of Bersin and Alvarado's *Blueprint*. Although her own learning about changes to the *Blueprint* had included information about why the changes had been made and their importance, Cavanaugh presented an extremely abbreviated version of the rationale to her staff. While observing the meeting, we noted that the principal covered all the important points—and even used much the same language she had heard at the principals' conference—but we also noted that Cavanaugh (2002):

> comes across as doing what she's supposed to do, in other words, explaining the party line. She doesn't allow or encourage a lot of conversation around it. It is just "This is what the *Blueprint* is. This is what we're doing. ..." She doesn't give a lot of her belief system of why we're even doing this. And I think that critique is consistent with the critique I feel when I listen to what teachers are saying. They had to move their libraries, but there was no conversation about *why*. So, they're just told to do things.

Opening the floor to questions or expounding on the reform more extemporaneously may have seemed risky to Cavanaugh. Sticking close to the party line enabled her to "control the conversation space," but it also narrowed her faculty's opportunities for meaning-making and deep learning.

Parker, too, tended to copy the language of her supervisors. She would open and close her faculty meetings with exhortations liberally sprinkled with terminology she had heard from top district leadership. For example, at several meetings we observed, Parker exhorted the faculty to become "powerful teachers," to "see reality in their classrooms," and to develop "a sense of urgency," all Bersin–Alvarado catchphrases. Similarly, when she communicated with the faculty in writing (memos), Parker used language and tones that were strikingly similar to what she had heard at principals' conferences and to the language her IL used during school walk-throughs. The use of similar phrasing is not necessarily bad; it may signal consistency and alignment with reform goals and the building of a common culture. However, in these (and other) cases, we sensed that the principals repeated phrases because they had no other language with which to explain ideas and concepts, a further indication that their own understanding of the reform was shallow.

Oliver, by contrast, had a greater command of early literacy, perhaps because of her prior experience with the Reading Recovery program. She was able to talk comfortably, deeply, and coherently about the Balanced Literacy program. However, she found it difficult to translate that knowledge into a form that would assist others. For instance, an administrative intern who worked for Oliver described the repeated efforts she and the school's peer coaches undertook as they tried to get Oliver to clarify points related to implementation of the framework:

> Sometimes, on the day before the Workshop is [to be] presented, I'd ask the peer coaches, "Do you understand what you're doing?" [Names one peer coach] says, "No." [Names the other peer coach] says, "No." So we give each other courage, and then we go back to Ms. Oliver [and ask]: "Ms. Oliver, can you tell me again what it is you want us to do?" She tells me, "You know what? Don't worry about it. I'll go home and type out an agenda." She writes an agenda for the staff, but then she'll write an agenda for the five of us (principal, administrative intern, assistant principal, two peer coaches) that's very detailed—it's even scripted at times. Usually, I get the courage to ask, "Well, gosh, can you explain it a little bit more?" and she replies, "Well, you know what, I'll write it out for you and it will be really clear for you." It's not always [really clear, even after Ms. Oliver writes it out]. In my mind, I'm still not clear about what I am about to present.

This exchange suggests that although Oliver knew the content well herself, she was less capable of helping others understand it. Her offer to "write it down" precluded spontaneous, two-way communication (i.e., an effective intersection encounter) between her and her support staff and thereby blocked any possibility of building a common understanding. Again we have a parallel with teachers. Principals, like teachers, must know details about Balanced Literacy, but they must also understand their "students" (in this case, the support staff), including how well (or imperfectly) they have grasped the material, possible strategies for learning the material (e.g., through reading or a "practice presentation" or by observing others), and how to scaffold their learning, instead of simply telling them or scripting it for them.

Organizational roles and the power differential between superior and subordinates also were important in the scenario the intern described. Both she and the peer coaches appeared reluctant to continue pressing Oliver to explain the instructional points she wanted them to make during the upcoming faculty meeting, despite their own awareness that they did not fully understand the material. When the meeting took place, teachers' questions soon revealed the support staff's limitations. They lacked the background knowledge necessary to move outside the script the principal had given.

In sum, school leaders appeared to have difficulty leading learning that required dialogue—that is, spontaneous, interactive communication—about the substance of the reform. Principals, in particular, appeared to be more comfortable transmitting knowledge than discussing it with groups. In trying to communicate the principles of the reform to teachers by relying on stand-and-deliver techniques and independent learning in small groups, school leaders were reshaping the reform to fit into their old frames of understanding and standard operating procedures. The use of more inter-active approaches to learning—the kind of approaches that formed the core of the Balanced Literacy framework—was infrequent. Rather, we observed procedures and heard language that had been "handed down" through the district's many organizational layers—from top leadership to ILs, from ILs to principals (see Chapter 7), and from principals to teachers.

Difficulties in Reaching Common Ground

We often observed meetings in which the school leader began with a specific focus but then found that teachers had other, more pressing needs they wanted addressed. For example, despite the best efforts of coaches and principals to maintain a focus on underlying principles of the frame-work, teachers often raised issues about which they felt deep concern but that had remained unaddressed by the district or the school, or they asked for detailed instructions on *how* to do something in their classroom, and in the process often obscuring the focus on *why* they were doing it in the first place.

An issue that confounded many faculty meetings at Scripps and Emmanuel Jackson elementary schools was how best to meet the needs of English-language learners. Teachers were upset with the district's insis-tence that all students be taught in English; they also felt that there was no "give" in the schedule, either for helping students to learn in their own language or for learning English. These issues often rose to the surface during faculty meetings. For example, during a meeting whose purpose was to develop teachers' understanding of the theory behind conferring (October 25, 2001), the school leader was leading a discussion about a videotape of a teacher conferring with a second-language learner. As the conference proceeded, it became clear that the child had not understood the book that he was reading and that he was struggling with a host of problems surrounding fluency, comprehension, and knowledge of how to select a Just Right book. The school leader had planned to ask teachers to identify the information that was gathered in the conference and then to talk about ways to use that information, in conjunction with a well-organized library, to design an appropriate instructional intervention.

Partway through the meeting, however, one of the teachers (who had been noticeably unhappy with the video) asserted that second-language learners were a "totally different ball of wax." These students' needs are very different from those of native English speakers, the teacher argued, and the Balanced Literacy framework did not address those needs. This led to a long discussion about the problems teachers were experiencing with this population of students and (sometimes ill-concealed) indictments of the district administration for not taking these children's needs seriously. The school leader acknowledged that these views were important and deserving of attention, but she felt that the current discussion was simply repeating many similar discussions that had already taken place at the school. She countered that there were other venues for working on "the biliteracy problem." From the leader's perspective, this discussion pulled the meeting off track and used valuable time that otherwise would have been devoted to accomplishing her goals for the session. From the teachers' perspective, this was a vital issue that was hindering their ability to move forward with the reform.

Teachers also insisted that their many pragmatic questions be answered during faculty and grade-level meetings, requests that often frustrated leaders. For example, during a second-grade teachers' meeting at Harvey Mudd, teachers were engaged in a book-leveling activity. Throughout the activity, the coach stressed that there was no simple formula for assigning the correct level to a book. Instead, he explained, teachers would have to read the books themselves and learn how to use their own judgment to match books with what they knew about *their* children. The teachers' first task at the meeting was to identify the simplest book in a pile of books and explain why it was the easiest book. The teachers found this task challenging. One asked why they could not simply continue to use the publisher-supplied lists that identify books' reading levels. The coach explained that these lists could be used only as a "guiding point." It was important for teachers to grapple with book leveling themselves because this would make them better acquainted with the books their children were reading and it would make them better able to identify the best books for individual children.

After the teachers had worked for a while but still had not been able to reach a consensus on the easiest book, peer coach Carl Richter explained why the book called *The Shopping Cart* was the easiest one. With little discussion about his conclusion, the teachers checked off the book on their lists and then launched into a discussion about which color sticker should designate which book level. Exasperated, Richter told them to use the same colors already in use in the school's Reading Resource rooms and tried to get the group back on topic. Throughout this session, the peer coach's attempts to focus teachers' attention on content were met with resistance and attempts to simplify the task.

Similarly, in a Scripps Elementary faculty meeting about conferring (October 16, 2001), immediately after the principal turned the meeting over to two coaches, they were barraged with questions, all of which were procedural in nature, including, "Can you call students over to your desk to confer, or do you have to sit alongside them?" "Can we [teachers] have access to the conversion chart [used in the past to translate reading levels from one system to another]?" "How often do you have to confer with each child?" "What should teachers do about a shortage of A/B leveled readers?" "Is it all right to send guided reading books home?" Many of these questions arose because, in the early days of the reform, teachers knew it was procedures they would be evaluated on, especially during walk-throughs. Hence, they felt they needed to know how to "do" the framework "right." They could not move to a deeper understanding of the rationale supporting practice until they had resolved practical issues related to their job evaluation during the principals' walk-throughs.

These exchanges, in which teachers and leaders participating in vitally important meetings ended up "talking past each other," exemplify for us an important theme of organizational behavior that we raised in Chapter 1— that of perspectival differences. From the point of view of leaders, the teachers were diverting attention from what they wanted them to focus on. From the teachers' point of view, they were acting in a predictable, rational way, attempting to extract from the meetings the information most important to them professionally. Perceiving the teachers' organizational behavior as a diversion may make sense from the perspective of top-down leadership, but it does not necessarily make sense from the teachers' perspective. These perspectival differences between teachers and leaders had many origins. The organizational press to make change rapidly, coupled with the centralized and comprehensive features of the reform, hindered the development of teachers' capacity to enact deep reform dimensions. Not surprisingly then, they were more concerned with the procedural aspects than the substantive aspects of the Balanced Literacy framework.

This returns us to the district's expectations regarding the role of school leaders. As leaders of instruction, principals, assistant principals, peer coaches, and literacy administrators were to teach the "meaning behind"

Balanced Literacy, thus enabling more effective instructional practice. We have seen how and why the principals and their support staff found it difficult to meet this expectation. Time was limited, and their own understanding of the reform was shallow. Moreover, it was often difficult to reach common ground when teachers were distracted by what they perceived as important unresolved issues or by their need to know as much as possible about areas on which they expected to be evaluated. Ironically, teachers face very similar challenges in their classrooms. They too often find time in short supply, and they may lack the in-depth knowledge needed to teach a particular topic. Finally, in classrooms where cognitively demanding tasks are prevalent, students often try to reduce those tasks to a set of procedures so as to remove any uncertainty about what the teacher expects them to do and how what they will be graded.

As we noted in Chapter 1, meaningful learning is time intensive; dependent on interactive discussion among individuals who trust one another but who possess different levels of experience, understanding, and knowledge; and tailored to the needs of individual learners. In the early years of the SDCS reform, these conditions did not prevail in faculty, department, and grade-level meetings. Instruction often was teacher centered rather than student centered. And, when more interactive forms of instruction were attempted (as in the previous peer coach example), school leaders often found teachers were not the "hungry learners" they might have expected but rather professionals more eager to vent their frustrations about district inaction on the issues that mattered most to them or anxious workers eager to learn what they needed to do to obtain a good evaluation. Thus, establishing a common ground for productive interaction was difficult.

We turn now to an examination of interaction during classroom visits—many of which occurred during walk-throughs—to assess the extent to which conditions more conducive to deep learning might have prevailed there.

Interaction during Classroom Visits

District leadership charged school leaders with the responsibility for interacting with teachers directly around their classroom practice. Discharging this responsibility took several forms, including walk-throughs, informal observations, modeling, and coteaching. In this section, we focus primarily on walk-throughs and examine the degree to which principals (and sometimes coaches) were able to use the walk-through as a mechanism for assisting *teachers' learning*. We also discuss walk-throughs in Chapter 7, focusing there on the role of the walk-through as a mechanism for assisting *principals'* learning.

Direct observations of teachers' practice represented a break from tradition. In most San Diego schools, teachers were accustomed to closing their doors and teaching as they saw fit. The idea that teaching practice was a professional activity to be shared, scrutinized, and improved was novel—and even threatening—to some. Many teachers were resistant. Even those who were ready for improvement were worried that their principals would "write them up" or use their weaknesses against them in formal performance evaluations.

The principals found adjusting to this new responsibility difficult as well. Many found it challenging to get into the routine of leaving their offices and visiting classrooms on a daily basis. Although we saw an increase of principal presence in the classrooms over our data collection period, each year we heard principals vowing to "do more" classroom visits the next year. At an end-of-year walk-through, one principal commented to her IL that she had made regular classroom observations of the literacy block during the year but that the observations were disjointed and that follow-up conferences with the teachers were inconsistent. She proudly showed her IL a much tighter schedule for the upcoming year, a schedule that had her observing each teacher at least once a week, with time budgeted for conferencing.

In addition to making it a habit to visit classrooms, principals needed to develop their skills regarding *what* to observe once they were in a classroom. During an interview early in the reform, Elaine Fink, "instructional leader of the instructional leaders," stated, "Very often principals get sidetracked [when they observe in classrooms] looking at the work kids are doing at their desks, ... looking at what is up around the room ... talking to kids, and [only] once in a while they'll focus on the lesson." But, she continued, "focusing on the lesson is exactly what principals should be doing." Although the theory of action guiding the reform (see Chapter 4) maintained that principals did not need to be literacy experts so much as experts in leadership, in practice they could not successfully "focus on the lesson" unless they knew how to teach reading. As Fink acknowledged, regretfully, principals who had never taught reading seldom were able to distinguish strong from weak instruction.

In terms of learning how to critically evaluate classrooms and how to guide teachers toward more meaningful implementations of the Balanced Literacy framework, the principals in our case study schools fared about the same as their colleagues districtwide. Like Fink, we noticed that especially early in the reform, when visiting classrooms, the principals tended to focus mainly on superficial aspects of the Balanced Literacy framework. For example, teachers at Harvey Mudd told us that their principal looked for very specific things, such as the wording on posters, prominently placed daily schedules with each component of the Balanced Literacy program identified, and the number of books in the classroom libraries. But these surface features often obscured teachers' actual knowledge about the purpose of reform strategies. For instance, as one IL pointed out, a classroom full of charts with no obvious organization was counterproductive; it would simply overwhelm students. "If I were a kid [in that room], I wouldn't know where to look for specific information" (Nolan, 2001). Similarly, an external consultant who conducted many teacher-training activities for the district stated,

> From what the teachers are telling me, it seems that some principals really don't know what they're doing [when they visit classrooms] because of the kinds of things they tell teachers to do. When people are told to hang up from the beginning of the year a chart with the comprehension strategies à la Stephanie Harvey [a textbook author] in their room, that doesn't make sense. *Why* would you hang them up in your classroom? But that's what they were told [to do]. (Thompson, 2002)

The consultant noted that because the teachers lacked an understanding of why these comprehension strategies could improve students' meaning-making of text, teaching the strategies tended to be viewed as simply another externally imposed inconvenience rather than as a valuable tool for learning.

Although many principals continued to focus on these kinds of readily visible—but not necessarily fundamental—aspects of the framework when visiting classrooms, as their experience and training deepened, most principals began to notice more meaningful aspects of the program. For example, in a walk-through in February 2002, we noted that the principal really knew the strengths and weaknesses of her teachers and also could identify the students in each class who were at or below the fortieth percentile on state-mandated standardized tests and thus needed to receive extra attention. The IL considered this a real sign of progress for this principal.

A continuing concern, however, was that principals appeared to be better at spotting what *should not be* than they were at knowing how to develop what *should be*. For example, Cavanaugh admitted during an interview that although she and her assistant principal were getting better at knowing when teacher practice was not good, they struggled with what to do about it. This dilemma emerged from several different comments Cavanaugh made. First, she talked about how long it had been since she had been a classroom teacher:

Whereas I'm not, this is my sixteenth year away from the class-room, so there isn't any way, I mean, I try and approximate it [give some general feedback] but I'd never give the down and dirty [specific suggestions]. So I think by looking at our teachers that I just, I know, I can tell by the progress of their students, I get it by watching them and then having conversations with them and the staff developers and sitting back, too, and listening when they have staff conferences or at grade-level meetings, hearing what's going on and the ones that come up with ideas to help others.

Second, Cavanaugh talked about her frustrations in trying to model her own behavior with students on her IL's interactions with individual children during walk-throughs. After marveling at how well the IL knew not only the books and individual children's needs but also "where to take the children next," Cavanaugh confessed ruefully, "We [she and her assistant] can sit down and we read with them and we know that they are getting it or not getting it, but we're not sure how to push them to the next level and she'll [the IL] know right away what to do." Third, in answer to a probe during an interview ("So it seems you are getting sharper at identifying what's not happening?"), Cavanaugh replied, "Right. But then how do you know what to do about it? That is always the trick."

Another principal, Cynthia Oliver, discussed a similar problem. During a walk-through, she noticed that her teachers did not seem to fully understand what it meant for students to be reading Just Right books. Her observation was reinforced a little later when she and her IL jointly conducted a walk-through. Oliver (2001) recounted to us what had happened during the walk-through she conducted with her IL:

> It was one of the common elements that we saw in the classrooms, and I think it was probably one of the pieces … we were still see-ing kids kind of turning pages and not really reading—and I mean—it's the core of everything we are doing. If kids are not reading, they are not improving. So, you know, the term "Just Right books" has gotten beaten to death, but it's the bottom line of what all the research is saying: kids have to be reading. They have to be reading at their independent levels so that they are making good meaning.

Although Oliver correctly identified the problem her teachers were having trouble with, the reason for the problem and the possible solution(s) both had eluded her. Donna Burns (2001), Oliver's IL, explained the matter this way: "What we were seeing in the classrooms was actually a result of Oliver teaching the structure [to her teachers] and *not* the understanding." Burns pushed Oliver to think about her next staff development meeting and to formulate a plan for how to improve teacher learning. When the two met again for this discussion, Oliver recounted for Burns what she had done so far to address the problem and together they talked through a plan, a strategy for her next steps.

Most of the high school walk-throughs we observed during the first year of our study focused on genre studies classes. Here, too, principals could detect problems, but often they were hard-pressed to devise solutions. As we described in Chapter 5, both enacted and structural features of the reform were notably absent from most high school academic classrooms. Physics, algebra, and history teachers (among others) continued using traditional, didactic ways of teaching and paid scant attention to their students' reading competence. These teachers, who typically lacked background knowledge of reading instruction, argued that teaching reading was the responsibility of English teachers. Even those experienced in teaching reading and writing were challenged by the reform, however. Many area high school students were newcomers whose native language did not incorporate the phonology or orthography of English. Their learning curve was steep, and for the English-language learners in tenth and eleventh grade, time was short. Exacerbating this situation was the fact that the Balanced Literacy framework was designed for elementary instruction; therefore, high school principals had few criteria to help them judge the best curriculum and pedagogy for their school's students.

The difficulties principals faced when they observed high school classrooms were obvious during a visit by a principal and her IL to a genre studies class at Martin Luther King High School in 2002. Both noted the absence of comfortable seating for reading, the presence of only a few charts or other signs of support for learning, and a sloppily arranged library. While leading the read aloud portion of the class, the teacher read for a long time without stopping to comment or ask students questions. He instructed students to retell the story on a work sheet and permitted paraphrasing or copying parts of the story from their books. After the observation, both the IL and the principal questioned the rigor and purpose of the lesson. "Was it just to get students to listen to the teacher read and then go back and retell?" the IL wondered, and then continued, "When you go back to the book and write from the book, page numbers etc., what skill are you learning? It's not just writing down from a book. It is supposed to be about making meaning of the text" (Johnson, 2002). Clearly, this teacher, who had not enacted even the more superficial features of the reform, was not prepared to teach Balanced Literacy reading strategies. The principal, however, could not recommend any practical steps this teacher could take to quickly improve his teaching and his students' learning. Only long-term, sustained professional development would suffice.

Thus, the major challenge for principals, after learning deeper aspects of the Balanced Literacy framework, was to identify ways to follow through and help teachers attain the next level of development. However, before principals could reasonably hope to achieve those goals, at least two additional elements were needed: a clear picture of the desired end-state of practice and a theory of how teachers' movement toward that end-state can be supported by more capable others. Although some principals (e.g., Oliver) appeared to have a vision of the end-state, few, if any, were clear about how to support teachers' development toward it.

Teachers' Perceptions of School Leaders' Assistance

Interviews with teachers and our notes from informal conversations with teachers suggest varied responses to the assistance they received from principals and coaches, but some patterns emerge as well. First, most teachers appeared to recognize and appreciate that they were being given an opportunity to learn new and worthwhile information—material that was important for them to know as professionals. As one first-grade teacher at Emmanuel Jackson remarked spontaneously at the close of a grade-level meeting that had been devoted to watching a video of an exemplary guided reading session (February 1, 2002), "It is incredible that teachers can get degrees without learning how to teach children to read." (We interpreted this statement to mean that in this teacher's opinion, he and others were just now learning this crucial element of "how to teach.") Other teachers in the room immediately agreed with him and began sharing opinions about their own inadequate training. The assistant principal chimed in, saying that she felt the training Emmanuel Jackson teachers were receiving was meeting a real need. Second, in recognition of how much "stuff was out there to be learned," many teachers expressed a desire for more information but with one caveat: that it be delivered by "experts." As a Harvey Mudd teacher told us at the end of the first year of the reform (June 20, 2001), "I feel like it is a waste of time to go to other teachers' presentations. … It is a much better use of my time to go to see a professional who is presenting on guided reading."

The sentiment that expertise is crucial—and that sometimes teachers were not in the best position to teach themselves or to teach one another—was echoed in the desire expressed by a Scripps Elementary teacher: "I actually think that the staff developers [peer coaches] should do a lot more *teaching* Guided Reading in small groups or *teaching* Shared Reading by videotaping themselves or Conferring with students and videotaping that. They keep wanting *us* to do it, but I mean, they're supposed to be the experts" (Oliver, 2001). Fulfilling this teacher's wish was almost impossible in the early years of the reform, given the often limited capacity of principals and coaches. Teachers were well aware of the variability in their coaches. Those who were "good" earned their respect; those who weren't good earned their disparagement. Indeed, when asked how helpful building-level staff development sessions were, one teacher replied, "It depends on who is hosting it. If [names a competent peer coach] was there, I got a lot out of it. The material that he was presenting was very helpful. If [names the principal] was doing it, to be honest with you, I got very little to nothing out of that."

Finally, when asked what did not work well with respect to their building-level staff development, many of the teachers expressed concern over their ability to translate what they learned in faculty and grade-level meetings to their own practice. A second-grade teacher at Emmanuel Jackson explained the problem this way:

> What didn't work very well in the professional development, I would say, in general, is that no time is given for how to practice, how to implement what you're learning. So the planning time isn't there. You're given lots of wonderful information, but no time to plan it out or practice it or collaborate in a—like a plan of action with your colleagues. So we, you know, it's like a bombardment of great ideas. I really think the literacy framework, it's best practice … [but] teachers weren't really given a medium to learn how to do it.

At least for this teacher, the link between theory and practice was never fully forged. At Scripps Elementary, the principal gave the teachers planning time with their colleagues to make just this link, but according to the peer coaches and the principal, teachers did not take advantage of this opportunity. They used the time to grade papers rather than to plan or work collaboratively with their colleagues.

District Responses to Principals' Professional-Development Needs

Because of the challenges principals faced while learning "on the job," district leaders concluded that all development of leadership capacity could not be done on the fly. Principals, they conceded, needed professional development *before* they assumed instructional leadership positions, as well as while they were leading reform activities. Principals agreed. It was too difficult to learn leadership skills while also having full responsibility for leading a school. Beginning in 2000, the SDCS added significant material resources to the professional-development equation, including ELDA, a program launched in partnership with the University of San Diego's School of Education. With support from the Broad Foundation, the University of San Diego offers an apprenticeship in instructional leadership for exemplary teachers or staff developers who are interested in earning the entry-level administrative credential needed for a principalship. ELDA participants take course work through the university and serve an internship in the SDCS. Each ELDA intern is supported by a supervising principal (considered by the district to be exemplary) while they get hands-on experience. One intern described the experience this way: "The internship was really good and really strong ... it was so focused on the actual work principals do. You know, whether it was writing up observations or how to do a debrief with the teacher, or how to read the budget, or what do you have to do when you do teacher evaluations; everything was specific" (Livingston, 2004). ELDA participants are virtually guaranteed an administrative position in the district after successful completion of the apprenticeship program.

Some content specialists who have worked as mathematics or science administrators have enrolled in ELDA to gain the leadership skills they need to be more effective literacy administrators. In addition, strong principals who have already received their entry-level credential, either through ELDA or through some other university, can enroll in ELDA's advanced program. Participants in that program are paired with a mentor principal for additional support. To date, ELDA has prepared four cohorts, graduating sixty-four individuals. Most have been placed as principals and some as vice principals; a few graduates returned to their positions as literacy administrators (see Hubbard, 2004, for details).

Summary and Conclusions

Consistent with recent national developments in the redefinition of the role of principal, district leaders in the SDCS sought to convert their principals from operational managers to site-based leaders of instruction. Consistent with recent research that suggests effective professional development occurs at the school site, during school hours, and in the context of hands-on classroom practice, SDCS leadership moved most of its teacher professional development away from summer workshops and autonomous university courses and into the work environment.

The two most salient activities in which school-site administrators exercised their new instructional leadership responsibilities were faculty, grade-level, and department meetings and classroom visits (also called walk-throughs). Recognizing that the vast majority of principals lacked experience as leaders of instruction, the SDCS reform added significant resources to assist them in supporting teacher learning at school sites, notably peer coaches and literacy administrators. These experts in Balanced Literacy usually assumed responsibility for conducting the substantive portion of meetings and for working one-on-one with teachers to improve their instructional practice.

Because the reform was to be implemented comprehensively and quickly, district leaders often had to hire coaches who were still in the process of developing their skills. As a result, peer coaches and literacy administrators varied in their expertise and capacity to assist principals in supporting teachers. Educators who came to these positions with background knowledge and experience in some form of literacy instruction—not necessarily even the Balanced Literacy framework—were judged to be more effective by teachers than those without extensive knowledge and experience in literacy or those who were learning on the job along with the teachers they were expected to coach. The effectiveness of staff developers also was compromised when teachers perceived them to be more evaluators than coaches. Practice on the ground was further complicated when the information coaches communicated to teachers contradicted or failed to reinforce messages sent to principals by their ILs.

The format of meetings in schools recapitulated the format of principals' conferences (see Chapter 7). After an opening address in which the purpose of the day's session was outlined and the urgency of the reform was reinforced, interactive work sessions ensued, followed by a carefully crafted closing address that often included a reminder of the reform's purposes. The content of meetings also recapitulated the content of recent principals' conferences. If, for example, an aspect of the Balanced Literacy framework (such as guided reading or conferring) was the focus of a principals' conference, it was likely to be discussed in a subsequent school meeting. By observing both the monthly principals' conference and that month's subsequent school meetings, we were able to trace the trajectory and transformation of the reform as it traversed SDCS organizational levels from district leaders to classroom interactions.

During our four years of data collection, we observed a shift in emphasis in faculty and grade-level meetings from the superficial, more structural aspects of the reform to its subtler, enacted aspects. Although that shift in emphasis was helpful in moving teachers to deeper levels of understanding about the goals, purposes, and rationales of the reform, one significant problem still had not been resolved by the time our observations ended: teachers reported being unsure about how to translate the elegant theory presented to them in meetings to the everyday practical realities of classroom instruction.

The classroom visit by principals (often accompanied by coaches or literacy administrators) was a new experience for many teachers. This new practice went against the grain of their standard operating procedures, in which autonomous teaching behind closed classroom doors prevailed. Direct observation of teachers was a new experience for principals as well. In particular, principals needed to learn how to judge instruction critically and guide teachers toward a meaningful implementation of the Balanced Literacy framework. Like the teachers, who tended to put the more superficial aspects of the reform in place before they enacted its more subtle features (see Chapter 5), principals looked more often for the visible, mechanical aspects of the framework—Word Walls, daily schedules, and the classroom library—than they did for the deeper aspects of the program, such as the substance of teacher–student interaction during conferring. We observed that principals, to their credit, who stayed at their posts for the four years of our study progressed in their ability to discern and guide the deeper aspects of the reform.

District leaders were not inattentive to these problems. Concluding that principals needed professional development before they assumed instructional leadership positions as well as on the job, the SDCS, in partnership with the University of San Diego, launched ELDA, an instructional leadership program that provides entry-level administrative credentials to aspiring principals and more advanced training for experienced principals.

In the next chapter, we turn our attention to the intersection encounter between ILs and school-based leaders (principals).

CHAPTER 7

Learning in Leadership Professional Development: The Enactment of Reform between School Leaders and Instructional Leaders

Introduction

In this chapter, we focus on the third oval of San Diego's nested learning communities (see Chapter 1, Figure 1.1), the intersection encounter between instructional leaders (ILs) and school-based leaders (principals). Despite being far removed from the classroom, the interactions between ILs and school leaders set the tone for what happened inside schools and classrooms in the district. This chapter, like the two previous ones, focuses on literacy because it was the first school subject to be addressed by the reform. Here, we examine the ways in which ILs supported principals in their efforts to learn how to help teachers assist students in becoming proficient and independent readers and writers. Consistent with the principles of our design research (see Chapter 2 for details), we present the reform from the point of view of its many participants, assess the differences in how school personnel experienced the reform, and link those differences to the participants' positions within the organization.

Ready for Reform

The San Diego City Schools (SDCS) district was well positioned to initiate a reform in 1998. Although Alan Bersin was an educational outsider, Anthony Alvarado had a tested theory of action. He was experienced in creating a community of professional learners who shared institutional norms and had a common language for understanding their practice. And, in terms of technical resources and political support, the prospects for reform seldom looked better. The State of California Department of Education, agitated over the long-term effects of social promotion, and the area business community, agitated over prospects of a labor pool that lacked competitive skills for a global marketplace, were encouraging educational change. The San Diego district leadership was successful in securing extramural funding for reform efforts.

Thus, the future looked promising for the SDCS on each of the dimensions of school change we introduced in Chapter 1—technical, cultural, and political. Nevertheless, district leaders knew that to succeed in a systemic reform, they would need to build capacity districtwide, with major attention focused on leaders at the top. In practice, this meant redefining the role and responsibilities of the district's area superintendents, transforming selected individuals into ILs. It would be these leaders' responsibility to teach and support principals, who, in turn, would be charged with leading instruction at their schools. Originally, the district chose seven individuals considered exemplar leaders and assigned each of these men and women leadership responsibility for a "learning community" consisting of approximately twenty principals, distributed over both elementary and secondary schools. The group of ILs grew to eleven when some of the original eight leaders took on additional district responsibilities and needed to reduce the number of principals they were supporting. Some of the added ILs were hired from outside the district.

Developing Leadership Capacity in San Diego

School districts throughout the country typically provide very little professional development for principals and assistant superintendents, apparently assuming that once these leaders have secured their positions, they don't need additional training. As we explained in chapter 4, the SDCS district believed otherwise. Their intention was to completely reculture the educational system and build capacity throughout. Professional development became the heart of the Bersin–Alvarado systemwide strategy for school improvement, and developing leadership capacity among its top leaders arguably became its soul.

To prepare high school, middle school, and elementary school principals for their new role, the SDCS provided several professional-development opportunities. These included visits to other schools, principal support groups, mentor–principal relationships, principal conferences, and walk-throughs led by ILs. These events were unique in the breadth and depth of support they provided for developing instructional knowledge and leadership capability. In this chapter, we focus on the two activities most salient for principals: the monthly principals' conferences and the school walk-throughs. Both events were strongly shaped by Elaine Fink, who joined the reform effort from New York City's Community School District #2 in 2000 and quickly became the ILs' coach (this position never appeared on the district's formal organizational chart, however; see Chapter 4, Figure 4.1).[1]

The IL position in San Diego was modeled after Fink's position in District #2, and each SDCS learning community was deliberately created to be approximately the same size as District #2. When she assumed the role of "instructional leader of the instructional leaders" in San Diego, Fink recognized the significant differences between the two districts (see Chapter 3 and Stein, Hubbard, & Mehan, 2003, for details). Initially, she focused primarily on the implementation of the Balanced Literacy framework (see Chapter 5) and provided instruction to the ILs mainly in planning sessions held before the principals' conferences and debriefing sessions held after the conferences. She used these occasions to coach ILs in their leadership skills and to improve their instructional knowledge. Fink also accompanied ILs on school walk-throughs with the principals in their learning communities to mentor the ILs in the conduct of effective walk-throughs. Because the training Fink provided to the ILs formed the basis of the training they provided to principals, we include information in this chapter on those aspects of Fink's work that intertwined with the main venues for IL–principal interaction. Each of these training venues is discussed next.

The Structure of Professional-Development Events for Instructional Leaders

We begin with a brief overview of the structure of the planning sessions, principals' conferences, and walk-throughs. Then we describe how Bersin, Alvarado, Fink, and the ILs used these professional-development venues to teach principals how to implement instruction and lead change at their schools.

Overview of Planning and Debriefing Sessions

Fink provided intensive professional development sessions for all ILs as a group, in monthly meetings held in her office. These sessions were coordinated with the monthly principals' conferences and included two components: a four-hour group planning session and a four-hour debriefing component. During the latter, Fink provided ILs with comments on and critiques of their performances at the previous month's principals' conference. She also scheduled one-on-one sessions with ILs, based on their individual needs and requests. Some ILs chose to meet with her individually or in pairs once or twice a month; a few chose not to meet with her individually.

The purpose of the planning sessions was to scaffold the knowledge and skills of ILs and enable them to construct principals' conferences that would be effective learning opportunities for principals. These conferences were expected to differ from the district's previous professional-development events which, in Fink's opinion, had amounted to "just sharing sessions" where principals traded stories about their work. Under Bersin and Alvarado, professional development required that principals spend a full day each month away from their schools, learning to lead instruction. Fink believed the ILs and principals needed some basic knowledge about the Balanced Literacy framework, but she did not expect them to become literacy specialists. Instead, she emphasized *leading* literacy instruction. Teaching the content of instruction to principals would be the responsibility of curriculum specialists, such as the district's literacy administrators, each of whom was teamed with an IL and peer coaches.

Fink defined her job as the ILs' coach, not their evaluator. Technically, Chancellor Alvarado was the ILs' supervisor, but this distinction was not always clear to the ILs. They felt accountable to Fink, as well as to Alvarado. They spent a great deal of time with her, and the quality of their interactions was intense. The ILs each felt pressure to ensure that the community of learners for whom they were responsible did as well if not better than Fink and Alvarado expected and as well if not better than their colleagues' learning communities.

Overview of Principals' Conferences

Principals' conferences typically followed a common pattern. Superintendent Bersin gave his opening remarks (approximately thirty minutes); next, Chancellor Alvarado presented his opening remarks (approximately thirty minutes); and then all the principals assembled in their learning communities to spend the rest of the day (approximately six hours) receiving instruction and support from their ILs. During these learning community "breakout sessions," the ILs usually built on the leadership theme Bersin and Alvarado had made the focus of their morning addresses. Often working with their literacy administrators, the ILs conducted two several-hour-long sessions focused on instruction and leadership and then ended the breakout sessions with a closing address. Frequently, all conference participants reconvened at the end of the day to discuss (for thirty to sixty minutes) operational issues such as budgets, transportation, and support staff policy changes. These pragmatic matters were always given less time and less emphasis.

Overview of Walk-Throughs

The walk-through, the second key SDCS professional development event, was modeled after a similar activity in use in District #2 (Fink & Resnick, 2001). Its main purpose was to build principal leadership capacity. Principals were required to conduct two types of school walk-throughs. One involved visiting each classroom on their own to observe their teachers' practices and then meeting with the teachers later to discuss the observation (see chapter 6). The other, the focus of this chapter, involved visiting at least one classroom at every grade level, accompanied by an IL (and sometimes Elaine Fink, as well). The principal and IL would confer before the classroom visits and again after the walk-through (see following text for details). The purpose of this type of walk-through was twofold—to help principals learn to conduct classroom observations and to enhance their ability to identify the needs of their teachers.

In addition to improving principals' leadership practice, the walk-throughs aimed to make instruction consistent and rigorous across all classrooms in the district. During the academic year, ILs typically conducted four walk-throughs at each of the schools in their learning community. Each walk-through lasted about five hours and included a preobservation conference, classroom visits, and a postobservation conference, followed by a written assessment of the IL's perception of the day's observations. In the preconference, the IL and principal reviewed the goals and objectives of the principal's work plan, a document crafted by the principal at the start of the year that outlined the school and staff needs and detailed how the principal would address those needs. The IL and principal also spent time in this meeting reviewing the strengths and weaknesses of each teacher and going over the school's most recent *Stanford Achievement Test, Ninth Edition* achievement data, disaggregated by grade level and by teacher. In analyzing the data, ILs and principals paid particular attention to the progress of low-achieving students.

ILs and principals tried to visit as many elementary school classrooms as possible, at all grade levels; in high schools, they visited literacy and mathematics classrooms. During the classroom visits, the principal and IL examined student work and assessed student engagement, frequently asking students about their learning. Especially in the early days of the reform, the leaders attended to the organization of the classroom. Specifically, they noted where the teacher's desk was located, if there were student-generated charts on the walls, and if leveled libraries and other artifacts that would support student learning were present. They also attended to the teacher's knowledge of and ability to implement the Balanced Literacy framework. They critiqued the rigor of the lesson, the level of teacher questioning, and the quality of student work; they also noted who dominated classroom conversation (teacher or students) and how responsive the teacher was to students' questions and answers.

During the walk-through postconference, the IL and principal drew conclusions from their classroom observations. ILs could also use this time to evaluate principals' job performance. The one-on-one experience enabled by the walk-through allowed the ILs to assess the extent to which principals were aware of teachers' strengths and weaknesses, their ability to create a plan to support each teacher, and the effectiveness of these intervention plans. After the event, the IL wrote a formal letter to the principal detailing their conversation and the plans they had agreed on during the visit. This document became part of the principal's performance evaluation, but as one IL stated, "Performance reviews should be no surprise if the walk-through activity is conducted with direct, honest feedback" (Burns, 2002).

Professional-Development Events: "It's All about Leadership and Instruction"

Professional-development sessions for the ILs provided particularly rich sources of information because they allowed us to observe participants making sense of reform ideas in the context of their daily lives and previously established routines. We begin by examining how Fink conveyed key elements of leadership to the ILs.

Leadership Instruction for Instructional Leaders

Responsibility for transforming the district's abstract theory of action into concrete practice fell primarily to the ILs. Fink arranged planning and debriefing sessions, aiming to turn ILs into effective leaders by bolstering their knowledge, skills, and dispositions. To model effective leadership strategies and encourage reflective practice, she videotaped and then analyzed the interaction that occurred between ILs and principals at the monthly principals' conferences. She insisted effective leaders should be "belief makers" who use a strong "voice" to explicate "who they are" and what they stand for (Fink, 2002b).

Part of developing a strong leadership voice, according to Fink, was explicitly establishing a purpose for the instructional breakout sessions ILs led at the principals' conferences. Videotapes of these sessions allowed ILs to hear their own words and assess if they had inspired principals to follow them. Their voice needed to convey a sense of urgency about the work, Fink explained; otherwise, principals could rightly wonder, "Why the heck am I sitting here wasting my day?" (Fink, 2002b: 7). Principals needed to understand the absolute imperative to close the achievement gap between rich and poor students. "Telling stories" that underscored the urgency of the situation would capture teachers' and principals' hearts and minds and reinforce the district leaders' message that the SDCS reform was based on values formed around social justice.

To this end, Fink taught ILs the importance of "seeing and changing reality." Only when principals saw the desperate circumstances in their schools could they become the "change makers" district leaders constantly called for in the opening addresses they delivered at the monthly principals' conferences (discussed later). Seeing the reality of inadequate classroom instruction required ILs to first engage in an honest critique of their own practice. Using the videotaped conference performances, Fink coached ILs to ask themselves "hard questions" about their practice and to think about what they said to principals. ILs reported that viewing videotapes of their instruction was painful, but most agreed exposing their practice to their colleagues and to Fink improved it. Johnson (2001) concurred, "They were relearning what it means to be a leader. Everything that they believed about themselves as leaders was not true and it was very painful. They became very insecure and their whole self-confidence was ripped apart. And then, as they attained skills, they started to come back—only they were even prouder and more [capable]."

Through Fink's coaching of the ILs, it was expected that the content, ideals, and values of the reform would make their way to the principals and ultimately to the classroom. Borrowing from Tichy (1997), Fink argued that the ILs needed to develop a "teachable point of view" that was based on knowledge and experience, and they should be adept at articulating that view in all their dealings with others. Teaching the ideas, values, and knowledge of the reform in all of their work with principals was what would make it possible for the principals to transfer this point of view to their teachers, who, in turn, would actualize it in their classrooms. The following example illustrates this process of learning and then transmitting a teachable point of view.

In preparation for a principals' conference in January 2002, Fink helped ILs understand the usefulness of conferring introduced previously as a Balanced Literacy strategy for teachers interacting with students (see Chapter 5). Conferring was a strategy that the ILs needed to firmly grasp the adult analog of because it would help them work effectively with their principals. The principals, in turn, needed to learn how to confer with their teachers to help them improve reading instruction at the classroom level. The teachable topic here was that conferring is a strategy useful in many exchanges. Fink showed a videotape of a conference between a district consultant (acting as a principal) and an elementary school teacher. In this mock preobservation session, the teacher told the principal that during the classroom observation that would occur later that day, she would see her teaching *inferring* during guided reading with her fourth-grade students. She was going to focus on inferring, she explained, because her students, although skilled at decoding, were not yet able to make meaning of their reading. The ILs then viewed the videotaped guided reading session conducted by the teacher and the principal's follow-up, which included conferring with the teacher in a debriefing session.

Analyzing the guided reading session and then observing the debriefing session in which the principal used appropriate language and identified particular strategies to improve the teacher's practice served two purposes. First, it gave ILs the opportunity to learn how a principal should confer with a teacher and to see the importance and utility of conferring around a particular pedagogical event. Second, at least in theory, it showed ILs how to replicate the practice of conferring around a particular practice with their own principals. Fink's lesson was intended to provide ILs with a strategy—conferring—that would both help them become more effective leaders and help them help principals to become more effective leaders. Conferring thus was both a guiding principle of leadership and a practical technique for improving teaching and learning.

Learning about Leadership at Principals' Conferences

The primary goal of professional development for principals was the same as for ILs; namely, to develop their leadership knowledge and skills. The principals' conferences were district leaders' vehicle for conveying key elements of their theory of leadership, including the importance of leading with a moral purpose, building capacity, developing teamwork, and making decisions based on empirical evidence.

Superintendent Bersin and Chancellor Alvarado used their opening addresses at the monthly conferences to impress on principals the need to develop the knowledge, skills, and dispositions of leadership. There are multiple and competing definitions of effective leadership (e.g., Berends & Bodilly, 1998; Datnow & Castellano, 2001; Hall & Placier, 2002). Bersin and Alvarado assembled their notion of leadership from three main sources: Fullan, who argued that leaders must have a "moral purpose" both in terms of contributions to society and in the development of a commitment to employees (Fullan, 2001a: 27), and Heifetz and Linsky (2000) and Tichy (1997), who offered a business model of leadership. According to these experts, leaders nurture the development of other leaders at all levels of the organization, have "teachable points of view about ideas and values, and have 'E-cubed'—emotion, energy and edge" (Tichy, 1997: 3). Leaders tell stories that engage listeners' minds and emotions; they also have "well-defined methodologies and teaching techniques" and "serve as effective role models" (Tichy, 1997: 4). They are able to clarify values, define their moral code, and "preserve a sense of purpose" (Heifetz & Linsky, 2000). Finally, leaders are both active and reflective; they observe and participate in what Heifetz and Linsky termed an "adaptive challenge."

Guided by this literature, Bersin and Alvarado defined their own jobs to include setting the district's vision and establishing goals and expectations for ILs and principals so that they could become effective leaders and change agents in their respective domains. The definition of leadership Bersin and Alvarado articulated in their speeches dovetailed with what the ILs were learning from Fink. This overlap, which ensured that principals would hear the same basic messages about leadership as their ILs had, was intended to further promote shared language and broad commitment to the same leadership goals. We analyzed twenty opening addresses delivered at principals' conferences held from January 24, 2001, through August 2002 and found that Bersin and Alvarado concentrated on nine elements of leadership. We present these next, in random order.

Moral Purpose Communicators
District leaders pointed out that the goals and the rationale of leadership were closely intertwined. They exhorted principals to embrace the "moral purpose" of the reform; namely, providing "a quality education for *every one* of San Diego's children." Superintendent Bersin (2002a) explained the moral imperative of leadership this way:

It's closing the gap that people say cannot be closed, but we will close it between children of color and from impoverished backgrounds and children with more advantages in life. That is our *moral purpose*. We will push children out of the bottom and we will push them into the top and it is the same effort that you lead that will accomplish both. (emphasis added)

Alvarado reinforced the idea that leaders need to have a moral purpose by arguing against blaming students for achievement gaps between low-income and minority students and their white middle-class counterparts. He maintained that students' poor academic record was the fault of the adults who were charged with teaching them. All SDCS leaders (including him) were failing kids. Alvarado asserted that it was an academic injustice to perpetuate conditions that do not produce success for all groups of students. All district leaders must instill in *all* educators the belief that *all* students can succeed and provide them with the leadership that will produce this outcome. "You're leading with a moral purpose ... about the justice of your work," Alvarado told the principals. "That is what it means to lead" (Alvarado, 2002b).

Change Makers
Bersin and Alvarado also stressed that principals must recognize that the reform was fundamentally about change. "Change is difficult," Bersin acknowledged, but "we must make it our friend in the City Schools because we understand that without change, the franchise of public education in San Diego is threatened and could be lost" (Bersin, 2002a). As adamant as district leaders were about what leadership *is,* they were equally unwavering about what leadership is *not*. District leaders claimed that leadership is not being a plant manager focused on operations, facilities, or bus schedules. It is about leading instruction, making everything in the school support the goals of teaching and learning. Bringing about this reorientation requires "coaching." "Our teachers actually coach our students to take responsibility for their own learning. Our principals, our site content administrators, our vice principals coach our teachers. Our principals coach their leadership teams and our instructional leaders coach our principals" (Bersin, 2003c). Bersin acknowledged some of the difficulties involved in coaching—that it demanded candidness, honesty, and diligence—but he maintained that without effective coaches teachers would not experience improvement.

Relationship Builders
Relationships between principals and teachers should be about "the work"; that is, about improving instruction so that children can learn better.

These relationships are not to be personal. They are to have an "edge," which according to Tichy (1997: 3) is "the ability to face reality and make tough decisions." Bersin (2002c) clarified that having an edge is "not mean spirited. Edge is not ugly. Edge is asserting the values of a system that insists on quality instruction for our children." Principals should be willing to have "difficult conversations with teachers," to tell them when they were doing something wrong, and, if necessary, to document their lack of progress. Having an edge might intrude on personal friendships, but such relationships were necessarily of lower priority than the goal of improving instruction.

Coherence Providers

Strong leaders should "provide coherence for those we lead. We must understand where we are, where the system is, how we can improve it, how we relate professional lives to personal lives and that coherence making at the end is what leadership is about in terms of conceptualization and communication" (Bersin, 2002a). That is, the SDCS reform demanded systemic change, and that imperative required that everyone be able to understand and use the same basic concepts.

Decision Makers

Effective leaders, Alvarado and Bersin asserted, must be *analysts* who study achievement data to improve the work of those they are leading. "This culture of working on the details of improvement is absent from our profession," Alvarado (2002a) told principals, explaining, "What instructional leadership does is to analyze data. ... It is going to hurt when you analyze your ability. ... It requires a level of ... functioning that you have never had to do. ... It gnaws at your self-esteem." Alvarado called the work that principals do when leading teachers the "guided reading of leadership." Leaders guide their teachers, offering them support based on their needs so that they can become more effective in the classroom. In general, instructional leadership "turn[s] a school culture into a performance-oriented culture ... [one that consists of] looking at performance and knowing that it is at the heart of improving results" (Alvarado, 2002a).

Reflective Practitioners

Both district leaders emphasized reflection as an essential element of leadership. During one principals' conference, Bersin (2002a) referred to his own efforts to be a reflective learner: "As I see leadership—it is evolving. I see it as a voyage of discovery. We need to discover new dimensions of leadership within ourselves to improve achievement. We engage in constant reflection." Alvarado (2002b) also personalized the work of the reform by reflecting on his own struggles as a reader tackling difficult texts. He admitted, "I actually need help with the strategies that I use about deconstructing text because it's such a darn challenge and I have to work hard, not only on language ... not only rereading, it is trying to figure out stuff." Following that speech, many principals whispered to each other about the personal connection Alvarado had made to the work and how his struggles resonated with them and inspired them.

Team Builders
The importance of sharing knowledge and team building were stressed. Bersin (2002a) instructed his audience at one conference to develop the kinds of relationships that permit "us to grow together and allow us to accept criticism of ourselves." "Be willing to be a learner," he urged, "even though some are not always willing to be taught. We need to look and document what we do, for we are on the road to building a learning community." Writing up principals' and teachers' practices following walk-throughs and tracking the changes in students' and schools' scores from state-mandated standardized tests were important components of this documentation process.

Urging principals to share knowledge, Bersin (2002a) said,

> [Thanks to the efforts of many, we have] a professional development system that increasingly is [about] sharing knowledge. Organizations must share knowledge. At every level across the district I think we are beginning to develop learning communities that are for real and not just rhetorical; that actually connect classrooms to principals' offices.

He also stressed that leadership involves building a "professional *system*":

> The effort you are leading, it is making a huge difference. We are so close to building a professional system. We are so close to having teachers take pride in what they are learning and what they know. We all have to [keep] working through the relationships and understanding the chain cycle, spreading knowledge, building relationships and providing coherence. (Bersin, 2002a)

Capacity Builders
At several principals' conferences and at a daylong high school principals' retreat, principals were pushed to reflect on their current school capacity and ask themselves questions such as, "What skills do my teachers and

staff developers have? What more do you need to do to make your leadership team effective?" At a 2002 conference, Alvarado asked the principals how they would assess the needs of each individual teacher. He reminded them that identifying teachers' needs and then taking this knowledge and "mak[ing] it actionable" was part of their job. He added, "There is no such thing as leading instruction until you are having, after analysis, a conversation with a teacher that is thoughtful, careful and accomplishes the goal [so that] when the teacher goes to teach again, she or he understands what they have to do to make it better" (Alvarado, 2002b).

Belief Makers

The last of the core elements of leadership we identified in analyzing Bersin's and Alvarado's conference addresses is beliefs. Alvarado argued that for principals to be strong leaders, they must make the organization's beliefs overt, explicit, and pervasive. In his view, communicating beliefs was crucial to the success of the reform: "If there's not good teaching, there's not good learning. Everyone in your school needs to get the message from you as the leader, all the time. So every time you talk to anybody, they need to know your belief system, they need to know what you believe, and you believe that all kids can learn" (Alvarado, 2002a).

Although Bersin was typically congratulatory and recognized the principals' achievements in his opening addresses, for Alvarado the principals' conferences were all about the work of improving student learning. Often, that meant giving principals a dose of reality: "Students are not achieving because the adults have continued to let them down. There is still enormous work to be done." Alvarado's uncompromising style produced mixed reactions. Many principals considered him "inspiring." Some criticized Alvarado's negativity. Others saw him as a tyrant who did not treat them with the respect they deserved as colleagues with expertise. Alvarado countered that his messages were aimed at the head and the heart. He summed up the moral and intellectual commitments involved in leadership this way:

> Leading is ... actually bringing the best out of people, out of teachers and out of students. It is an intellectual task. It is about struggling over how you do things, how you solve problems, how you analyze, and how you come up with solutions that actually move the agenda [forward]. It needs to be felt as deeply personal and it needs to be understood as deeply intellectual because that's what you have to accomplish in order to do this work. (Alvarado, 2002b)

Learning about Instruction at Principals' Conferences

In addition to teaching principals leadership skills, the principals' conferences aimed to provide professional development in instruction. District leaders considered the conferences the single most important vehicle for teaching principals how to implement the reform. Developing a better understanding of the Balanced Literacy framework usually dominated the breakout portion of the conferences, when the ILs and principals met in their learning community groups. During these breakout sessions, ILs and principals analyzed the strengths and weaknesses of various implementations of the Balanced Literacy framework, and they discussed topics such as how to choose "Just Right" books, build a classroom library, level books, and construct a classroom environment that would support learning.

Explaining how to teach literacy was challenging for many ILs. By their own admission, they were learning right along with those they were charged with teaching. When they reviewed the work they had done at the principals' conferences, particularly in the early days of the reform, they often recognized their own mistakes: they had missed many opportunities to provide support to struggling principals, they had used misleading language, or they had delivered ambiguous messages. These problems were also made clear when Fink and the ILs viewed videotapes of their teaching. At one conference, for example, the ILs introduced principals to the use of "accountable talk," a literacy strategy involving classroom discussion designed to help students make meaning about what they have read. Principals needed to understand this teaching and learning strategy well enough to model it for their teachers. The teachers, in turn, would be expected to use accountable talk with their students. Following this conference, Fink (2001b) commented, "It's pretty clear to all of us that we weren't one hundred percent sure of what accountable talk was. And, even if we did think we knew what it was, we did not get the principals to [the point where they could] have an accountable talk session with their staff."

On a different occasion, when an IL attempted to explain the importance of "moving the teacher's desk," the principals interpreted the instruction literally and missed the implicit underlying theoretical message—that such a physical move had the potential of changing pedagogy and improving student learning. If teachers were no longer center stage, if students were engaged in discussions with one another and the teacher was more of a facilitator, then deeper learning would occur. Because the IL could not find a way to express the meaning behind the directive "move the desk," the principals' confusion mounted, making them resentful rather than supportive. This incident exemplifies the challenges faced by a district that tried to build the plane while flying it. Building capacity without having capacity is hard work.

Deepening Principals' Learning about Leadership and Instruction during Walk-Throughs

The stirring messages and instructional sessions provided at the principals' conferences were intended to prepare these leaders to return to their schools to address problems and improve practice. Still, all concerned recognized that additional, individualized, and site-specific guidance was needed to translate the district's theory of action into concrete and consistent educational practice. Walk-throughs enabled ILs to meet principals' needs for tailored guidance and deepen the leadership and instructional knowledge introduced at the principals' conferences. Walk-throughs also could serve as professional development for ILs. Elaine Fink often accompanied leaders during these events, offering advice and critiquing the walk-through strategies the ILs were using with their principals. Here, however, we focus on the walk-through exclusively as a professional-development event for principals. During the walk-throughs we observed, ILs particularly emphasized two facets of leadership: developing "the principal's voice" and "increasing capacity for schoolwide improvement." We address each separately in the following sections.

Learning to Develop a Leadership Voice

Fink explained to the ILs that teachers needed to be aware of their principals' beliefs and commitments. In the language of the reform, they needed to hear "the principal's voice." "You need to tell them [teachers] that we're here for the kids," she coached (Fink, 2001a). Following Fink's lead and recapitulating messages delivered at the principals' conferences, ILs insisted that their principals develop a voice that conveyed a sense of *urgency*. Principals must lead with a passion and pace that would exact success quickly. ILs reiterated top leaders' contention that students were failing and that failure was the responsibility of the adults who were teaching them. During one walk-through, for example, the IL pointedly reminded the principal, "About half the school is below and in the bottom quartile, which means those kids have no reading skills" (Fink, 2001a). The message was clear—failure was not acceptable, and it was the job of the leader of the school to move quickly to improve educational outcomes.

IL Laura Turner's approach to developing a sense of urgency in her principals' voice was evident during a walk-through on December 11, 2001, at Emmanuel Jackson Elementary School. Although Principal Dorothy Cavanaugh had led the majority of her teachers to use Balanced Literacy strategies successfully, a few—all third-grade teachers—remained resistant. These holdouts had learned just enough about Balanced Literacy to appear as though they were using the framework whenever the principal or IL visited their classrooms. During this walk-through, however, closer observation revealed that their practice had changed little.

Problems quickly became apparent when Turner asked a student to read to her, a practice ILs and principals commonly employed to assess if children were being exposed to books appropriate for their individual reading level. This child was reading a book that was much too challenging; moreover, when the IL accompanied the child to the classroom library to select a different book, it became clear that this student did not know how to select a Just Right book (see Chapter 5 for a discussion of Just Right books). Turner also learned that the third-grade teachers avoided professional-development sessions devoted to Balanced Literacy and appeared determined to continue using their traditional practices.

The IL reminded Principal Cavanaugh that if teachers did not avail themselves of the learning opportunities she provided or refused to change their practice, then she needed to hold them accountable. Together Turner and Cavanaugh designed a strategy that would provide support to the most recalcitrant of these third-grade teachers (e.g., have the teacher observe in an exemplary classroom and work with a peer coach to improve her understanding of Balanced Literacy) while also documenting this teacher's level of engagement and changes in practice. It would be up to Cavanaugh to make her expectations regarding improvement clear to the teacher. If the teacher continued to resist, the principal would document the resistance and remove the teacher from the school.

Adopting a "voice of urgency, pace, and passion" was not easy for Cavanaugh because confrontation was not a natural part of her leadership style. Turner (2001) helped her reframe the issue as "what is best for kids" rather than "what is good for adults." By the end of the walk-through postconference, Cavanaugh appeared to be comfortable with the plan. When we interviewed her nearly one year later, she said the teacher had continued to be resistant, but in the face of Cavanaugh's ongoing demands for improved performance, the teacher had eventually left the school voluntarily. Cavanaugh's newly adopted voice of urgency inspired her staff, gave her the strength of conviction to deal with recalcitrant teachers, and seemed to have improved student learning, as well. By the end of the next year, test scores at Emmanuel Jackson had risen, and Cavanaugh was recognized as an exemplar principal and hired as a mentor principal in the Educational Leadership Development Academy's apprenticeship program (see Chapter 6).

Learning to Build Capacity

In stressing the importance of the principals' role in improving teaching and learning at schools, Fink (2001b) likened their responsibilities to those of a company CEO:

> When you are leading that company, you need to go in and find out what's not working. No one's going to do that for you. You are heading it. It is your responsibility to know what's going wrong and what's going right, to figure out how to teach the people that work for you, how to make it better, get rid of those who can't do it. ... You have to problem-solve all the time. Analyze, problem solve, act. ... And persuade others to come along with you.

In the everyday lives and routines of principals, resolving problems at their school sites required "always focus[ing] on what the problems are and how to solve them." A principal's job involved helping teachers "swallow their egos and [be] continual learners" (Fink, 2002a). Problem solving most often meant figuring out how to build capacity among the teaching staff. During twenty walk-throughs in six schools from 1998–2002, we observed ILs help principals cluster problems so as to attack them more efficiently, use more capable teachers to assist less capable teachers, revise and improve professional-development plans, evaluate teachers' performance, and—in extreme cases—arrange for the removal of poor performers.

During a walk-through at Scripps Elementary in 2001, IL Donna Burns helped Principal Cynthia Oliver categorize teachers to "fix the problems" that were blocking improvements in student achievement at her school. To assist the principals in her learning community to see common rather than individual challenges, Burns recommended they place teachers along a continuum ranging from "beginning," through "developing," to "proficient," to "advanced." Applying this strategy, Oliver could assess similarities in her teachers' needs and then use proficient and advanced teachers to lead beginning and developing ones. Burns (2001) also claimed that classifying teachers this way was a more objective approach: "This procedure has really helped all of my principals to get more accurate. ... They started keeping their documentation letters [written to teachers in the aftermath of a walk-through] to talk to me and conversations started occurring, you know, around the kind of supports that are actually [needed] and ... how to improve skills."

Like Burns, Fink advocated building capacity by pairing less capable teachers with more proficient ones. After a walk-through at Harvey Mudd Elementary School that included an IL, Principal Constance Parker, and Fink, Fink (2001a) reminded Parker, "You don't buddy teachers because they are friends, you have to buddy them based on what you know about them." On the basis of her classroom observations, Fink felt there was little evidence of teacher collaboration at the school: "When I walked into these classrooms, everybody was doing their own individual thing and there was no sense that anybody was working with anybody and that they had learned anything. So if they were [learning], it didn't go deep enough" (Fink, 2002b). Fink used the information she gathered from the walk-through to help Parker purposefully pair her teachers to scaffold their knowledge about instruction and encourage deeper forms of learning.

Improving instruction for English-language learners challenged everyone in the district. All biliteracy teachers—but especially those at Scripps and Harvey Mudd—struggled to help students transfer their knowledge of reading and writing from Spanish to English while retaining their Spanish proficiency. During walk-throughs at these two schools, the ILs and principals devised professional-development plans for teachers that would address these challenges. They deployed peer coaches to help struggling teachers and arranged for the schools' literacy teachers to plan lessons together.

Walk-throughs also presented opportunities for ILs to challenge principals' existing professional-development plans. At Hunter High School, the principal had arranged for his staff developer to work intensively with two teachers who, despite a great deal of potential, continued to need help. On the basis of a walk-through, the IL concluded that this semiprivate coaching strategy did not provide enough support for the other teachers in the school. She maintained that the principal's plan was "expensive" and that his talented staff developer "should work with more teachers." After the walk-through, the principal concurred with his IL's assessment and decided to chart a different course of action.

Learning to Evaluate Teachers' Performance
The SDCS reform required all teachers to improve their practice to improve their students' learning. Walk-throughs provided principals with opportunities to record both positive and negative aspects of the classroom practice they observed. As one IL said bluntly, some teachers do not belong in the classroom, and it is the principal's job to identify, document, and remove such individuals. This evaluative responsibility and its association with walk-throughs is clear in a discussion between an IL and a principal during a walk-through postconference about a teacher whose practice was not improving. The IL told the principal to act aggressively. During the walk-through, the IL noted, "The teacher was in the back of the classroom doing nothing. It was awful." "Visit her classroom every single day," the IL

advised the principal, "and write up something every single day and get her out. The kids are not learning anything" (Fink, 2001a).

Learning to Understand Balanced Literacy More Deeply
In addition to deepening principals' leadership skills, walk-throughs were used to deepen principals' knowledge of Balanced Literacy. As we showed in Chapter 5, the Balanced Literacy model placed very heavy learning demands on teachers, but it also placed heavy demands on principals, who had to differentiate strong from weak pedagogy and diagnose and recommend appropriate support for teacher improvement.

In the early days of the reform, principals, like teachers, seemed to devote more attention to Balanced Literacy's superficial aspects (e.g., charts and schedules posted on walls, classroom libraries stocked with leveled books) than to its substantive ones (see Chapter 6). The need to critique teachers' use of the reform's deeper, more interactive features (see Chapter 5) was not being met. For example, a crucial feature of Balanced Literacy that Fink and the ILs wished their principals could see was the role of "strategy work." According to Fink, teachers needed to teach students to make meaning of texts rather than training them to recite the facts books contain. She insisted that strategies such as visualizing, inferring, and predicting could be applied to students' meaning-making efforts no matter what books they were reading. The fact that many teachers did not understand how to teach these strategies to their students indicated to Fink either that principals were not clear about strategy work or that they had not yet taught it adequately to their teachers. Hence, a focus of many of the walk-throughs we observed was the quality of classroom practice with regard to teaching strategies for comprehending text.

Our observations of walk-throughs indicate that *both* of Fink's suppositions were true. Principals did not fully understand Balanced Literacy strategies, and they had not been able to teach the strategies to their staff. We believe that a significant part of the principals' difficulties in grasping the more complex aspects of the framework were an artifact of their ILs' didactic teaching style. Research on student learning shows it improves when students learn to think critically, solve complex problems, dialogue with teachers, and engage in hands-on learning (Freire, 1967; Meier, 1995; Rosenstock & Steinberg, 1995; Vygotsky, 1978). Sawyer (2004: 14) described learning as "a creative improvisational process" and argued that when classrooms are "scripted and directed by the teacher, the students can not construct their own knowledge." Research on adult learners offers similar findings. Adult learning improves when the process is active and dialogic (Bransford, Brown, & Cocking, 1999; Comings, Garner, & Smith, 2000; Cunningham & Cordeiro, 2001; Stein & Gewirtzman, 2003).

Unfortunately, especially in the early days of the reform, the pedagogy we observed most often resembled didactic teaching—what Freire (1967) termed "banking," where knowledge is deposited into the heads of passive learners. ILs rarely engaged their principals in debates or in problem-based learning. Although almost all educators would be quick to agree with Schön (1987: 39) that it is a mistake to assume "that existing professional knowledge fits every case ... [or] that every problem has a right answer," the urgency and fast pace of the San Diego reform may have prompted ILs to judge deep learning techniques such as dialogue and creative improvisation as too time-consuming. Opting for the relatively faster traditional lecture-style transmission of information entailed significant drawbacks, however. The experiences of Principal Dorothy Cavanaugh are illustrative.

Cavanaugh had a good relationship with her IL, Laura Turner, whom she saw quite frequently. She took what Turner offered and put it into place, faithfully following directions. For the most part, this approach appeared to be successful. Test scores at Emmanuel Jackson rose, and Cavanaugh's school was honored for this achievement. When asked why she thought the students had been so successful, Cavanaugh responded by crediting her IL: "Because our teachers are doing it. It's [the work with Turner] building our capacity, because we're seeing how it really happens in classrooms and we're seeing the students and how they are progressing. So I think that accelerated our learning, because we are actually seeing it work."

Despite these outward signs of success, our analysis of *how* Cavanaugh learned from Turner reveals the relatively shallow nature of her learning. In most cases, Turner diagnosed the problems and told Cavanaugh what to do to fix them. During many of our observations at Emmanuel Jackson, it appeared to us that Cavanaugh hungrily grabbed whatever Turner offered and implemented it "to the letter." Our hypothesis regarding the depth of Cavanaugh's learning was reinforced by her (2002) own comments during an interview:

> The first time she [Turner] was here, she said, "Gotta' buy chapter books, that's what's going to move you." And so maybe that afternoon, we started ordering all the chapter books and what a difference that made. Every suggestion she's given us, we carry it through. And it always has worked, with all of them. I think it's that knowledge base she has.

Later in that same interview, Cavanaugh expressed a similar thought: "She'd give us an idea or something to do. We'd run out, immediately do it, make sure it was implemented in the classroom, not just because to prove to her we were doing it, but because we wanted to see if it worked. ... And she has been right every time."

Cavanaugh's learning style appeared to be directly linked to her IL's didactic approach to teaching, thus confirming our expectation that deep learning will be suppressed when novices feel they must follow instructions exactly. When Turner coached Cavanaugh on how to confront resistant teachers, for instance, the language she used, as well as the language she "gave" to Cavanaugh to use, assumed teaching as active and learning as passive. Cavanaugh was instructed to say, "Here I am providing the professional development, and that's my role as a principal to do that, but it doesn't end there. It's your role as a teacher *to take that on* and implement it" (Turner, 2002). Notice that Turner's wording says much about the *teaching* the teacher should do but mentions nothing about the *learning* the teacher needed to do to actively construct meaning about the reform.

Turner expressed a similarly directive philosophy about teaching and learning when describing an incident at another school. She reported (2002) that after a disappointing walk-through, she told the school's leadership team the following:

> Either you didn't do anything with that knowledge [that I had provided to you at my last visit] and *give* it to the teachers, or you *gave* it to the teachers and you're not making sure it's being carried through or implemented ... what you teach, you need to make sure that your teachers implement it. ... I'm teaching you this. This is what we're learning, so now let's focus on this. I'll come into your classroom. I'll put in a peer coach, do a staff development. I'll do all those other things, but you have a responsibility to approximate what has been taught.

Here, Turner equates instruction with knowledge transfer. ILs provide principals with knowledge. Principals receive that knowledge and then pass it down the instructional corridor to their teachers. In this banking model, learners are told very little about how to make meaning of the received information, how to go about connecting it to their present situation, or how to help others understand the information.

In other situations we observed, the ILs appeared to have established more collaborative relationships with principals. As a result, the learning accomplished by both parties deepened. At Scripps Elementary, for example, Principal Cynthia Oliver told us that Donna Burns, her IL, always attended to the "unique problems" of Scripps's staff and students Oliver was comfortable sharing ideas with her IL and, in turn, received support from Burns for her thinking. An especially clear example of Burns's willingness to accommodate the specific needs of Scripps Elementary occurred when Oliver was deciding when to implement the district's new writing initiative. Although most of her colleagues were following the district plan by putting it into place immediately (in September 2002), Oliver decided to wait until later in the year. Burns not only supported her for making a decision that best met the needs of her school but also encouraged Oliver's increasing assertion of responsibility for leadership. When we asked Oliver why her IL was removing the scaffolds, she answered (2001),

> She knows her schools. She came back when we met one day in our learning community and she said, "Now some of you need to be thinking about where this is going to fit, and is it going to fit in September, or are you going to have it fit someplace else?" And we had a day where we shared out our plan for bringing this to our site and I stood and told everyone that "I am not going to roll this out until February. ... I was just starting units of study in reading. I can't stop that because [it would be difficult to incorporate writing in time devoted to reading]. ... And she's fine with that ... she supported that.

We believe Oliver's feeling of increased freedom as opposed to the feelings of anxiety and even anger some of her colleagues expressed is highly correlated with the interactive, collaborative, and problem-solving approach to the walk-through she and her IL established. And the development of collaborative relationships seemed to be correlated with ILs' assessment of the progress principals and their schools were making toward realizing district goals. Because Burns was sensitive to the special circumstances at Scripps, she knew when to grant Oliver autonomy. As a result, both principal and IL achieved deeper learning. When we questioned Burns (2002), she said, "In the beginning I did a lot of modeling. ... At the end of the year, I was doing a whole lot more questioning of her than I was at the beginning of the year, so I learned how to, you know, really question her and get at her thinking and then kind of ponder [and step] back so that it wasn't like I had all the answers."

Consciously changing her teaching strategy from didactic to dialogic allowed Burns to learn from Oliver; they built knowledge jointly. Burns mentioned specific areas of joint learning, such as "classroom instruction and whether the principal's teaching is actually changing anything." She went on to say, "But I think there's this other parallel that I have. I am also observing how the principal is [acting]—either problem solving around the issue, or analyzing instruction or whatever we are doing—[and] that reflects on my teaching." This is an important acknowledgment. Burns recognized that teaching and learning is a joint accomplishment—an accomplishment that reflects on *her teaching* as well as the learners' efforts. Studying her principals' strengths and weaknesses led her to reflect on her own leadership and to alter her style to be more closely aligned with the individual needs of her principals.

Learning to Build Trusting Relationships
Building relationships of trust seems to be an essential component in successful reform, but top-down leadership coupled with fast-paced change is seldom associated with high levels of trust (Bryk & Schneider, 2003). When ILs did forge a trusting relationship with principals in their learning communities, however, both principals and ILs agreed that this bond advanced the instructional and learning goals of the SDCS reform. And relationship building was directly tied to the teaching strategy ILs used during professional-development events such as the walk-through. In comparing her own experiences with those of her colleagues, another principal in Donna Burns's learning community offered this revealing contrast:

> It's real interesting to talk with other principals about how I am able to communicate at all different levels with [my IL] and that their relationship is a little bit different. And it depends on each IL sometimes, too. I have talked with one other principal who is really frustrated and not knowing how to deal with the communication [issue] and so I kind of helped her think about how to communicate her concerns. I could have just called Donna and said, "Look, ... I am doing some thinking" whereas [in my colleague's case] it needed to be a little bit more formal. I'm not saying that Donna's and [my] communication isn't always on a formal basis, but [our] relationship is stronger. (2002)

This principal pointed directly to the trusting relationship she had developed with her IL. Even though the IL continued to demand that this principal express and justify the rationale for any alternative problem-solving ideas she proposed, the principal felt she was constructing a school environment that was increasingly conducive to learning. Her perception of her IL as providing strong support seemed linked to the IL's willingness to acknowledge the principal's mastery of reform topics and increasingly honor her competence to make decisions.

Principals' Reactions to Their Professional-Development Opportunities

Principals' reactions to professional-development activities ranged from gleeful exuberance to cautious acceptance to doubtful resistance about how to convert abstract theory into concrete practice. They were often stimulated by the challenges that lay ahead but exhausted by the frustrations posed by the enormity of the work. Principals recognized that the success of their efforts rested primarily on knowing how to lead, but they faced a number of daunting challenges. These challenges included (1) connecting instruction with leadership, (2) translating the district leaders' abstract theory of leadership into concrete leadership practices at their school sites, (3) understanding the rationale for the district's choices, and (4) resolving the apparent contradictions between the supportive and evaluative dimensions of professional-development opportunities. For analytical reasons, we address each of these concerns separately. In practice, of course, they are inextricably interwoven (McDermott, 1980; Star & Bowker, 1997).

Connecting Instruction with Leadership

Although district leaders insisted that principals did not need to be literacy specialists, they did need to learn enough to (1) identify weaknesses in instruction, (2) help improve the teachers' practice, and (3) organize schoolwide support that would address teachers' needs and build capacity at their schools. This level of expertise demanded that principals know *how* to instruct, *how* to lead, and *how* to integrate instructional knowledge with leadership skills.

Despite the frequent reminders leaders issued at principals' conferences that school leaders' core responsibility "is your leadership practice and leading instruction at your school site" and that these should be the "focus in all of the work we do" (Johnson, 2001), principals remained confused about exactly how to enact the reform's ideas. As we explained in chapter 6, many principals lacked a deep understanding of the Balanced Literacy curriculum and the pedagogy associated with it; hence, they did not know how to lead their teachers to enact the framework. Principals pointed this problem out repeatedly and requested more guidance in understanding where the weaknesses in teacher practice existed, the reasons for these weaknesses, and suggestions for how to fix them.

Principals who turned to their ILs for concrete instructions or requested these leaders' help in devising appropriate leadership strategies to work with their teachers sometimes found their needs unmet: "They view your videotapes of your planning session or the faculty conferences. Then, they are supposed to help you critique them and help you plan more efficiently with more content or whatever … but it's so few and far between, and they have so many people" (Parker, 2001a). One solution was to turn to colleagues. Many principals concurred with a principal who told us, "I get more support from my colleagues [than from the IL]. I have some colleagues that I work with, and I think through on my own with my VPs and my peer coach" (Parker, 2001a). This strategy had drawbacks, though. Vice principals and peer coaches were learning along with principals, but the gaps in their knowledge had somewhat less serious consequences. All school leaders were learners—but principals bore the additional burden of being formally charged with the responsibility to lead instruction at their sites.

Of course, principals varied in their levels of expertise, but we found that most struggled to learn the reform strategies thoroughly enough to teach them to their faculties in a way that would allow the teachers to implement the strategies effectively in their classrooms. The ILs tried to respond to principals' concerns. For instance, when it was apparent that the instructional breakout session on accountable talk described earlier had left many school leaders more confused than enlightened, the ILs attempted to teach the strategy again at a subsequent principals' conference. Unfortunately, even after a second exposure to the technique, many principals remained unsure how to guide their teachers in its use.

We believe that a key reason why the ILs' efforts to teach the reform strategies were not always effective was their didactic approach. On the surface, interactions within the range of professional-development activities the district provided appeared to be collaborative because participants were often grouped for discussion, participated in question and answer sessions, and analyzed videotaped lessons together. However, close analysis of these events shows that most discussions followed a similar pattern. The leader of the professional-development event asked very guided questions, with specific answers in mind. The other participants responded if they felt they had the "correct" answer, an instructional practice that has been referred to as "the search for known answer questions" (Mehan, 1979). The need to come up with the right answer limited discussion and debate and, arguably, impeded learning.

Translating Theory into Practice

The proper practice of leadership also remained murky in the minds of many principals. They had been instructed to lead with an edge, but they were not clear what this no-nonsense approach should look like in practice. They worried that so seemingly confrontational an approach would not mesh with the more collaborative culture common in most schools. And they were increasingly aware that "leading with an edge" needed to be backed up by a high level of knowledge about the reform—a degree of expertise many principals feared they did not yet possess.

Guidance from ILs sometimes worsened rather than improved this situation, as an example from a principals' conference breakout session illustrates. An IL who had just recently learned the Balanced Literacy strategy of conferring tried to instruct his principals in the use of this technique, saying,

> Some teachers ... really don't understand the importance of conferring. That is a reality we have to face. ... If I know that as principal, I have to make some decisions. ... I need my teachers to understand the theory of conferring ... [some ways to achieve that include] having some accountable talk about it ... looking at other professional texts. ... I can observe conferring myself ... [then] make a decision and put it into action. (Johnson, 2001)

This IL's principals were no clearer on how to put the general theory of conferring into concrete practice after listening to his presentation than they had been before it. Principals came away from this and other professional-development opportunities without a deep enough understanding to successfully undertake any of the three steps the IL outlined. Many had learned the language of the reform, but few had acquired the necessary theoretical understanding to translate their knowledge into practices their teachers could implement.

At the same breakout session, the IL told principals to observe independent reading and get "decent answers from kids on the books they are reading." But the notion of a "decent answer" remained elusive. Principals drew up a list of questions teachers might ask students to elicit a decent answer and determine if they were reading Just Right books. When they shared the list with teachers, the response was disheartening. The teachers felt that the principals were out of touch with classroom realities and that they were overly concerned with theory and not concerned enough with practice.

In fact, as we have noted, most principals were very concerned about connecting theory and practice. What they lacked were explicit instructions in how to do so. When their ILs offered suggestions such as "What we need to do is reflect on who our teachers are, what they need to know, and what expectations I have" and "[It's all about] asking the questions, doing the analysis, and coming up with a plan, rather than, 'Oh, here's the rule,' " principals rightly countered with "But how do I work with my teachers?"

"What questions could I ask that would lead me to a plan?" "How do I get to know my teachers?" "How do I construct a faculty conference that will lead to a change in teacher practice?" Such questions clearly show that the challenge for successfully implementing the reform was to make the implicit explicit for the principals.

Understanding the Rationale for District Leaders' Choices

Another set of penetrating questions principals (and teachers) raised concerned the rationale for district leaders' choices: "Why *this* instructional content, why *this* model of leadership?" "Why is the method of instruction associated with Balanced Literacy better than what we have been doing?" "Why are district leaders *telling* us what to do instead of *asking* us?" Questions such as these persisted even though, in virtually every opening and closing address they gave at principals' conferences, Superintendent Bersin and Chancellor Alvarado specified closing the achievement gap as *the* rationale for the reform. The message that all children deserved academic success and that providing the means to that goal was the responsibility of all educators in the district was reinforced by all ILs in their introductory and closing remarks during breakout sessions and in nearly every walk-through. Thus, the topmost level of the district's leaders repeatedly demonstrated that they had no trouble answering the question, "*Why* are we doing this reform?"

Some principals (and many teachers), however, posed this question with an important change. They asked, "Why are we doing *this* reform?" The admirable social justice goal of improving the learning of all students did not satisfy those who wondered how and why they should implement the Balanced Literacy framework or why they should adopt the district's model of leadership to close the achievement gap. They also asked, "Why is the method of instruction associated with Balanced Literacy better than what we have been doing?" "Why are district leaders *telling* us what to do instead of *asking* us?" From their point of view, neither the district leaders nor the ILs provided convincing, detailed rationale for the specific interventions they required principals to assist their teachers in implementing. As a result, many principals complied blindly with district directives rather than acting from a commitment to or deep understanding of the reform's ideas. Reflecting on this situation, one IL told us, "Where we need to get to is not compliance with ground rules, but an understanding of why we need to do some of the things that have been imposed. We will never get the change we need to get if we are only doing things because someone told us we have to" (Simpson, 2001).

*Resolving the Contradictions between Evaluation and
Support in Walk-throughs*

The six principals we studied closely, and many other principals in the district, told us informally that they learned considerably from the walk-throughs. The ILs had an almost uncanny ability to identify teacher needs and to home in on the essence of their problems. Harvey Mudd principal Constance Parker was typical of those we interviewed who considered walk-throughs "wonderful training" and wished the visits were more frequent. Another principal commented, "The walk-through is phenomenal support … it's probably the greatest time dedicated just to me, and that I really am able to kind of think aloud about things that have been on my mind, but also have my thinking pushed and clarified where I need to go next." Although principals regretted that the walk-throughs and accompanying pre- and postconferences did not afford them as much time as they would have liked for discussing site-specific issues, they believed the special time set aside just for them did make it easier to solve their problems.

Interestingly, the same principals who told us they looked forward to walk-throughs as an opportunity to work intensively with a knowledgeable mentor also described walk-throughs as a "mixed blessing" because they combined support with evaluation. "The walk-through *is* evaluative," Principal Parker emphasized. "Am I implementing? Am I supporting change? We spend a lot of time at principals' conferences learning how to coach. Am I coaching my teachers? Am I creating a change of instruction in this classroom? Because if I'm not, I'm not doing my job. And I'm held accountable for that" (Parker, 2001b). She went on to point out, "There isn't a time when, if your boss is with you, that you're not thinking of being evaluated and everything your boss sees goes into your brain."

Not all district leaders agreed that walk-throughs involved performance evaluation, however. One IL clarified that walk-throughs are not about assessing teachers but about providing support.

> It is not about individual teachers; it's really about the [principal], to help her to see where she needs to go next. It's not about assessment—that's the old model. It's about coaching and how to see what teachers are doing so we can have staff development that meets the needs of the teachers. [Walking through] classes are a data-gathering point. This is also [an attempt] to move [teachers] from compliance to commitment—to give them the rationale. (Burns, 2001)

This eloquent defense of the supportive function of walk-throughs notwithstanding, principals experienced these events as both evaluative and supportive—and they found these two functions fundamentally contradictory. Fink noted that most principals felt the walk-through was "very pushy, and they knew that they were going to be pushed. On the other hand, they also looked forward to it. ... I think they really wanted to be pushed" (Fink, 2002b). Other ILs concurred—during walk-throughs, principals tried hard "to show their very best." They wanted to do a good job, and they wanted their ILs "to be proud of them" (Burns, 2001). Because ILs held principals accountable for their actions, in addition to providing them with deeply appreciated support, a complicated arrangement that colored the relationship between principals and ILs ensued. Principals worried, for example, that an IL's infrequent observations "may not get the full flavor" of any given teacher's practice—or the IL might visit on a teacher's "off day" and then erroneously conclude that the principal's supervision of staff was not up to par. In large schools, the issue of the amount of time devoted to a walk-through was especially salient. ILs could not possibly visit a sufficiently large sample of classrooms to reach empirically sound conclusions about instruction, a situation that left principals "not feeling good."

External factors added to principals' anxieties, as well. School test score data was prominently reported in the local newspaper. In the first year of the reform, several principals were relieved of their positions because their schools were not improving (see Chapter 9 for details). Some of these removals generated a strongly negative response from the community. Thus, in addition to their IL's scrutiny, principals worked in the shadow of highly charged political events.

Somewhat to our surprise, some principals viewed the ever-present tension in walk-throughs between appreciation for the support ILs provided and anxiety over being evaluated as motivating. One principal described the odd sensation of feeling simultaneously pressured and excited this way:

> I think I need a massage after every walk-through [laughter] because of all the tension that's created. ... I am trying to be consistent and have a specific focus for my teachers, so I go in with that focus and I give them feedback, and then when I go in with Donna [and her] lens is, like, wide angle. And so it's like, "oh, my gosh, I have so much to do." And that's where that tension is. So it's helpful that I get my questions answered, but it's also that *urgency* because that push, through her questions, is driving my next steps. (Oliver, 2001)

ILs seemed to purposefully play off this tension to instill a sense of urgency in both teachers and principals. "The only thing that gets you to move is that tension," one IL explained. "If there is no tension, there's no need for you to feel an urgency to work on something, and that's what I try to leave people with, a real feeling of a real desire to do it—and the knowledge to go forth and do it."[2]

Instructional Leaders' Responses to Principals' Concerns about Their Professional Development

ILs may have found the number and intensity of principals' complaints and concerns unsettling, but to their credit they neither downplayed nor ignored this feedback. The SDCS, and the ILs in particular, responded forcefully to their principals' concerns in technical, cultural, and political terms.

Enhancing Principals' Learning by Technical Means

ILs recognized that their biggest challenge lay in teaching principals *how* to instruct their teachers: "The biggest hurdle that we've heard time and time again is, '*How* am I going to teach my teachers more ... so that they can better figure out what students need so that they can produce a better classroom?' " (Johnson, 2001). ILs also were aware that confusion reigned among teachers about how to implement the instructional content of the Balanced Literacy framework. One IL summarized some of the questions she heard from teachers: "Is this right? Is this allowed? Can we do it this way? If a principal walks in, will she say I am not supposed to be doing it this way?"

Adding and Rearranging Human and Material Resources
Realizing that instruction was neither deep nor explicit enough, beginning in September 2002, ILs added technical resources, both human and material, to the equation. The ILs began teaming with literacy administrators (the district experts on literacy instruction) to discuss reading strategies and how to distinguish fluent readers from emergent and beginning readers. They engaged principals in more hands-on activities during walk-throughs to help them learn how to match a student with a Just Right book. They asked principals to read academic literature, such as chapters from Fountas and Pinnell (2001), Elmore (2000), and Fullan (1999), to improve their knowledge of content and leadership. Principals from schools designated as "vulnerable" met monthly with their ILs to discuss the readings and the applicability to their own practice. ILs also refined their role-playing exercises to better expose problems and to model conversations with teachers that would lead to solving students' learning problems.

Adapting Resources for Practical Use

ILs deployed several innovative strategies to make the additional human and material resources useful to principals as they learned about instruction and leadership. They showed principals "reality" videotapes of SDCS teachers who had volunteered to be taped as they put various Balanced Literacy components such as guided reading, shared reading, and conferring into practice with their students. Then the ILs helped principals compare these with tapes of expert teachers conducting a lesson (sometimes with the same students and frequently with the same lesson). Strong practice was distinguished from weak or less effective practice to make effective pedagogy explicit to the principals.

Principals' conferences were reconfigured to identify common problems across schools and to provide structured opportunities for principals' professional development. To better prepare principals to confront the vexing problem of building teacher capacity schoolwide, for example, ILs focused a conference on how to write and implement a work plan. (As noted earlier, the principals' work plans detailed their course of action for addressing the needs of their teachers.) ILs also worked closely with school leaders in venues other than the principals' conferences, often in meetings held in the evenings or before school started, where they would go over the principals' descriptions of teaching practice and student achievement at their sites. With coaching from the ILs, the principals learned to formulate the steps they should take to improve instruction and increase student achievement.

ILs increased their reliance on learning strategies grounded in well-established pedagogical theory and practice (Cole, 1996; Lave & Wenger, 1991; Tharp & Gallimore, 1988; Vygotsky, 1978). They provided more specific guidance to principals about connecting less capable teachers with their more capable peers—expert teachers, literacy administrators, or staff developers—to improve teachers' practice. Although pairing teachers was a common strategy designed to support less experienced teachers, principals varied in the strategies they used to construct pairs. Some pairs were more successful than others.

In addition, ILs increasingly encouraged principals to confer with their teachers to learn the status of their practice and to move them to a deeper level of knowledge and skill. Finally, they taught principals how to critique professional-development events such as one-on-one conferences with teachers and grade-level meetings. ILs developed a rubric to guide principals in this work and presented this tool at a principals' conference. They used the rubric to assess a video of a conference between a principal and one of her teachers, comparing that conference to one conducted by an expert (a district-hired consultant). This exercise enabled principals to return to their schools better prepared to model the same practice with their teachers.

Professional development organized as a group activity was not an entirely adequate venue to raise principal competency. The rigorous expectations of the SDCS reform demanded some intimate, one-on-one interaction between the ILs and each principal in their learning community. In many cases, despite their already overburdened schedules, ILs took on this added responsibility. They helped their principals plan staff conferences, including reviewing scripts of opening addresses and consulting on the content of an instructional day. In some cases, the benefits were profound (see Hubbard, Beldock, & Osborne, 2003). Many ILs and principals made considerable progress as their knowledge and experience grew. Unfortunately, however, this well-intentioned effort also contributed to the uneven implementation of a reform that privileged consistency. Principals lucky enough to have ILs who were willing and able to do extra work profited from coaching that was not available to other principals. This in turn affected classroom practice, because better-coached principals were better able to help their teachers.

Enhancing Principals' Learning by Cultural and Political Means

The district's willingness to allocate additional human and material resources to solve serious problems was helpful, but this technical assistance unwittingly generated some nagging problems in the cultural and political domains. For example, arranging for planning time with already overburdened ILs, content specialists, and literacy administrators posed logistical problems. Moreover, each of these professionals had her or his own organizationally defined work roles, institutional norms, impossibly impacted work schedules, and strong sense of personal place in the hierarchy of the school system. Developing a team approach to principals' leadership development demanded that attention be paid to institutional culture and the micropolitics of status arrangements.

Power struggles surfaced between ILs and literacy administrators over who was to lead principals' learning. These power relations had to be negotiated, as did differences in theoretical backgrounds and orientations to the work. For example, literacy administrators prided themselves on knowing how to teach the Balanced Literacy framework and were critical of ILs they judged as lacking this knowledge. ILs occupied a higher position of authority within the district, but the literacy administrators were responsible directly to Alvarado, not to the IL with whom they were paired. These conflicts over institutional authority undermined the good intentions of using a collaborative approach to intensify professional development.

Fortunately, ILs invested the effort necessary to overcome these practical–political organizational problems. They sorted out organizational responsibilities, reconfigured pairs who were temperamentally mismatched, and became more adroit at assigning responsibilities to their literacy administrators. ILs also became more adept at scripting presentations to ensure that all participants spoke a common language and that the substance of their talks was consistent with that of district leaders. Last, to enhance commitment to district-sanctioned norms and values, ILs emphasized to the principals their beliefs about the work of the reform and assisted principals in learning to convey their own beliefs and further specify organizational norms and values to their teachers.

Summary

In this chapter, we outlined the dialogue that occurred between top district leadership and principals regarding the reform. Superintendent Bersin and Chancellor of Instruction Alvarado initiated the dialogue by presenting their theory of leadership in broad strokes, including statements about reform goals, rationales, and strategies for accomplishing goals, to the principals at monthly conferences. The district leaders' presentations about leadership and instruction were then reinforced by ILs during the breakout sessions they taught at the principals' conferences and in school walk-throughs.

Principals' responses to leaders' statements ranged widely, from faithful and enthusiastic implementation to confusion about how to connect theory to practice. ILs responded to principals' concerns by providing greater specificity about goals, strategies, and rationales through the use of videotapes, role-playing, and other activities. Although the more rigorous professional-development opportunities were helpful, when we stopped observations in 2002, principals were still trying to understand how to unite leadership with instruction. As a result, the district's theory of action was applied unevenly in practice.

Both SDCS principals and ILs were taught to believe that strong and effective leadership required individuals to have a deep commitment to a moral purpose. District leaders insisted that social justice, defined as closing the achievement gap between rich and poor students and between white students and students of color, was their moral purpose. To actualize that moral purpose, principals were told by ILs in conference breakout sessions and during walk-throughs to speak with a voice of "passion, pace, and urgency." They were expected to acquire and deploy a dizzying array of talents, including building relationships, sharing knowledge, analyzing data, reflecting on practice, and building capacity. Principals were also told to become knowledgeable about instruction, particularly the Balanced Literacy framework's reading strategies, to lead their faculty toward improved student learning.

Under Fink's tutelage, ILs learned to use the walk-through to help principals improve the leadership skills and deepen the instructional knowledge introduced to them at principals' conferences. ILs also used walk-throughs to assist principals in using scaffolding and modeling strategies to improve their teachers' classroom practices. More capable teachers were assigned to coach less capable teachers; struggling teachers observed exemplary teaching. Principals also learned that leadership involved evaluation. ILs and principals praised and encouraged teachers to move to the next plane of competence, but if ILs and principals concluded that teachers' practice was not improving, then they used walk-throughs to produce evidence to remove teachers. Walk-throughs were, arguably, instructive and evaluative for both principals and teachers.

Without question, principals' leadership skills and knowledge of instruction improved as a result of this injection of material and human resources. However, not all professional-development events were equally effective in passing on district leaders' intended messages and developing a common culture of practice. The pressing needs of the diverse population of San Diego students, the focus of Balanced Literacy on young learners, and high school teachers' perceptions of themselves as disciplinary specialists not reading instructors contributed to differences in reform implementation in elementary and high school classrooms.

Because ILs added even more human and material resources in response to principals' concerns, over time principals were better supported in their work with teachers. Many principals were empowered by the ILs' heightened commitment. We found, however, that for many principals, ILs' teaching did not go deep enough and their language still was not sufficiently explicit. These principals continued to leave the myriad professional-development opportunities provided to them wondering how to connect theory with practice. All the while, the clock of test score accountability ticked on. District leaders had successfully constructed and communicated a *theory* of leadership, but when it came to the operational *practice* of leadership, principals were left asking the familiar question, "What do I do on Monday morning?"

****

In Chapters 5, 6, and 7, we have shown that the time, energy, and person power required to provide adequate learning opportunities for teachers, principals, and ILs was underestimated and that many of the effects of the reform's deliberate break with the standard operating procedures of the district were unanticipated. In Chapter 8, we expand on our explanation for why the district's possibly unprecedented commitment to the professional development of the educators was not as successful as envisioned. We find answers in the conflicts that the district's comprehensive, centralized, fast-paced approach to reform created both within the taken-for-granted, deeply entrenched culture of the schools and between the district and its constituents.

CHAPTER 8

Demystifying the Gap between Theory and Practice in the San Diego City Schools Reform

Our examination (presented in Chapters 5 through 7) of learning at intersection encounters, from teachers with students to instructional leaders (ILs) with principals, shows how difficult it is to change an institution as large and complex as a school district. The San Diego City Schools (SDCS) seemed to have all the ingredients for success: innovative leaders who had a tested theory of action (the Balanced Literacy framework), significant human and material resources invested in a wide range of professional development activities that went beyond the traditional summer workshop approach to encompass activities that were embedded in the work at the school site, and dedicated mentors who were close to the action. Despite these positive enabling conditions, the instruction-based reform of the SDCS had neither penetrated deeply into middle school and high school classroom practice nor improved students' test scores significantly by the time we stopped closely monitoring the reform in 2002.

In this chapter, we try to explain why the district's theory did not translate smoothly into practice. We propose that a dynamic combination of technical, cultural, and political factors threatened the consistent, coherent application envisioned by district leaders. For analytic purposes, we treat these interwoven dimensions separately. Accordingly, we begin with an examination of the technical considerations that limited the reform from the outset and then consider the cultural and political clashes that threatened even the successful practices as the reform unfolded.

The Technical Limitations of the Reform

Teachers and their classroom practices are considered by most policy makers and reform experts to be integral to educational change. It is not surprising, then, that most reform efforts are directed at teachers (Darling-Hammond et al., 2005; Fullan, 1991; Heckman & Peterman, 1997; Hubbard & Datnow, 2002; Sarason, 1982, 1996; Wideen, 1994). Reformers often add resources such as labs or equipment, or they change curriculum, or they attempt to expand teachers' capacity to teach by providing professional-development activities. That is, they lead with *technical* means to achieve reform goals. Unfortunately, in the case of the SDCS reform, introducing these technical changes did not lead to improved student achievement, which was the overarching goal used to justify the massive reculturing and restructuring of the district.

Rearranging Standard Operating Procedures

The SDCS reform was built on two tightly interrelated assumptions about teacher quality and student achievement: SDCS students' poor achievement was a direct result of their teachers' ineffective teaching, and effective teaching can be learned, especially through systematic professional-development efforts (see Chapter 4).

Convinced that students—especially those from low-income neighborhoods—would not survive in college or the world of work unless their literacy skills improved, district leaders mandated the Balanced Literacy framework in all elementary, middle, and high schools. As we have documented in previous chapters, the Balanced Literacy framework required an intense commitment to an entirely new instructional model between teachers and students. In addition, this reform initiative required considerable changes in the standard operating procedures of schools. Every school day was expected to include two to three hours of literacy instruction. Because their schedules were not rigidly segmented into time blocks, elementary school leaders could accommodate this required technical change in their standard operating procedures, albeit with some difficulty. High school (and middle school) leaders, however, faced much larger challenges. Their school day schedules were rigidly divided (typically, into 50-minute or

120-minute periods); meeting the technical demand to institute a two- or three-hour literacy block required rearranging master schedules, teaching assignments, and other standard operating procedures. To accommodate literacy instruction, electives were pushed to the margins of high school course offerings.

The technical capacity of teachers to teach Balanced Literacy posed another challenge. Increasing the number of hours devoted to Balanced Literacy in elementary schools required a level of sophistication about students' reading and writing that few teachers possessed. Adding more genre studies courses in high schools required more teachers conversant with literacy instruction. Teachers in high school English departments typically teach literature, not literacy, and they had neither the inclination nor the training to change that practice. In squabbles over who would teach the mandated literacy courses, it was the newest teachers, with the least experience, who often ended up with these assignments, and in extreme cases teachers were recruited from other disciplines.

ILs also faced structural problems that limited their capacity to implement the reform as intended. Perhaps the most daunting was the number of schools for which they were responsible. With twenty schools in a typical learning community and 180 days in a school year, ILs could visit any given school only a few times per year. And with an average of twenty classrooms in a school, a maximum of six hours per visit, and time needed for conferences before and after walk-throughs, they could visit any given classroom for ten minutes, at most. The empirical basis for ILs' evaluations of principals and principals' evaluations of teachers thus was hardly robust. The maximum amount of time a principal and IL would have had in classrooms was thirty minutes per year. Because teachers and principals are at work a minimum of 480 minutes per day, for a minimum of 180 days per year, the ratio of time devoted to evaluation compared to time devoted to teaching was seriously skewed. Moreover, in practice, even the thirty-minute annual maximum could not be maintained, because ILs had responsibilities in addition to site visits. Also, field trips, fire drills, special assemblies, and other unforeseen events periodically forced the cancellation of walk-throughs, further constraining ILs' and principals' capacity to translate theory into practice.

Finally, the ILs leading high school principals had to motivate them to address recalcitrant teachers who frequently chanted that "high school is different" and "elementary school teachers should teach reading, not high school teachers." To convince high school teachers that they had a responsibility to teach disciplinary knowledge and reading strategies, principals had to be prepared in the theory of action that supported their work, and they had to be able to make the rationale for the reform explicit. But ILs often were not prepared for either of these new responsibilities. The result was gaps in communication and understanding across intersection encounters. One technical reason ILs faced this problem was that with respect to the Balanced Literacy framework, their resources were insufficient. Balanced Literacy had not been tested or proved effective at the high school level—so ILs did not have an empirical base on which to build their knowledge and substantiate claims of efficacy.

The Debate about Students' Achievement

Superintendent Alan Bersin and Chancellor Anthony Alvarado asserted from the outset that the effects of their reform would be seen in improved student achievement. But between 1998 and 2002, the district's record in this area—the quintessential technical–academic consideration—was not unequivocal. The absence of an outstanding record of student achievement was a particularly troubling technical constraint on the reform.

The primary, publicly available instrument for measuring students' academic achievement from 1998–2002 was the state-mandated *Stanford Achievement Test, Ninth Edition* (SAT9). The SAT9 is a standardized test of basic skills that compares California students' performance with that of students nationwide. Some applaud the use of this high-stakes test because it provides evidence reformers can use to focus attention on low-performing schools (Haycock & Navarro, 1997; No Child Left Behind [NCLB], 2001; Simmons & Resnick, 1993). Others criticize the SAT9 because it is norm referenced rather than criterion referenced, is not well aligned with district instructional goals and programs, absorbs too much instructional time for its administration, does not produce results quickly enough to assist teachers in diagnosing students' learning needs, and demoralizes test takers who are not fluent in English. In the absence of better instruments, however, and under pressure to demonstrate accountability to supporters of the reform—especially those in the business community and state and federal officials—San Diego educators had to rely on the SAT9 for achievement data, while at the same time deflecting criticism of the test's methodological and pedagogical limitations.

The standards and accountability department of the SDCS was admirably diligent in tabulating results of students' test performance and transparent in presenting them. Results were posted on the district's Web site within days of their receipt from the California State Department of Education. The data were presented in the form of the number and percentage of students at or above the national average on the math and reading sections of the SAT9, and the number and percentage of students in each quartile of test takers. This information was made available to the press and presented to community groups, including the United Front and the Business Roundtable for Education.

For our purposes, the relevant results are the student test scores from 1998–2002. The district released this information to the public and the press in August 2002 (SDCS, 2002) and also presented the results at a public meeting sponsored by the Business Roundtable for Education in September 2002 (Bersin, 2002d). Highlights of the SAT9 scores include the following:

- The number of students reading at or above grade level in 1998 was 37,744; in 2002, it was 45,241, an increase of 10,500 students. The number of students at or above grade level in math in 1998 was 39,163; in 2002, it was 51,369, an increase of 12,000 students.
- From 1998 to 2002, the number of students in the highest quartile in reading increased by 5,704 students, and the number of students in the lowest quartile in reading decreased by 4,582 students.
- From 1998 to 2002, the number of students in the highest quartile in math increased by 8,513 students, and the number of students in the lowest quartile in math decreased by 6,112 students.
- Gains on the SAT9 by grade level showed elementary students (grades two through five) with the greatest gains (11%), middle school students (grades six through eight) the next highest (6%), and high school students with the least (1%) from 1998 to 2002.

Second-grade students received special attention, because they had been educated in classrooms guided by the reforms for three consecutive years. That data showed a 12% gain in the number of students in the highest quartile and a 17% decrease in the number of students in the lowest quartile for math and reading.

The August 2002 release and the September presentation by the superintendent also provided test score data for ethnic groups. In these reports, the achievement gap was defined in terms of gains in scores within prominent ethnic groups: African American students improved by 10%; Filipinos, 9%; Hispanics, 8%; Indochinese, 19%; and whites, 7%. Information on the percentage of students by ethnic group who were at or above the national average was also provided: 37% of African Americans, 72% of Asians, 62% of Filipinos, 29% of Hispanics, 47% of Indochinese, and 74% of whites. That presentation showed the standing of students in prominent ethnic groups relative to each other. By calling attention to the gains within ethnic groups but not the performance of low-achieving groups to high-achieving groups, the SDCS was able to claim that the "achievement gaps among racial/ethnic groups continue to narrow in reading" (Bersin, 2002d; SDCS, 2002: 8) (see Figure 8.1).

The San Diego Union-Tribune (Spielvogel & Moran, 2002) interpreted the district's report as showing an increase in achievement "in nearly every grade and subject since 1998. The greatest growth has been in reading among its youngest students, whose entire education has been guided by the reforms." Citing "local educators," the newspaper attributed the drop-off in improvement among middle school and high school students to a variety of factors, "including the possibility that older students may be years behind or that teenagers don't take the test seriously." Other commentators received the district's presentations with less enthusiasm. For example, school board member and persistent reform critic John deBeck compared SDCS students' gains on the SAT9 to California students as a whole. He concluded that the gains in achievement were not strong enough to warrant the district's expenditure of funds on the Bersin–Alvarado initiatives (deBeck, 2002).

Because of the often acrimonious debate about student achievement, in 2002, the San Diego Dialogue, a local civic group based at University of California, San Diego, convened a group of prominent local educators (including the presidents of the San Diego Community College District, San Diego State University, University of San Diego, and University of California, San Diego) and area education scholars and researchers to review the data on student achievement. This "achievement forum" was charged by the Hewlett Foundation to provide an impartial analysis, one that would rise "above the clash of personalities, the shouting on the school board, the struggle for power between the teachers' union and the superintendent—and help the public focus on what really matters" (Nathanson, 2002: 1).

The group's October 2002 report, presented at a community forum, summarized main trends in SAT9 achievement but was careful not to make causal attributions to the Bersin–Alvarado strategy (the *Blueprint*) or to any other reform effort, such as class size reduction. Sensitive to the limitations of the SAT9, the forum also presented trend data on other measures, such as drop-out rates, the high school exit exam, and college preparation. The SDCS drop-out rate for Latinos was 17%, and for African Americans it was 21%, compared to the district average of 14%, the forum reported. Moreover, whereas 40% of students, on average, completed the courses necessary to apply to a University of California or a California State University campus, only 25% of African American and Latino students completed the necessary courses. "Most disturbing," the report concluded,

San Diego City Schools
2002 STAR Program Test Results

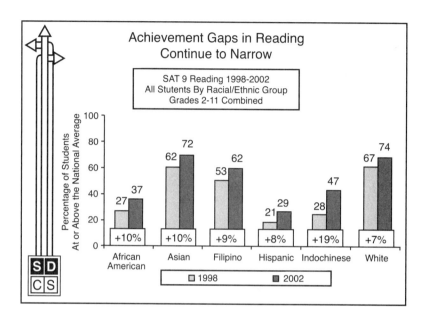

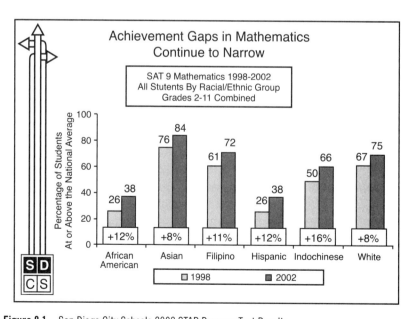

Figure 8.1   San Diego City Schools 2002 STAR Program Test Results.

were the results of students' performance on the state's high school exit exam: "About 50% of this year's 11th grade students have not passed one or both sections of the exam." Although applauding students' performance in elementary school grades, the forum also concluded, "Our survey of student achievement data often found troubling levels of performance in the district's high schools" (San Diego Achievement Forum, 2002: 3).[1]

Much to the chagrin of the San Diego Dialogue leadership, this civic-minded effort did not get wide press coverage. The *Union-Tribune* carried a report on the Opinion pages of its Sunday edition (October 27, 2002), but the forum's work did not receive coverage on the news pages. This empirically based attempt at mediation between sparring groups may not have gained traction in the wider community because the findings were not astonishing and therefore not newsworthy.

Measuring student achievement is complicated. Because the district leaders did not tie the general goal of improved test scores to any specific number, a small upward tick or a giant jump in test scores could each equally be said to constitute (or not constitute) "increased" student achievement. Furthermore, any single measure, be it a state-mandated standardized test, a locally generated assessment, or term grades, gives an incomplete picture of students' performance and development. This is why reputable education groups have called for multiple and diverse evaluation measures.[2]

Unfortunately for the reform's design team, as well as for civic-minded groups such as the San Diego Dialogue and members of the general public seeking useful information, no widely respected portfolio of data for San Diego's schools was available. This imprecision regarding how the district and the community would assess the efficacy of the reform contributed mightily to its contentiousness. This suggests to us that the debates were as much about staking out and defending political positions as they were about understanding student achievement.[3]

The Cultural Limitations of the Reform

The relations within social organizations, such as the central office of school districts, and the entities they deal with, such as the schools within their districts, parent groups, unions, and state and federal governments, are sometimes messy, sometimes contentious, often conflicted, even chaotic. The capacity of social actors in these organizations to process information is constrained by a variety of economic, cultural, and political circumstances. To adapt to the practicalities of messy organizational decision-making situations, these "practical actors" employ routines and standard operating procedures, and they do so within an organizational culture that is infused with deep-seated beliefs and implicit norms and values about *who* should be educated and *how* they should be educated.

Research also has shown that for a reform effort to be successful, teachers must buy into it and feel ownership over it. The process is complicated, because as Hargreaves (1994: 256) pointed out, "Teachers' beliefs and practices are grounded not only in experience and altruism, but also in structures and routines to which they have become attached, and in which considerable self-interest may be invested." Hargreaves's insights apply equally to all other educators within an educational system (Fullan, 1999: 64; Healey & DeStefano, 1997: 10–11; Stein & Gewirtzman, 2003: 2ff). That is, ownership of an innovation must be spread widely through the system. In the San Diego reform, more than a generic buy-in was necessary. The Balanced Literacy framework required an unusually high level of acceptance and commitment from all concerned to succeed.

Clashes over Norms, Beliefs, and Standard Operating Procedures

Instructional practices and standard operating procedures both reflect and construct teachers' ideas about education. Just as teachers' dispositions and perceptions are evident in their practice, so too are their practices continually shaped by their beliefs. A school district that is unable to change the beliefs, norms, and practices of its teachers and obtain their support is not likely to achieve systemic, enduring change. This reculturation is not a simple task, however. As Deal and Peterson (1999: 4) pointed out, "School cultures are complex webs of traditions and rituals that have been built up over time. … Cultural patterns are highly enduring, have a powerful impact on performance and shape the way people think, act, and feel." In San Diego, reculturation stalled. The SDCS district leaders failed to achieve significant buy-in from teachers and other educators because what they asked the educators to do flew in the face of their perceptions of good teaching and learning and required significant changes in their habitual procedures and practices.

From Private Practice to Public Practice

The district leaders' attempt to convert schools into "learning communities" was one of the most visible cultural changes attempted by the reform. A prevailing belief in public education, especially in high schools, is that teachers are relatively autonomous agents. Despite parental pressure, state and local laws, and district policy, all of which increasingly limit the type and range of acceptable classroom activities and tie money to classroom implementation of specific programs, teachers believe they are in charge of the teaching and learning that occurs within their classrooms.

As we described in Chapter 7, district leaders attempted to reculture (Hargreaves, 1994) teaching from private practice to communities of public practice (Elmore, 1996) by opening classroom doors to principals' and coaches' scrutiny, emphasizing collaborative work with peers to solve common problems and developing common thoughts, beliefs, and language about skills, practices, and accountability. Many teachers—and all of the San Diego Education Association (SDEA) leadership—resisted these changes initially because they challenged their belief that they had earned autonomy, or the right to teach as they saw fit, when they received their teaching credentials. Teachers in general, but high school teachers in particular, resented walk-throughs, coaches, and other calls for public practice as an attack on their professional integrity (American Institutes for Research [AIR], 2002, 2003; California Teachers Association [CTA], 2002).

Walk-throughs, especially, challenged teachers' beliefs that they had earned the right to practice their craft in private. The walk-through was intentionally structured to expose teachers' practice to principals and district administrators (ILs). District leaders believed that making classroom practices public encouraged the sharing of ideas, thereby leading to a coherent theory enacted consistently in practice across all schools in the district.

Disciplinary Specialists or Reading Specialists?

Another significant culture clash—this one over teachers' beliefs about their instructional role—was generated when district leaders, especially ILs, tried to persuade high school principals to persuade their faculties to teach reading strategies. Principals knew their teachers were reluctant to undertake instruction in areas other than their academic specialties. They insisted that high school teachers knew how and wanted to teach biology, algebra, and English (literature), but they neither knew how nor wanted to teach reading strategies.

Responsibility for Students' Learning: Teachers Teaching or Students Studying?

Deep-seated cultural beliefs associated with the teaching–learning process were challenged by the reform. Many high school teachers understood their jobs as involving the presentation of information; it was the students' responsibility to learn—to "get it." If a student didn't get it, then it was the student's fault. It was not the teacher's responsibility to change instruction to meet students' needs. This notion of "students' responsibility" overlies assumptions about students as learners that are quite different from the assumptions guiding district leaders. From these teachers' perspective, students are active agents who can choose to accept or reject information. They are not passive recipients who succeed or fail as a result of their teachers' expertise.

This perspective also incorporates assumptions about older students' knowledge base. Despite obvious evidence to the contrary, many high school teachers firmly believe that their students have already—or, more precisely, should have already—learned the basics. So, it is not a high school teacher's responsibility to fill in the gaps, if gaps exist. This returns us to the issue of school culture and differences by grade level. Assumptions about what students should already know—what a teacher simply has to presume they do already know to proceed with the curriculum—differ significantly by grade level. Asking high school teachers to undertake literacy training with their students not only requires skills the teachers do not have but also violates basic assumptions embedded in high school teachers' culture.

District leaders—from the superintendent to those at school sites—asserted that all children can learn and that it is the teachers' responsibility to see that they do. The presumption that teachers' high expectations and instruction can improve students' academic performance challenged yet another belief widely held among educators (and supported by certain interpretations of the sociological literature); namely, that social factors outside the school, such as students' impoverished conditions, their lack of mastery of the English language, and their frequent movement between schools, are reasons why students do not learn. Some teachers and the SDEA leadership complained that the district's focus on instruction as the means to close the achievement gap blamed teachers for students' failures (CTA, 2002).

Instructional versus Operational Leadership
A fourth set of clashes based on institutional culture erupted over one of the most basic tenets of the reform: that the new ILs and principals make operational responsibilities subservient to instructional ones. This demand challenged some ILs' and principals' strongly held beliefs, school norms, and standard operating procedures about the leadership role. Teaching the reading process is difficult for any educator; communicating the intricacies of the Balanced Literacy framework further complicated matters. The challenge was especially great for those ILs and principals who had not learned to teach reading in the manner advocated by the district and those who had never received any training in reading development (e.g., high school principals). "Leveling" books, conferring for the purpose

of understanding if students were in Just Right books, and conducting guided reading sessions were concepts no more familiar to high school principals than they were to high school teachers.

Uncertainty about Collaborative or Centralized Leadership
Important research supports the idea that reform models that incorporate distributed leadership and collaboration positively affect systemic or organizational change (Elmore, 1999; Heifetz, 1994; Heifetz & Linsky, 2002; Kotter, 1996; Portin, Beck, Knapp, & Murphy, 2000; Sergiovanni, 2000; Stein & Gewirtzman, 2003). In a claim consistent with this research, the district said that the community of learners the reform cultivated included shared, distributed decision-making responsibilities. One confirmation of this commitment to shared leadership came at a principals' conference (August 22, 2000) at which ILs and principals studied and discussed Elmore's (1999) argument for distributed leadership, which encourages a collaborative approach and an atmosphere of knowledge sharing. At other principals' conferences, ILs helped principals learn how to create an atmosphere of knowledge sharing at their school sites. They promoted the idea that a school leader not only delegates and harnesses the expert knowledge of the staff but also engages teachers in developing and learning new ways of thinking. ILs coached principals in how to pair less skilled teachers with more capable teachers to build on individual strengths and address individual weaknesses. They encouraged principals to visit other school sites to learn from more experienced colleagues and to work closely with mentor principals who could offer guidance that would improve their work (see Chapter 7).

Unfortunately, district leaders' messages were often inconsistent. Messages supporting distributed leadership theory were contradicted by messages supporting centralized decision making. Many of the latter messages were derived from Tichy (1997). For example, during a breakout session at a principals' conference (August 22, 2001), ILs and principals focused on General Electric corporate leader Jack Welsh, who, as Tichy recounted it, turned the company around by inculcating in his employees the values he espoused and by requiring that leaders be accountable to him. In this business-inspired discourse, leaders have "clear ideas, energy, edge, and tell stories that touch people's emotions" (Tichy, 1997: 20). Some SDCS principals, like some education researchers (Sergiovanni, 2000), objected to this application of a business model to the education arena. They argued that their responsibilities as school leaders supporting children's learning were very different from the responsibilities of business leaders selling products.

Another Tichy-inspired dictate promoted by district leaders—that school leaders need to have an "edge"—created more confusion and even anger, as many principals assumed that now they were expected to become tough and abrasive leaders. Explicit efforts by Superintendent Bersin (2002a, 2002c) and some ILs to dispel this misunderstanding by explaining *edge* as a willingness to make difficult decisions when (and only when) the situation demanded did not fully convince principals (see Chapter 7). Many continued to believe that they were required to be tough.

Guest speakers who addressed principals' conferences were another source of mixed messages about leadership. Some speakers seemed to support *both* shared decision making and the use of mandates, a combination that confused principals who were trying to determine how to lead at their school sites. For example, when Michael Fullan (2001b) addressed principals, he asserted,

> Individualism and collectivism must have equal power. Neither centralization nor decentralization works. There has to be a connection with the wider environment. That's critical for success. Every person is a change agent. You can't mandate what matters, that's McLaughlin's finding. We've actually modified that a little bit. You have to have some things mandated.

This call for "some" mandates was hard to reconcile with Fullan's (2001b) emphasis, later in the talk, on shared leadership and the skills and resources of individual leaders:

> Shared leadership is preferred. The main goal of the principal is to build school capacity, which requires building knowledge, skills and the disposition of individuals. Building a professional community. Building program coherence. Building technical resources. … Some schools do well because they had initial capacity and they have strong school leadership. The principal is the key.

Far from seeing themselves as independent "change agents," valued as "the key" to the reform, many principals believed they were expected to implement district directives precisely and without question at their school sites. As a result, they felt marginalized and certainly not part of any collaborative effort. They complained that the district, by mandating a Balanced Literacy curriculum, establishing two- and three-hour literacy blocks, and cutting teachers' aides, undercut its own messages, frequently repeated at principals' conferences, about "sharing knowledge," "team building," and "creating a professional system" (see Chapter 7).

These examples, which are representative of a myriad other complaints we and other observers (e.g., AIR, 2002, 2003) collected from principals and teachers, speak to the importance of the social–political dimension of leadership. Even though district leaders claimed that personal relationships were vital to the work, principals felt the district did not do enough to cultivate them. The moral of this story is that although adding material resources and building human capacity—which we have included within the technical dimension of change—may be necessary for initiating a reform, unless beliefs are widely shared and trusting relations are firmly established, a reform will not penetrate deeply into the culture and structure of the system.

The Political Dimension of the Reform

The Influence of State and Federal Policy on the San Diego Reform

The San Diego reform did not unfold in a political vacuum. Federal government and California state policies constrained district actions. The federal NCLB Act of 2000 resulted in significant new funding, but it also presented challenges and contradictions. The NCLB calls for tougher accountability for consistently low-performing schools and expands the federal government's role in education by requiring states to test students annually. In addition, the NCLB is fundamentally different from the state's accountability system. California's Public School Accountability Act (passed in 1999) is a growth model that measures student achievement progress or decline *over time*. The NCLB, in contrast, is an accountability program based on a *snapshot* picture of test scores measured against a national target. This means that previously low-performing schools are not given credit for making progress.

California State Proposition 209 eliminated the use of non-English-speaking students' native language as a medium of instruction (often called "bilingual education"). Although the legality of the proposition was immediately challenged in court, its initial passage influenced the organization of the Balanced Literacy framework, especially in classrooms with significant numbers of English-language learners. Teachers had to take special care in how they distributed instructional time in Spanish and English, for instance. The SDCS *Biliteracy for Spanish Speakers Model–Revised* details the number of hours recommended for Spanish literacy at each grade level and describes English literacy and other subject areas. The revised plan requires a strict distribution of language instruction time (see Figure 8.2).

The policy supported an attempt to maintain and build on Spanish literacy in the early grades. After third grade, the amount of instruction in

BILITERACY PROGRAM FOR SPANISH-SPEAKING STUDENTS

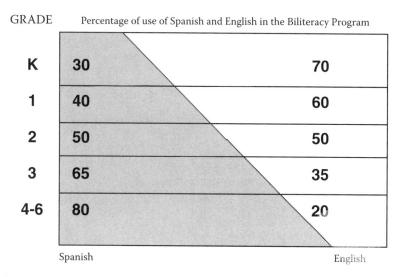

GRADE — Percentage of use of Spanish and English in the Biliteracy Program

GRADE	Spanish	English
K	30	70
1	40	60
2	50	50
3	65	35
4-6	80	20

Figure 8.2 Percentage of use of Spanish and English in the SDCS Biliteracy Program.

Spanish decreases progressively. By grades four through six, only one to one and a half hours of instruction in Spanish is recommended, and none is recommended in middle or high school.

The use of the SAT9 as an assessment instrument in the state's standards and accountability scheme also constrained the district between 1998 and 2002. Another limiting factor was the state board of education's pro-phonics position. Although the Balanced Literacy model does not ignore phonics (it has a word-study component), the systematic study of phonics does not drive the program in the way that many phonics advocates believe is necessary. San Diego leaders had to learn how to modify and describe their literacy efforts in a way that allowed them access to state resources oriented toward phonics without betraying the underlying philosophy of the Balanced Literacy model.

State policy regarding school finances was another very important source of limitations on district actions. The State of California faced a $38 billion shortfall for the 2003–2004 fiscal year.[4] This predicted shortfall required that the district make decisions about reform priorities starting in 2001–2002. In addition, the general downturn in the economy that started when George Bush became president had residual effects in California, notably by depressing the amount of revenue the state collected in the form of business and personal income tax. Finally, the state ratcheted up spending during the 1990s, when the California budget climate was flush, which made all the more painful the curtailing of investments in medical care, education, and environmental protection that began in 2002–2003 (and are continuing through 2005–2006). The district's response—in the form of drastic cost-cutting measures—is a topic we explore in Chapter 9.

Business Community and School Board Politics

San Diego's business community was visible and reliable in its support of the Bersin-initiated reforms. Business leaders helped select Bersin as superintendent, provided vocal and financial support to elect school board members who would support Bersin's reforms, and bankrolled Alvarado's peripatetic leadership (e.g., underwriting the costs of airfare and a condominium) during the first year of the reform. The business community also staved off a potential schism over school vouchers. Some of the leaders of a voucher initiative placed on the 2000 ballot were members of the San Diego Business Roundtable for Education. Although they implored the Roundtable as a group to support the initiative, members voted *not* to do so, on the grounds that such support would undercut their stated commitment to the Bersin–Alvarado reform effort (Hovenic, 2001).

Although business support of the SDCS reform was strong, especially in its formative stages,[5] it produced difficulties. The strategic decision by Bersin and Alvarado to move the reform quickly to maintain the support of the business community antagonized many teachers and certainly alienated the SDEA, which complained bitterly that the reform was top-down and imported and that it ignored the voices and expertise of local educators.

The Chamber of Commerce (the Roundtable's parent organization at the time) was found guilty of violating tax and campaign-finance laws for using its charitable fund-raising arm to support San Diego school board candidates in 1996. Contributions totaling $11,000 were illegally funneled to a political action committee of the Chamber of Commerce to support Ron Ottinger, Ed Lopez, and Frances O'Neill Zimmerman. Ottinger and Lopez became unflagging supporters of Bersin's initiatives (Berliner & Magee, 1998). Four years later, the SDEA severely criticized the business community for unduly influencing the fall 2000 reelection bid of O'Neill Zimmerman—a strident critic of the reform. A group of wealthy businessmen bankrolled an opponent to the tune of $500,000, an unusually large sum for a school board election. To many critics in the media, this was unprecedented interference, and when O'Neill Zimmerman won anyway, the reform's business supporters had egg on their faces and Bersin had a newly aggrieved as well as vocal critic on the board (Magee, 2000d; Perry, 2000; Whitaker, 2000).

If locals found much to complain about in the San Diego reform, outsiders did not. Superintendent Bersin acted as advisor on education issues for both California governor Gray Davis and President George W. Bush and garnered compliments across the state and the nation for his work in public education. The American Federation of Teachers awarded Alvarado their Quality Standards in Teaching Award in 1999 ("Teachers union honors Alvarado, Riley," 1999). Kati Haycock, a nationally prominent educational reform expert who promotes the standards and accountability movement, praised the SDCS for its elementary school students' gains on standardized tests from 1998–2002: "San Diego's scores clearly reveal a pattern we hope to see in any community as diverse as this one: an 'everybody wins' scenario in which scores rise for all groups while gaps between groups get narrower" (Haycock & Jerald, 2002).[6] Numerous articles casting a generally positive light on the reform appeared in *The Wall Street Journal* ("San Diego Charger," 2002), *The New York Times* (Goodnough, 2002; Hartocollis, 2002; Lewin, 2000; Sengupta, 1998; Whitaker, 2000), and *The Washington Post* (Mathews, 2001).

Further enhancing the prestige of the reform was the attention of private foundations and funding agencies. Applied Microcircuits, Atlantic Philanthropies, the Broad Foundation, the Carnegie Corporation, QUALCOMM, and the Wiatt Family Foundation made sizable gifts and grants to the district. The district also benefited greatly from $22.5 million in grant funding provided by the Bill and Melinda Gates Foundation and the William and Flora Hewlett Foundation. This and other less tangible forms of support for the reform seem to stem from the determination of public education supporters to take a stand against the rising tide of privatization. For some government and progressive funding agencies, the reform in San Diego and similar reforms (i.e., ones that tout high standards, accountability, and the power of instruction to close the achievement gap) in other large urban districts, such as Boston, Chicago, Seattle, and Sacramento, represent the last stand before the invasion of the vouchers.

Ironically, local hostility toward the reform ran so deep that this national endorsement was used *against* the SDCS administration. The Gates and Hewlett foundations and Atlantic Philanthropies grants caused controversy because the awards were conditional on the continued service of Bersin and Alvarado as district leaders (Magee, 2001b). Prominent critics, including school board member O'Neill Zimmerman and John Warren, the editor of the newspaper *Voice and Viewpoint*, the voice of San Diego's African American community (Warren, 2001), saw this condition as further evidence of the heavy-handedness of Bersin and Alvarado and ongoing efforts by the business community to wrest control of the schools from parents and voters. "The school board is supposed to have control over monies that come under its oversight," O'Neill Zimmerman pointed out. "You either want to have your elected representatives be responsible for your school district or you don't. This is about privatizing education through these grants" (quoted in Magee, 2001b).

The school board was consistently divided three to two in favor of the Bersin–Alvarado reforms. This split produced many long and contentious board meetings and public disagreements that detracted from the reform's goal of improving instruction. For example, the board's three to two approval of the *Blueprint* in 2000 came only after a raucous six-hour meeting marked by teacher and community group protests (Magee, 2000d). In 2002, another three to two vote gave Bersin a second four-year term as superintendent (Magee, 2002c). In an episode emblematic of the discourse consistently marking board meetings, the majority bloc of Board President Ottinger and trustees Sue Braun and Ed Lopez praised Bersin for delivering bold initiatives to classrooms and strengthening teaching quality, whereas the board minority of deBeck and O'Neill Zimmerman countered that Bersin alienated the public, sacrificed comprehensive education for a narrow literacy focus, and politicized the school system (Magee, 2002a). Other highlights (or lowlights) include the (then) school board president Braun fantasizing in an e-mail message about shooting the two members of the board minority[7] and the board president's formal rebuke of O'Neill Zimmerman because she signed campaign literature during board meetings (Ottinger, 2002).

Teachers' Hostility and Union Disputes with the District

In promoting the progressive ideal of closing the achievement gap, the district leadership called attention to the poor performance of students in certain schools, almost all of which were "South of 8" (the freeway that serves as the symbolic and material border between more affluent and less affluent neighborhoods in San Diego). They also appropriated Haycock and Navarro's (1997) finding (replicated locally; Mehan & Grimes, 1999) that low-performing schools tend to be in low-income neighborhoods and tend to have teachers who have the least teaching experience and the least professional qualifications (such as degrees and credentials). Airing these "social facts" was intended to rally the community, especially parents of color. By admitting that the public school system had not served the children of these parents well, the district hoped to stimulate parental support for a more rigorous curriculum and higher quality instruction.

This rhetorical move was accompanied by another. Guided by Resnick's (1995: 56) assertion that "effort actually *creates* ability," the leadership of the SDCS attempted to actualize the idea "that people can become smart by working hard at the right kinds of learning tasks." Bersin and Alvarado were well aware of the sociological literature (e.g., Coleman et al., 1966; Jencks et al., 1972, 1978; Jencks & Phillips, 1998) that says the socioeconomic conditions students bring with them to school influence their academic outcomes more than what happens inside schools. They were impatient with such findings, however, dismissing poor socioeconomic conditions, language status, and ethnicity as unacceptable excuses not to educate all students to the highest level possible (Bersin, 2000b; Bersin & Alvarado, 1998). They implored teachers to work with each and every child, and, they argued, each and every child's learning would improve.

The idea that effort can create ability also did important rhetorical work. Bersin and Alvarado used it to block critics' statements about the constraints imposed by students' socioeconomic conditions. The district leadership often chided critics when they invoked students' impoverished conditions, their lack of mastery of the English language, and their frequent movement between schools as reasons why students do not learn (e.g., Bersin, 2000b, 2005). These conditions were dismissed as unacceptable excuses for not engaging students in rigorous instruction. However, these rhetorical moves, intended to be a call to arms, spawned an unfortunate side effect, especially among some members of the teaching corps. Teachers (and some parents and students) felt that they were being unfairly blamed for the achievement gap. For example, Emma Dannin (2000: B9), a San Diego High School student, wrote an editorial protecting her apparently low-performing school and complimenting her teachers for being good and motivating. Adding to this negative perception was another: the sense that local teachers' knowledge didn't count, that only the expertise of people from New York and New Zealand (the origin of the Balanced Literacy framework and materials) mattered. This impression had an empirical base. AIR (2002: V-10), in their district-funded survey of SDCS teachers, principals, and peer coaches, reported that 88% of the 1,294 teachers responding, 48% of the 130 peer coaches and staff developers responding, and 25% of the 109 principals responding said they were not involved in decisions about the implementation of the *Blueprint*. AIR (2002: V-14) also reported that only 38.5% of 1,294 teachers responding felt respected by district staff.

These findings are troubling in light of the literature on the importance of teacher buy-in and "relations of trust" (Bryk & Schneider, 2003) for successful school reforms. Datnow (2000), for instance, studied the implementation of twelve separate reform designs in twenty-two school sites and concluded that new programs are not successful without meaningful involvement of teachers in their adoption and implementation. The process of adoption, Datnow said, echoing Fullan, is as important as the reform. There is a world of difference, she said, between compliance with the rules of a particular solution and genuine support for its principles.

The SDEA coalesced these rebuffs and expressions of disrespect and rejection into planks in a political platform opposing the reform. Although the teachers' union was initially supportive of Bersin's hiring Alvarado because Alvarado had established a record of school improvement, once the two leaders began the reform without explicitly including the union in decision making, the union became a voice of opposition. The SDEA (Knapp, n.d.) often cited a membership poll in which the vast majority of respondents reported feeling that they did not have an influence over district decisions and that they did not have confidence either in the *Blueprint* or in the superintendent (CTA, 2002: 4). During the run-up to the November 2002 election, the State of California Educational Association pledged $24,000 (Magee, 2000d) to support the reelection of deBeck—and the election of Jeff Lee—both of whom opposed much of the Bersin–Alvarado reform.

The SDEA's opposition to the SDCS reform was detailed in an extensive article in the *California Educator,* the magazine of the California Educators Association. "Administrative meddling"; "terror in management"; "top-down dictatorship"; "one-size curriculum and professional development"; "dumbed down" science curriculum; elimination of art, social sciences, and music; and a general disregard for teacher expertise were primary among the litany of complaints and criticisms chronicled in the article (CTA, 2002).

Community Concerns, Strategies, and Outcomes in Affluent Neighborhoods

In discussions of the political dimensions of educational reform, the "community" is often considered—but usually only as a monolithic entity. San Diego is no different from other large cities in that it has a variety of communities—many of which have affected the San Diego reform, albeit in different ways. In the following two sections, we present the concerns of community members in more affluent and less affluent neighborhoods, the strategies they employed to modify reform initiatives, and the outcomes they achieved.

Parents and community leaders in virtually all neighborhoods applauded the district's successful campaign in 1998 to pass a $1.51 billion bond referendum for school construction, repairs, and renovation (Proposition MM) and its "San Diego Reads" book drive to put more books in schools and classrooms. Parents in San Diego's affluent neighborhoods, however, were much less supportive of the pedagogical dimensions of the reform—particularly as they affected their neighborhood high schools. One particularly virulent line of criticism concerned curriculum content and instruction. Parents in well-to-do neighborhoods complained that the two- and three-hour literacy blocks watered down instruction, forced more valued elective courses off students' course rosters, and restricted the creativity of teachers. Parents in wealthy neighborhoods also lambasted the district's new high school physics program. They said the course textbooks lacked the rigor needed for a college-prep curriculum, and they objected to the program being required for all ninth graders.

Schools in well-to-do neighborhoods successfully sidestepped some and directly challenged other district reforms. For instance, in La Jolla, a powerful combination of parents, teachers, and community members applied political pressure through a variety of channels, including face-to-face encounters with district leaders, to exempt La Jolla High School from the *Blueprint* requirements. As a result, the high school was designated a "pilot school," which enabled site leaders to organize curriculum and instruction according to local needs.

The cooperation wealthy parents gave their children's teachers during these disputes is noteworthy. This solidarity was partly due to the teachers' own disgruntlement, but it also reflects the different kinds of relationships wealthy and poor parents have with educational institutions. Parents in well-to-do neighborhoods tend to see their children's schools and teachers as an extension of their families and their personal interests. They take steps to establish close home–school relationships. Parents in less well-to-do neighborhoods tend to view most aspects of their children's education as the responsibility of schools and teachers (Lareau, 1989, 2003). They usually do not forge strong connections with school personnel, and most lack the requisite cultural capital to influence district leaders.

Community Concerns, Strategies, and Outcomes in Less Affluent Neighborhoods

Parents and community activists in San Diego's less affluent and predominantly ethnic neighborhoods voiced different concerns, adopted different strategies of engagement, and achieved different results than did their more affluent contemporaries. First some background. The district's schools are "majority minority." In 1977, when the *Carlin* desegregation case (the San Diego desegregation case that required the SDCS to achieve a racial balance in its elementary, middle, and secondary schools) was settled, the district's overall enrollment was about 70% white and 30%

nonwhite. When the Bersin–Alvarado reforms were introduced, nonwhites accounted for 72.6% of the district's students: Latinos, 37.5%; African Americans, 16.5%; Filipino, 8%; Indochinese, 6.3%; Asian, 2.7%; Pacific Islander, 1.0; and Alaskan/Indian, 0.6% (SDCS, 2001a).

Spokespeople for various components of these minority communities asserted that politics had not followed demographics. San Diego County superintendent of education Rudy Castruita maintained, "We don't have equal access, and that's what the minority population is frustrated about" (quoted in Farnsworth & Kendricks, 2001: 83). This same article references a study conducted by Viewpoint America that reported 77% of African Americans and 53% of Latino residents in San Diego see "a lot of or some" discrimination against them with respect to equal access to a good education. Conversely, 78% of Asians and 81% of Caucasians said they feel little or no discrimination in this area.

For nonnative speakers, the state and district policies mandating standardized test taking in English were an especially frustrating example of unequal access. Parents and teachers of students who are English-language learners cited the demoralizing and demeaning effects of testing on students who cannot even read the questions but must take the tests nevertheless. Similarly unpopular in many San Diego communities was Proposition 209's "English Only" mandate. Farnsworth and Kendricks (2001) cited a poll indicating that 62% of San Diego parents believed bilingual education improves non-English-speaking students' school performance.

The Latino Coalition, a particularly vocal group within the Latino community, initially supported the *Blueprint* because of its promise to close the achievement gap but withdrew its support after eighteen months. Coalition leaders said the SDCS reforms were not meeting the needs of the English-language learners, the management and school leadership profiles did not reflect the diversity of the students in the school district, and the district was diminishing due process and respect for parents by excluding them from decision making about curriculum, instruction, and governance issues (Latino Coalition, 2001).

In addition, with support from the school board minority, a combination of community groups, notably the District Advisory Council on Compensatory Education (DELAC), complained vociferously about the process of decision making in the district from 1998–2001. These critics accused the district of making administrative decisions "top down"—with no effort to consult parent or community groups. Examples cited include the removal of district administrators in 1999, removal of school principals each year of the reform,[8] and removal of Title I aides from classrooms in 2000 (Gembrowski, 2000). "It should be frightening to you and other citizens," one especially irate parent warned in a posting on the Web site of a local TV station, "that here in the 21st century, in what we believe to be the most democratic country on earth, we have a blatant dictatorship in one of our public institutions" (Escmilla, 2001).

Unlike the affluent parents in La Jolla, parent and community groups in less affluent neighborhoods did not succeed in squeezing concessions from the district through negotiation. When talks regarding instruction and management decisions stalled, they resorted to walkouts, lawsuits, and appeals to the U.S. and California secretaries of education—most notably to reinstate fired principals and Title I aides (Magee, 2000a). For example, incensed that the principal of Johnson Magnet School for Space Exploration had jettisoned a direct instruction reading program in favor of the Balanced Literacy framework, made decisions about students' participation in the gifted and talented education program without consulting parents, employed too many substitute teachers, and had too few textbooks, parents staged a two-day walkout. More than 160 of the school's approximately 450 students cut classes. Parents resorted to this tactic, they said, because the district administration had not responded to requests made through traditional channels (Magee & Daniels, 2002).

Resorting to legal means, parents and staff of Sherman Elementary and DELAC filed Uniform Complaint #534 with the board of education, alleging that on numerous occasions, the district had made administrative decisions on curriculum, instruction, and personnel without parent or community consultation, violating provisions of the *Blueprint for Student Success*. In a letter to the district released on June 13, 2000, Assistant Education Secretary Michael Cohen praised the city schools for implementing the reform strategy, which is "in keeping with the kind of school reform that we wish to see school systems across the country put in place." Rebuffed by the federal government, parent and community groups then approached the state. After a fourteen-month investigation, the California Department of Education concluded the district had done nothing illegal when it used federal funds to pay for the reforms, but they criticized the district for failing to consult with parents, as federal Title I law requires (Magee, 2001). Theresa Creber, parent and chair of DELAC, was quoted as being pleased about the result: "Parents want to help their children achieve and I feel the district also wants [that]. They just left parents out of the loop, and it's important to have [a] partnership of parents and teachers with the district" ("Blueprint for Student Success under Fire," 2001). Bersin (2002d) announced that U.S. Secretary of Education Ron Paige also had approved the district's use of Title I money for teachers instead of aides. Indeed,

Bersin reported Secretary Paige as predicting that San Diego's approach would become a model for other districts.

Also resorting to legal measures, the fifteen principals and vice principals who were removed from their assignments in June 1999 filed suit that year, asking to be reinstated and to receive compensation for the abrupt and undignified manner in which they were fired. (The principals were put on administrative leave the very day that the school board voted to reassign them; they were escorted to their offices by police officers and ordered to remove their belongings immediately.) In a two to one ruling, a panel of the Ninth U.S. Circuit Court of Appeals said that the SDCS officials had done nothing illegal in reassigning the principals and vice principals, although they did reprimand the district's use of police escorts as "an unnecessary affront" (Moran, 2003b). But the superior court reversed that decision in 2004, ruling that the fired principals should get their jobs back, as well as lost pay and benefits (Magee, 2004b).

In sum, teachers, parents, and community members with different types of social and cultural capital deployed different strategies to exact concessions from district leaders, and they enjoyed differential success. Groups from more well-to-do neighborhoods applied political pressure primarily through face-to-face encounters—and they obtained desired results, including exemption from the district's centralized reforms. Groups from less well-to-do neighborhoods, frustrated by the lack of response to their overtures to administrators, resorted to legal and extralegal tactics. They did not often obtain the results they desired.

In addition to highlighting the importance of social and political capital, these cases also underscore the role of social position. Many teachers in low-income schools were new to the profession and to the district and tended to be more supportive of the reform. In addition, they stood to personally gain—the reform was providing them with extensive professional development at the start of their careers, infusing their classrooms with material resources, and so forth. Teachers in affluent schools, by contrast, often stood to lose as a result of the reform. The reform restricted their classroom autonomy, exerted pressure on them to comply with pedagogy they did not necessarily agree with, and so forth.

The reaction of the district to parents and teachers in different social locations is also telling. The deferential treatment of parents and teachers in well-to-do neighborhoods versus the stonewalling or nonresponse to parents, teachers, and principals from low-income neighborhoods, suggests that the district calculated each constituency's relative power. They responded promptly to affluent groups, courting and mollifying well-to-do parents while leaving low-income parents and community groups to pursue their grievances slowly and unsatisfactorily through legal channels.

Summary and Conclusions

This analysis of the district's attempt to introduce wide-ranging and innovative changes reinforces what could be called "Sarason's Law": introducing innovations into complex systems such as school districts is treacherous because the existing system pushes back in sometimes predictable albeit always mysterious ways. What is mysterious is the fact that over and over those who seek change tend to ignore or overlook what is already known about the kind of change they have in mind.

Throughout this book, following Oakes, we have claimed that engaging the technical, cultural, and political dimensions of change facilitates the enactment of educational reforms. Engaging the technical dimension involves allocating a district's material resources, including time, to developing strong leaders, improved instruction, and better curriculum. Engaging the cultural dimension involves developing a common language and beliefs and a coherent vision, as well as establishing trusting relationships between individuals in a professional community. Engaging the political dimension means not only galvanizing important political constituencies outside the system but also building productive professional relationships within the system.

Technical factors, factors rooted in organizational culture, and factors embedded in community politics contributed to the gap we observed between theory and practice. The major technical factors hampering the reform were an uneven record of student achievement, teachers' lack of capacity to teach Balanced Literacy, administrators' lack of capacity and time to lead teachers in this sophisticated learning system, and the Balanced Literacy framework's unproven record at the secondary level.

One culturally based reason for the gap between theory and practice concerned the meanings educators in various contexts within the educational system attributed to changing norms, beliefs, and standard operating procedures. The district leaders' desire to convert the area superintendents' and principals' roles from operational to instructional, to make all their teachers capable of teaching literacy, and to transform teachers' practice from private to public collided with many educators' long-standing and deeply held beliefs about leadership and teaching roles. Another culturally based reason for the gap between theory and practice resided in the manner in which instruction was organized across intersection encounters. Although the district professed adherence to a collaborative theory of action in which all members of learning communities would learn from one another, the actual interactions across intersection encounters (constrained by lack of capacity and no critical pedagogy) often belied this claim.

Political reasons for the gap between the district's theory of action and its actualization in practice emerged from the power dynamics within the local San Diego context. Although the district leaders extended impressive energy in infusing human and material resources into their district's transformation, they invested more heavily in building political alliances with powerful community groups than they did in building personal and trusting relationships with educators up and down the line. The latter would have been more consonant with the preexisting culture of schooling and the "reform as learning" organizing principle of the reform. As a result, the local teachers' union, a vocal school board minority, and advocacy groups based in well-to-do and less-well-to-do communities voiced loud and consistent opposition to the district's content-driven, comprehensive, and centralized reforms.

In the final analysis, the SDCS reform stalled because district leaders envisioned school change as the implementation of ideas they generated from the top of the system. This approach relegated the job of carrying out the plans to people in learning communities; that is, completing the predetermined goals and objectives of the design team. In this "grammar of implementation," the causal arrow of change travels in one direction only—from active, thoughtful designers to passive, pragmatic implementers. Galvanized by the moral, political, and practical reasons described in Chapter 4, district leaders underestimated the extent to which the actions taken by educators throughout the system influence the reform. Far from being passive implementers, educators are active initiators in local contexts. Classrooms are local contexts, of course, but so are the intersection encounters we have investigated: district leaders with ILs, ILs with principals, principals with teachers, and the all-important interaction between teachers and their students. Whatever actions educators in these contexts take—including passively complying, faithfully enacting, actively enhancing, aggressively subverting—shape the reform.

That *shaping* is a vital part of what is meant by the co-construction of reform (Datnow, Hubbard, & Mehan, 2002). The co-construction of reform also means all participants "work together within the richness and against the limitations of multiple knowledge domains to create new knowledge" (Stein & Gewirtzman, 2003: 7). And, we add, "all participants work together against the limitations of institutional cultural practices and political constraints." To engage in the co-construction of reform, all participants must develop trust in each other's expertise (Bryk & Schneider, 2003) and must be committed to reaching shared institutional goals. Both are continuous and long-term processes. Once reform leaders recognize that the arrow of change can fly in many directions and that reform is a messy, dialogic, convoluted, and politically influenced process, not a linear, direct, and rational process, then they may actively engage participants from all local contexts in the co-construction of reform, instead of trying to impose on people what they, as leaders, are certain are good ideas.

CHAPTER 9

Changes in the Reform:
Influences of Technical Constraints
and Cultural and Political Conflict

As we related in Chapter 8, technical constraints and conflict within the San Diego City Schools (SDCS) and between the district leaders and valued constituencies pressured district leaders. The reform's fast pace, centralized control, and commitment to raising student achievement won the district leadership early support of the powerful local business community, the national press, and granting agencies. It did not secure teacher buy-in or win significant union, community, or school board support. The resulting political and cultural conflicts pulled the SDCS reform in new directions. Other factors were important, as well. These include technical constraints (e.g., insufficient capacity to transform operational managers into instructional leaders, the Balanced Literacy framework's unproven track record in middle and high schools, and an undistinguished record of student achievement) and a devastating state budget crisis.

Calls for collaboration by business and opinion leaders accelerated change. Ginger Hovenic, executive director of the Business Roundtable for Education, an early supporter of the Alan Bersin–Anthony Alvarado reforms, changed her position as the political discourse grew more corrosive.

211

In 1999, while endorsing school board members who supported Bersin's vision of reform, she said, "[Bersin] needs support, he needs to have the backing of the [school] board. He needs to have the board in support of his activities and the agenda he has going" (quoted in Magee, 1999: B1). But in 2001, she called for more open lines of communication between the district office, teachers, parents, and the school board. In an editorial in the *San Diego Daily Transcript,* a business-oriented newspaper, she (Hovenic, 2002) recapped the first three years of the Bersin–Alvarado administration in positive terms and praised the district's efforts to ensure passage of Proposition MM. She then turned her attention to the reform process:

> Let me be very clear: My concern isn't with the *Blueprint* itself, rather with the hasty process with which it became enacted. There needs to be far wider district and community-level collaboration on something as massive and high stakes as [this] program. ... While teachers have said they support the teaching strategies in general, they've barely had time to learn how it works, much less to see how it affects their students in the big picture. They need time to look at the blueprint comprehensively and objectively—to ask questions and even offer refinements or suggestions about how best to implement the many strategies. With no time for reflection or the opportunity to provide meaningful input into the program, the district risks losing the level of understanding and support on the part of teachers needed to make the *Blueprint* strategies truly effective in San Diego's classrooms. Support from teachers and the business community is [just] as vital.

Like business leaders, editorial writers for *The San Diego Union-Tribune* strongly supported the reform. In September 2001, the editors urged the school board to renew Bersin's contract with the headline, "Schools Chief Merits Four More Years." But as relations between the district office, teachers, and the union continued to deteriorate, the *Union-Tribune* adopted a decidedly critical stance—even calling on Bersin to fire Alvarado:

> It's time Bersin shows he can persuade and lead or find a strong-willed deputy gifted in communications skills to help him. He should replace Tony Alvarado, a now expendable target of angry teachers. Otherwise San Diego's televised school board sessions (beginning Jan. 8, 3–8 p.m., ITV) could become the first San Diego soap opera to go network. (Morgan, 2001)

External evaluators also were beginning to change their opinion. The first edition of a multiyear independent study of reforms in the schools

(American Institutes for Research, 2002) praised the district for its bold approach to literacy instruction and its commitment to raising student achievement, but the report also assailed the district for fostering a "climate of fear and suspicion." In her verbal presentation to the school board on February 12, 2002, lead researcher Beverly Farr urged the board to direct the superintendent to collaborate more with teachers and parents or risk missing the goal of helping students learn—especially those struggling the most. Farr's recommendations were endorsed by *Union-Tribune* editorial writers, who implored Bersin and Alvarado to "take the initiative in bridging the communication gap" ("End the Sniping," 2002).

Calls for reorienting the theory of action guiding the reform mounted as new installments of test score data failed to show clear gains in student achievement. Had the business community and the parents of historically underserved students been able to see the kinds of improvement Bersin and Alvarado promised and repromised, both constituencies' support would likely have grown, not diminished. Perhaps similar support would have been forthcoming from skeptical teachers and harassed principals, as well. Had the reform been a more robust success in terms of students' achievement, then its moral aspects, fast pace, and heavy-handed top-down control might have seemed legitimate, or at least worth the pain. The budget crisis would have been difficult regardless of improved gains in student achievement, but it would not have been as crippling had the reform delivered on its purely technical and academic goals.

The district leadership was not wholly unprepared for resistance, including political conflict. They anticipated that engaging in rapid reculturation—"jolting the system" is the way Bersin and Alvarado described their strategy—would arouse passions and produce negative reactions. They believed, however, that such conflict was necessary to move the system forward. "You have to break a few eggs to make an omelet," Bersin would frequently say, expressing his conviction that fast change involving some conflict was preferable to the slow process entailed in building consensus. Alvarado (2001: 37; quoted in Gribble, 2001) tended to legitimate the need for speed on moral grounds:

> When people say to me, "Tony you are moving too fast; [these changes are] just too demanding," it is always a question about the impact upon the adults. What drives the pace and the sense of urgency, frankly, is keeping in mind the results on kids. In public education it takes so much time to get change. People say, "Well, change takes time." [What does that mean for the kids who are in today's classrooms?] Were they born too soon? Do we just say, "I'm sorry, you just didn't get into a good enough system?"

By the start of 2003, a combination of technical constraints and political and cultural conflicts (see Chapter 8) forced district leaders to significantly modify the reform agenda. The new approach was more incremental in scope and differentiated by site (reform elements would be implemented differently in different schools and not implemented in every school), decentralized in direction (school sites would be more responsible for generating reform ideas that would improve their schools), and slower in pace (not all schools would make changes at the same time). These adjustments lessened the reform's contentiousness by addressing contextual differences among schools and simultaneously increasing collaboration among participants.

The shift to a more incremental, differentiated, and collaborative reform was especially evident at the high school level. Beginning in 2003, comprehensive high schools, pilot schools, charter schools, and alternative high schools were no longer required to be on the same timetable or to enact the same strategies for reform. These modifications, which emphasized local solutions to general educational problems guided by a set of fundamental, jointly agreed-on assumptions about teaching and learning in high school, added a decentralized dimension to the new incremental theory of action. The high school reform plan is decentralized in that each high school, or affinity cluster of schools, is recognized as having its own needs. For so-called challenge schools, the need is to close the achievement gap between white and underrepresented minority students; for "community engagement schools," the need is to return white, middle-class students to classrooms in their neighborhoods; for the big comprehensive schools, the need is to personalize students' everyday school experiences. All high school leaders were charged with devising plans to meet these school-specific needs while at the same time remaining true to the districtwide commitment to instructional quality.

The remainder of this chapter focuses on the changes made at the high school level beginning in 2003. We examine the effects of a dramatic change in district leadership, a significant modification of the theory of action guiding the reform, and the introduction of mechanisms intended to make the district more responsive to teacher, parent, and community concerns.

Changes in District Leadership

The pressures on Superintendent Bersin to modify the SDCS reform were many. Test scores remained relatively flat or even declined in some cases (see Chapter 8 and Table 9.1), educators were increasingly vocal in their rejection of a one-size-fits-all approach, and community members had grown tired of dysfunctional school board and union–district relations. Emboldened by new, structurally based reform ideas from the Gates Foundation and the Carnegie Corporation, Bersin removed Alvarado from the leadership of the reform and changed its direction.

The Removal of Anthony Alvarado

The most dramatic single change in the SDCS reform was the removal of Alvarado as chancellor of instruction. Although his termination was not complete until July 2003, the superintendent reduced Alvarado's responsibilities early in 2002 and asked the school board to renegotiate his contract in December 2002. Bersin explained the change to all district employees as follows (Bersin, 2002e):

> Change can be difficult. We also know good often accompanies change, and I believe as we move forward with our work on improving student achievement, it is time for change in the leadership of the Institute for Learning.
>
> The design genius embodied in the *Blueprint* is recognized throughout the country, thanks to Chancellor of Instruction Tony Alvarado. His work has rightfully earned the praise of all, even his adversaries, who have never taken issue with the point of the *Blueprint*, but rather with its implementation. Over time, his immense contributions to the children of San Diego and to our school community will become even more apparent.
>
> We have heard from principals and teachers that the *Blueprint* is good for children, but they need to have more discretion on how to implement it and how to make it work for the children in your school. We believe it is with the implementation of the *Blueprint* that we must strive to improve ourselves. While we can certainly credit Chancellor Alvarado as the architect of the *Blueprint*, it is our principals and teachers who are responsible for its continued successful implementation.
>
> It is on that note I share with you what I shared with principals today at their monthly instructional conference; I will be going before the Board of Education next Tuesday December 10, to ask for permission to renegotiate the contract of our Chancellor of Instruction, Anthony Alvarado. We will evaluate both the scope of his responsibilities and the nature of his contract with the district. This will result in a proposal to be brought before the board in the first quarter of 2003 as we discuss with him a continued relationship with the district on terms that benefit all of us.

As we continue down the path of improving student achievement, I ask that you support Mary Hopper [newly appointed Chief Academic Officer; previously Alvarado's Chief of Staff] and our instructional leaders who will lead this effort at the side of principals, along with their faculties. There will be more discussion, but I wanted to share this with you as we bring it forward for the Board's consideration and as it continues to become public knowledge in the San Diego community.

For our students,
Alan D. Bersin

A "Design Genius" and a "Lightning Rod for Controversy"

Bersin's message to district employees acknowledges Alvarado as a "design genius," whose "work rightfully earned the praise of all." But, in addressing principals and ILs, he characterized the change as a "phasing out" of a "controversial leader" to "ease tensions" and "give teachers the autonomy they crave in the classroom" (Magee, 2002b). After the school board restructured Alvarado's contract, Bersin again praised his former chancellor of instruction for his "genius" in "designing educational reform" but noted that Alvarado was a "lightning rod" who had made the process of change more difficult (Moran, 2003a). In these formulations, Bersin implied that political pressure exerted on him from within the organization had compelled his painful decision to remove Alvarado. For instance, achieving a more harmonious relationship with teachers required that Bersin turn away from Alvarado's hallmark idea that teachers earn autonomy through improved teaching practice rather than acquiring autonomy along with their teaching credential or gaining autonomy as the result of a politically negotiated compromise.

Bersin also alluded to political pressure to oust Alvarado as emanating from outside the organization. In his address at the December 2002 principals' conference, he called for a "truce in the ongoing feud between the business community and the teachers union" (Magee, 2002b). The powerful hand of the business community can be felt in this echo of the *Union-Tribune* editorial (Morgan, 2001) that had urged removing Alvarado and making peace with the union. Perhaps because the earlier strategy of funding the campaigns of proreform (and against the San Diego Education Association [SDEA]) school board candidates had failed rather grandly (recall that Frances O'Neill Zimmerman, staunchly opposed by business interests, won reelection anyway) and had become divisive, business leaders changed course, preferring to encourage Bersin to improve the reform's image by removing the "lightning rod for controversy."

The Limitations of Dual Leadership

In their dual leadership arrangement, Bersin "faced out" to the communities and Alvarado "faced in" to the organization. Bersin shielded Alvarado from political squabbles and enabled him to concentrate fully on improving instruction; Alvarado (a hot commodity in the field of education when the SDCS recruited him) buffered Bersin from criticisms that he knew little about education when he took over as superintendent.

The clear advantages of this arrangement blurred its associated disadvantages, however. Facing inward blocked Alvarado from developing his own bank of social capital (the currency that accrues to people who are positioned within influential social networks) with San Diego's communities—a feat that, as we showed in Chapter 3, he managed very well in New York (Resnick & Fink, 2001; Stein, Hubbard, & Mehan, 2003. Focused within the SDCS district office and schools, Alvarado did not personally connect to relevant constituencies outside the schools. This made it hard for him to draw on the social capital he did have when political circumstances called for it. Moreover, he was often physically absent from the district. During his first eighteen months of service, Alvarado repeatedly returned to New York to smooth the transition for his replacement. This contractual necessity, combined with his inward facing leadership role, exacerbated his disconnection from San Diego communities. It also made him a more attractive target for criticism. After all, it is easier to attack ideas associated with a disembodied apparition than those embodied in a charismatic person. The lack of tangible and personal connections to Alvarado and his reform ideas enabled critics to attack abstractions, rightfully anticipating no effective rejoinders.

Alvarado's image as a controversial and contentious outsider who was insensitive to the knowledge and expertise that existed in the San Diego community haunted his tenure. In his final interview with us, he lamented that he hadn't spent sufficient time building "a series of very strong relationships" (Alvarado, 2003: 14) with educators throughout the system—especially school board members, the union president, and classroom teachers. Spending time, adding his personal touch, and conveying his deep knowledge of the reform might have won over his critics, he mused. Referring to one staunch critic, he said, "I should have met with her three times a week. I would have asked her for her help, and I would have taken her to classrooms all of the time to see what this [the reform] was about and talked to her about it" (Alvarado, 2003). Equally important, building relationships of trust (Bryk & Schneider, 2003) would have enabled him and his colleagues to better gauge the progress of the reform, make necessary adjustments, and encourage good ideas to bubble up from the field and become integrated into the reform initiatives.

Our analysis of the circumstances surrounding the departure of Alvarado should not be construed as an indictment of the dual leadership arrangement. That it did not work in this instance is attributable to several factors, including some that could not have been foreseen (e.g., the California budget crisis, teacher union–district squabbles). The potential usefulness of a dual leadership arrangement remains. Large urban school districts are so complicated that shared responsibilities and a division of leadership are ideas worthy of further exploration.

Changes in the Theory of Action Guiding High School Reform

Changes in the theory of action guiding the SDCS high school reform accompanied Alvarado's departure. The Alvarado-inspired plan was comprehensive in scope (all schools were expected to implement the same reform uniformly), centralized in direction (reform ideas emanated from top district leaders), and fast in pace (a "boom" approach; see Hightower, 2002). As noted earlier in this chapter, the theory of action that emerged starting in 2003 is incremental in scope and differentiated by locale, decentralized in direction, and slower in pace. These modifications make the reform less contentious and more consensual in orientation. They also make San Diego's plan look more like the reforms in large urban districts around the country.

Allowing Some Schools to Be Free Agents

In Chapter 8 we described the complaints teachers, principals, and parents associated with La Jolla High School, in San Diego's most affluent neighborhood, lodged against the reform. These included objections to the two- and three-hour literacy blocks, to an activity-based and allegedly nonrigorous physics program required of all ninth graders, to a narrowing of electives, and to assorted limitations on teachers' creativity. After months of rancorous debate in 2002, during which reform opponents repeatedly challenged the utility of the Balanced Literacy framework for high-achieving high school students, district leaders relented and agreed to free La Jolla High School from the strictures of the reform (Bowman, 2002). Granting pilot school status to this high school was an unplanned rupture in what had previously been put forth as a nonnegotiable feature of the reform—its districtwide, systemic implementation.

Three other schools—Hoover High School, Monroe Clark Middle School, and Rosa Parks Elementary School—all located in the midcity section of San Diego, had been exempted from the mandates of the reform in 1998. Wealthy philanthropist Sol Price, as part of his project to revitalize the midcity area, had forged an alliance in 1998 among San Diego State University (SDSU), the SDEA, and the three midcity schools to create a learning laboratory to improve education. Designated as "community schools," Hoover, Clark, and Parks provide students with comprehensive health and social services; SDSU provides the teaching corps (including support for novice teachers from the university's education faculty).

Other deviations from the systemic feature of the San Diego reform also preceded the broader community-based political struggles that culminated in 2002. In response to the elimination of affirmative action in the college admissions process, the University of California, San Diego planned to build (on its own campus) a college-prep charter high school exclusively for low-income students (Rosen & Mehan, 2003). The school would provide up to eight hundred students with a rigorous course of study supported by scaffolds such as a longer school day and school year, tutoring from college students, and mandatory parent involvement. The planning culminated coterminously with the appointment of Bersin as superintendent in 1997. Initially wary of allowing a high school to define its own mission, design its own curriculum, and establish its own admissions criteria, Bersin finally relented in 1998, citing the lessons that other schools in the district could learn from this mold breaker (Bersin, 2003c).

A similar rationale was provided for the approval of charter status to High Tech High. Launched in September 2000 by an industrial and education coalition led by QUALCOMM founder and president Irwin Jacobs (later a contributor to the efforts to unseat reform opponent O'Neill Zimmerman from the school board), High Tech High occupies a newly designed learning space at the former Naval Training Center in San Diego. A small, diverse learning community of approximately four hundred students, High Tech High is founded on three design principles: personalization, adult-world connection, and a common intellectual mission (Kluver & Rosenstock, 2002). High Tech High's innovative features, which include performance-based assessment, daily shared planning time for staff, state-of-the-art technical facilities for project-based learning, internships for all students, and close links to the high-tech workplace, is serving as a model for other public high schools in San Diego and elsewhere (Kluver & Rosenstock, 2002).

To win approval to set their own course of action, supporters of these schools made use of their significant social capital and also successfully exploited the twin resources of growing parent interest in and district distress over charter schools. The compromises forged for these schools foreshadowed the district's later move toward a more decentralized and differentiated reform strategy.

School-Based Initiatives Guided by Nonnegotiable Principles

Early in 2002, the SDCS embarked on a reform targeting its sixteen comprehensive high schools. The organization and implementation of the high school reform has differed from the rollout of the SDCS reform that began in 1997. Overall, the old and new reform processes diverge in three significant ways: (1) principals participated from the earliest stages in planning the high school reform; (2) although principals' responsibilities as onsite leaders of instruction look much the same as they did in the original reform, principals are now expected and encouraged to tailor the reform to their own schools' needs; and (3) rather than being districtwide, the high school reform initiatives are being implemented on a smaller scale.

These differences suggest that the district leadership has modified its reform strategy in response to technical, cultural, and political considerations. On the technical dimension, the district was unable to build capacity fast enough either to transform schools into communities of learners or to tailor the Balanced Literacy framework appropriately for use in middle and high schools. High school teachers were the most vocally upset by the structural changes the genre studies classes entailed. The new high school reform, in directly addressing teachers' cultural concerns as well as technical and academic factors, helped shape the district's systemwide move toward consensus. Other important enabling conditions include satisfactory compromises on political factors, especially educators' insistence that "one size does *not* fit all," and the availability of funding from the Carnegie Corporation for the construction of small learning communities and from the Gates Foundation for the design of small schools.

The earliest stages of the decentralized or site-specific high school reform effort started in 2001–2002, under Alvarado's guidance. District leaders selected six schools they deemed as most poised for change, in large part because of their strong leadership. A small planning group composed of top district leaders and the principals of the six schools identified assumptions they considered fundamental, indeed unalterable, to high school reform— academic rigor, personalization, and leadership. Academic rigor means that all high school students should successfully complete a course of study that makes them eligible to enroll in the University of California or the California State University. Personalization means that all high school students should have meaningful connections to faculty and staff to reduce the alienation and anonymity associated with large schools. Leadership at the school site means that principals guide and direct instructional improvement, enhance the skills and knowledge of school staff, create a common culture of expectations for student achievement, unite faculty in a community, and hold individuals accountable for the collective result (SDCS, 2001a: 2).

With these fundamental assumptions in place, principals were encouraged to analyze each school's needs, set goals, and develop strategies to meet those goals. The strategies proposed were quite different. For example, the principal of one high school concluded that the large number of English-language learners and recent immigrants at her school necessitated special consideration. She proposed and received approval for an on-site language academy. This is a prime example of a call for help from below being heeded from above, or, to phrase this slightly more elegantly, this was an instance of "organizational learning." Just as reform-minded teachers modified their practice in response to their students' needs, so too did district leaders modify their practice in response to locally felt and expressed needs.

Because the strategies the principals proposed were expected to be sensitive to their local context, any given fundamental feature of the reform might be addressed differently at each school. For example, personalization is an unassailable assumption of the high school reform effort. But the strategies under consideration to reduce the impersonalization associated with large, comprehensive high schools varied considerably. They included "looping" (the practice of linking teachers and students for successive years), homerooms, "link crew" (the practice of assigning older students to mentor younger students), and theme academies within schools (such as the language academy mentioned previously, a maritime academy, a technology academy). Thus, the new high school reform effort not only tolerated but also encouraged local variation and the independent design of that variation.

Further Differentiating the Approach to High School Reform

Despite the district's investment in improving its high schools, student achievement, as measured by state-mandated standardized tests, did not show a consistent pattern of improvement (see Table 9.1).

The superintendent convened groups composed of the principal, parents, and community members at each high school and asked them to identify their school's needs.[1] The district's newly designated instructional leaders for high schools then analyzed the local conditions, leadership capability, and level of improvement at each of their schools and arranged the schools into groups with similar strengths and needs. "Challenge schools" were to develop a school accountability contract based on the state accountability system, coupled with additional district-specific targets to close the achievement gap between different ethnic and socioeconomic groups of students. "Redesign schools" were to convert large comprehensive high schools into smaller, more personalized high

Table 9.1. Academic Performance Index (API) Scores of San Diego City Schools High Schools, 1999–2002[2]

School	1999	2000	2001	2002
Crawford	537	541	541	528
SDHS	538	564	545	529
Kearny	557	575	554	605
Morse	604	628	616	633
Lincoln	477	485	481	485
University City	707	728	741	718
Point Loma	665	700	672	664
Scripps Ranch	750	unavailable	746	753
Serra	665	708	692	669
Performing Arts				
Mira Mesa	719	730	724	715
Patrick Henry	691	704	693	698
Mission Bay	599	625	627	604
Madison	601	604	575	575
Claremont	595	638	613	590

schools. Each small school on a site would have its own theme—such as architecture, art, law and public policy, or marine biology—intended to provide a common intellectual purpose for the curriculum. "Community engagement schools" were to address the problem of "white flight." Situated in well-to-do neighborhoods, these schools would work with the middle schools and elementary schools in their cluster to raise expectations for students and improve academic quality through curriculum units of study linked to state academic standards to reattract neighborhood students. Principals and teachers from four "alternative schools" were to form a learning community to refresh their purpose, develop a long-range plan for improving academic rigor, apply learning issues to acceleration and graduation, develop site-specific measures for monitoring student progress, and develop special relationships with local community colleges that will enable high school students to earn college credit (Hopper, 2003b).

Last, Superintendent Bersin's plans called for the construction of new freestanding small schools. Like the small schools within the large comprehensive high schools, these new small schools would have a theme intended to provide a common intellectual purpose for the curriculum. Both the redesign and the new small schools clusters reflect an infusion of new ideas linked to outside funding. The district's decision in 2002 to accept an $8 million grant from the Carnegie Corporation's "Schools for a New Society" initiative and an $11.4 million grant from the Gates Foundation in partnership with new American Schools strongly affected Bersin's revised theory of action for the high schools. Both funding agencies think student engagement is a decisive factor in school improvement. The grants they award are designed to underwrite educational change that promotes such engagement. Specifically, these agencies award grants to districts willing to develop "small learning communities" and "small schools." The emphasis in this kind of reform thus is on structure, as opposed to the emphasis on content that was a hallmark of the original Bersin–Alvarado reform plan.

In addition to making the district eligible for much-needed outside funding, the cluster school approach—grouping the high schools according to the strengths and weaknesses they shared—was intended to enable each school to address structural, personalization, and engagement issues according to its local needs. Each cluster is expected to have a different relationship with the district, but all schools remain responsible for meeting the same district goals of improving student achievement and enhancing instructional quality through leadership development and personalization of students' learning experience. The expertise of the principals and teachers in each school type (challenge, redesign, community engagement, etc.) is acknowledged and built on; administrators and faculty members are expected to think creatively about how best to achieve the district's overarching goals (Hopper, 2003b).

As of this writing, *all* SDCS comprehensive high schools, regardless of how well "poised for change" or how strong a leadership role their principals may have taken in the past, are participating equally in this new effort at reform. This is not a variation on Alvarado's model of the gradual release of responsibility but rather a complete break from it. Because the goal now is to create a variety of school *structures,* the principals' job seems likely to need revamping; likewise, classroom teachers' practice no longer seems to be the bottom line for achieving high-quality student performance. And those "external factors" (e.g., poor socioeconomic conditions, language status, transience) that earlier had been seen as having no significant effect on learning—provided teachers and students worked sufficiently hard—are front and center in a structural reform as opposed to a content-driven reform.

This thinking marks a sharp departure from the theory of action that prevailed from 1998–2002. Indeed, it is almost a full circle, if the administrations of former superintendents are taken as the baseline (see chapter 3). Bersin's predecessors established and maintained relatively harmonious relations with the SDEA, and no previous superintendent had attempted to initiate systemic, districtwide reforms. Each school or area had been allowed to determine its own improvement goals and course of action to meet those goals. There had been few centrally imposed constraints. This kind of environment has advantages, but it also leads to lack of coordination across the system and to difficulties in maintaining quality control.

The parallel between the changes in the reform plan and the movement over time that occurred within our case study schools (see Chapter 6) is striking. After years of principal- or coach-led staff development, teachers in many schools eventually persuaded their leaders to use professional-development time for teacher-run grade-level meetings. Although many of these meetings were put to good use, the majority of our observations contain examples of teachers using this time to talk about noninstructional issues and to grade papers. Without boundaries to constrain the work, an atmosphere of "anything goes" began to pervade our case study schools; there was little or no coordination across classrooms within each school, and there was no quality control.

When Bersin initiated the reorganization of the reform, he insisted that improving instructional quality for all students remained central to the district's vision. But the superintendent also claimed that improving student achievement and enhancing student engagement requires reshaping school structure *before* attempting to improve instruction. More specifically, he said that because high schools have students with diverse interests, they need diverse reform efforts, with high quality standards maintained at each site (Bersin, 2003a).

In sum, the new version of SDCS high school reform appears as a portfolio of reform elements rather than as a cohesive plan with a single theory of action. The underlying assumptions for redesigning schools in some ways are the mirror opposites of those informing the Alvarado–Bersin reform. Rather than factors external to the classroom being assumed to be of negligible importance, these factors (especially those related to differences in the school population, school culture, and neighborhood dynamics) now are assumed to have a definitive, overarching impact on education. Funding agencies played a decisive role in the pastiche of initiatives represented in the high school reform effort. Grant support from the Gates Foundation and the Carnegie Corporation—especially at a time of diminished state funding—influenced the superintendent's decision to restructure large comprehensive high schools into smaller, presumably more personalized, ones.

Organizational Changes Accompanying High School Reform Strategies

Significant organizational changes in the central district office and between the central office and school sites accompanied the high school reform.

Reorganizing the District Office

The district office has been reorganized twice since the departure of Alvarado. Effective July 2003, Mary Hopper was appointed chief academic officer, assuming many of the responsibilities formerly carried out by the chancellor of instruction. Alvarado's main organizational innovation, the Institute for Learning (described in Chapter 4), was reorganized and renamed the Office of Instructional Support. Six major divisions were under its auspices: Student Services; Special Education; School Supervision and Support; Standards, Assessment, Accountability, and Compliance; Instruction and Curriculum; and Teacher Preparation and Support. Other changes included creating the Office of School Site Support and assigning responsibility for financial operations, business operations, and facilities management to the chief administrative officer (see Figure 9.1).

The responsibilities of instructional leaders also changed in this reorganization. High schools were no longer included in learning communities with middle and elementary schools. In addition, the newly reorganized learning communities would have a single source to consult regarding curriculum and instruction. One particularly knowledgeable instructional leader was given responsibility for all curriculum and instructional areas (literacy, mathematics, sciences, social studies, history, etc.) at the elementary and middle school levels. This consolidation aimed to both answer complaints that the district office issued conflicting messages (see Chapters 5, 6, and 7) and increase the coherence of information as it progressed up and down instructional corridors (through interactions among and between instructional leaders, curriculum specialists, principals, and teachers).

The high schools and the district office forged a different organizational relationship. Two new positions—high school reform administrator and director of secondary school innovation—were created. A well-regarded high school principal from a neighboring district accepted the first position and assumed responsibility for *administrative* aspects of the newly conceived community engagement and challenge schools in July 2003. The job includes leading and overseeing curriculum development, AVID (Advancement via Individual Determination) program strategies, and the development of smaller learning communities within the high schools in

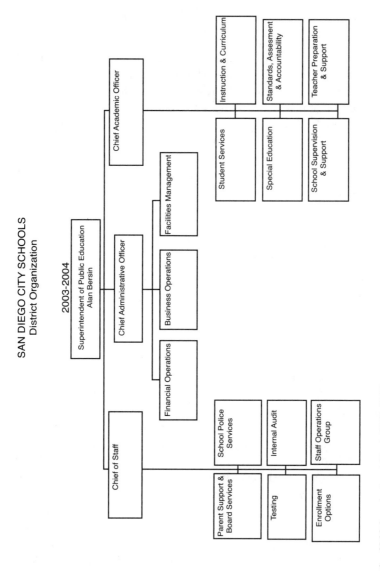

SAN DIEGO CITY SCHOOLS
District Organization

2003-2004

Figure 9.1 SDCS Organizational Chart, 2003–2004.

these two categories. The new director of secondary school innovation leads the high schools in the redesign, alternative, and new small schools categories, all of which were then under the auspices of the Gates Foundation grant to the district. Incumbents in both new positions reported first to the chief academic officer and next to the superintendent. Thus, these changes represent material as well as symbolic ones.

A second round of central office reorganization occurred in fall 2004. Hopper became chief *administrative* officer, responsible for business operations; facilities; financial operations; human resources; instruction and curriculum; special education; standards, assessment, and accountability; student services; and support of teacher preparation. A deputy superintendent was placed in charge of instructional leaders, the high school reform administrator, and mentor principals.[3] A new chief of staff assumed responsibility for legislative services, communications, community relations, the general counsel, labor relations, and school choice, among other functions. This new arrangement increased intraorganizational communication by streamlining interrelations between the superintendent, the chief administrative officer, the deputy superintendent, and the chief of staff (see Figure 9.2).

Only time will tell if these reconfigurations signal a return to the traditional split between teachers and administrators and whether the "we are all learners" and "we are all focused on the same goal" notions persist or fade.

Cautious Moves toward Decentralization
What we have characterized as the *centralized direction* of the reform, the district's critics characterized as a *top-down control* of the reform that excluded valuable constituencies (see Chapter 8). Starting with the 2003–2004 academic/fiscal year, Superintendent Bersin began loosening the central office's financial control. He recommended that some school sites be given more discretion in the expenditure of Title I funds. Schools had been receiving 20% of their Title I allocation as discretionary funds; Bersin asked the school board to raise this limit to 50% for the 2003–2004 school year. Reiterating a theme from the letter to the SDCS faculty and staff in December 2002 in which he explained the dismissal of Chancellor Alvarado, he said, "It is timely and appropriate to provide sites with greater flexibility as they continue their efforts to improve student achievement" (Bersin, 2003b).

This increase in school-based discretionary funding helped the district address the budget crisis (see Chapter 8) and gave Bersin some much-needed political capital with schools and the community. In an

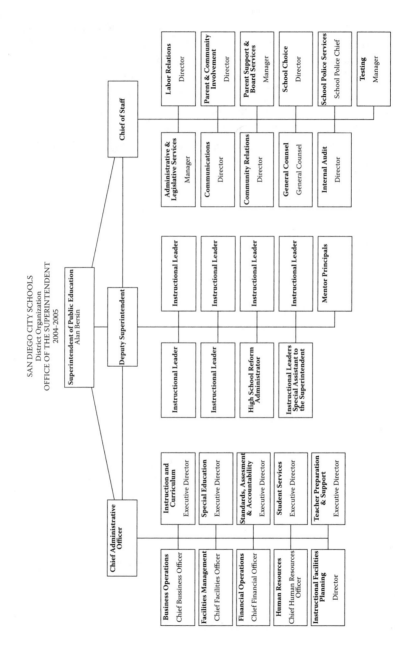

SAN DIEGO CITY SCHOOLS
District Organization
OFFICE OF THE SUPERINTENDENT
2004-2005

Superintendent of Public Education
Alan Bersin

Figure 9.2   SDCS Organizational Chart, 2004–2005.

accompanying memo to members of the District Advisory Committee, principals, and chairs of the School Site Councils, Chief Academic Officer Hopper (Hopper, 2003a) asked the school board to approve other changes in the use of Title I funds. These included the following:

- Increasing literacy block class size from twenty students per instructor to twenty-five students, for grades six, seven, and nine
- Eliminating the three-hour literacy block at grade
- Eliminating supports for retained students
- Restricting summer school offerings to Title I schools and high schools
- Restricting extended day care to certain schools

Financial decision making was shared even more extensively beginning in 2004–2005. Bersin gave principals and their parent and employee advisory groups the power to decide where cuts should be made at their schools. To help balance the district's $1.1 billion budget, the average-size elementary school had to cut an estimated $42,000; the average middle school, $265,000; and the average high school, $380,000 (Magee, 2004a). The irony of decentralizing decision making just in time to allow school-site leadership teams to make difficult budgetary choices was not lost on some principals: "I agree with the idea of giving principals more power," Mary Martel, principal of Roosevelt Middle School, observed. "I hope that when we are in good budget times, we still have the power" (quoted in Magee, 2004a).

Another example of decentralization involves schools under No Child Left Behind (NCLB) mandate to restructure because of chronic under-achievement. When four of the eight affected schools asked the school board to allow them to reform as independent charter schools, the superintendent and his staff did not discourage the proposal (Gao, 2005a). The new school board (installed in January 2005) is not supportive of the proliferation of charter schools, however. Members voted (by a four to one margin) against schools that wanted to reopen as charter schools in fall 2005 (Gao, 2005b)[4] but reversed their position, voting five to zero in March 2005 to approve the conversion of four schools to charter status under the provisions of NCLB.

By devolving decision making on budgetary matters to the schools, eliminating the wildly unpopular three-hour literacy blocks, and allowing low-performing schools to reorganize as charters, Bersin provided tangible evidence of a new willingness to be more flexible in his leadership. These actions indicate a loosening of the comprehensive, centralized approach to school reform that characterized the first phase of the SDCS reform and a shift toward a more differentiated, decentralized approach.

Cautious Moves toward Collaboration
At the heart of the calls for collaboration and negotiation is a debate over democracy in the local context. To what extent are decisions about school governance to be made by "the community" or the school board? And to what extent is the district to be managed by the superintendent (and his staff) after election by the school board? When some members of the community and advisory groups such as District Advisory Council on Compensatory Education and the SDEA called for shared decision making, the superintendent and the school board majority were not swayed. They asserted that the superintendent had been hired because he was a strong leader and that his responsibility to improve the school district included making unpopular decisions when they were necessary. Many of the superintendent's critics, although separated geographically and by their traditional political interests, were united in their agreement that decision making should be shared. They insisted that their input should be included in hiring and firing as well as curriculum and instruction decisions.

After a series of feedback sessions conducted independently of the district in fall 2000 and summer 2001 among teachers, parents, principals, and district administrators, Daniel Yankelovich, a nationally recognized and respected arbitrator (Yankelovich, 2001), called for regular meetings among stakeholders so that district decision makers could be informed about the progress of reforms in schools and classrooms and take mid-course corrections as needed. In his opinion, institutionalizing these dialogues would build the trust, communication, and confidence necessary to sustain the reform. Ginger Hovenic (2002) of the Business Round-table for Education endorsed Yankelovich's proposal in an editorial in the *San Diego Daily Transcript*: "In the minds of many, input from parents, teachers and others is the *Blueprint*'s only chance for success."

Notice that for both Yankelovich and Hovenic, responsibility for major decision making belongs with district leadership. They leave the basic design principles and assumptions of the reform unchallenged and consign parents, teachers, and principals to a reactive "input" and "feedback" role. This position is consistent with recent research on San Diego parents' attitudes toward their children's schools. Most parents indicate that they do not want complete control over schools, but they do want opportunities for input and feedback (Jones, Yonezawa, Grimes, 2002).

The question we consider here is this: Have any practical consequences or changes in courses of action emerged from the heated debates over decision making? We think so. Evidence of promising practices concerning collaboration began emerging as the reform took new directions. In an e-mail message to all SDCS employees, the superintendent (Bersin, 2002b) responded in a conciliatory way to the many criticisms of the reform aired in the *California Teacher* (see Chapter 8). After dismissing the SDEA complaints enumerated in the article as misinformed "myths," Bersin called on all members of the San Diego educational community to "work together to make constructive and real attempts to improve the reforms." Accepting some responsibility for the perception that his administration has perpetuated a "climate of fear," Bersin said, "I pledge to continue the district's efforts to gather important feedback, and act upon it where appropriate, as part of our work to make informed mid-course corrections to our reforms."

An agreement reached between the SDEA and the superintendent to work together on the district's 2003–2004 budget was another tangible sign of collaboration. Terry Pesta, who became president of the SDEA in summer 2002, signaled a new willingness to cooperate: "It's an opportunity to work together on this issue, and hopefully it will lead to much better relations in the future" (quoted in "Schools Cease Fire," 2003). Applying his signature motto ("There are two kinds of employees in the district—those who teach and those who support instruction") to the budget crisis, Superintendent Bersin, working closely with President Pesta, preserved teachers' jobs at the expense of other kinds of positions. No teachers, counselors, or nurses were laid off, but 412 staff positions (including those of 24 managers, 12 supervisors, and 2 top business officials) and 189 teaching assistant positions were eliminated.[5] In addition, on July 24, 2003, the school board unanimously voted to end several magnet school programs, close the charter school office, cut spending on athletics by 10 percent, cancel summer sessions at dozens of campuses, curtail after-school reading programs, and cut back bus routes (Moran, 2003d). The network of literacy, science, and math administrators, peer coaches, and instructional leaders remains largely intact, although the board reduced the instructional leader positions by two in 2003–2004. Personnel previously assigned to the central office to lead and oversee the Balanced Literacy framework were assigned to school-site leadership positions.

Summary and Conclusions

The SDCS has made significant organizational changes in response to powerful political forces, unplanned fiscal constraints, and deep-seated cultural conflicts. The back draft from teachers, parents, and various community and opinion leaders seemed to make the district more responsive to local contexts and helped bring about a movement toward building consensus to carry the reform rather than jolting the system into new practices. The district leaders also modified their professional-development practices so that efforts to build leadership capacity would take place prior to placing leaders in positions of responsibility. The leadership coped with fiscal uncertainties by trimming jobs and remanding the toughest fiscal responsibilities and belt-tightening to individual school-site principals. Leaders also appear to have recast the reform's theory of action in ways that made it appealing to foundations and other funding agencies. The net result has been a significant alteration in the design features of the district's theory of action.

As the district began moving forward with its theory of action in 1998, leaders cited moral, pragmatic, and political reasons for implementing the Balanced Literacy framework quickly. Speedy implementation was legitimated morally by saying a whole generation of students could not be asked to wait until an entire system was ready to provide the support they needed to learn. Pragmatically, the leadership asserted that significant change could not be accomplished piecemeal, because organizations as large as the district have a way of absorbing innovation. Politically, the reform had to be implemented quickly to ensure ongoing support from the business community.

The need for speed has been overtaken. Particularly at the high school level, by as early as 2002, a combination of technical, cultural, and political forces were pushing the reform model toward a slower-paced, more incremental, locally sensitive approach. Lack of capacity, cultural conflicts within the district, and political pressure from the multiple constituencies we described in Chapter 8 continued to intensify. Eventually, Superintendent Bersin elected to sacrifice the architect of systemic reform—the person who was simultaneously a "reform genius" and a "lightning rod for controversy"—to reduce that pressure. Today, to sustain the content-driven reform in the lower grades, teachers must accept a stripped-down version, shorn of much of its moral urgency and commitment to educational equity, as well as lacking multiple, intensive forms of professional development.

The district leaders also seem to have concluded that a centralized and comprehensive reform effort does not capture and use the expertise that exists in the district and community; indeed, it can repel colleagues and foster resistance. Equally important, what critics called the reform's one-size-fits-all approach does not appear to meet the needs of the very large and very diverse student body of the SDCS. Successful restructuring and reculturing of schools, district leaders now believe, require that principals, teachers, parents, and community members be involved in planning changes and participating in the resulting programs and activities.

Coping with Fiscal Constraints and Opportunities

The goal of redesigning its large, comprehensive high schools into independent, flexible, small high schools with smaller learning communities presents the SDCS leaders with formidable financial challenges. Some constraints, such as state budget decisions, lie outside the district's control. The California budget crisis has significantly reduced the funds available for all schools, which also adversely affects school redesign efforts.

As of this writing, the long-term effects of the statewide budget cuts on the reform are uncertain. The district actively encouraged retirement as a cost-saving measure. How the resulting decrease in personnel will affect capacity—a grave concern during the Alvarado-inspired content-driven reform—is not yet clear. The reform might gain momentum, if entrenched educators (veteran teachers, vice principals, and principals), who often were opponents of the reforms, leave and are replaced by newcomers who have been trained in district policies and practices and are more receptive to the reform. On the other hand, the reform might lose momentum because of the tremendous loss of institutional memory, leadership, and stability. In either case, the institutional resources required to confront the budget crisis diverted energy and effort critically needed to meet the academic needs of students. The California budget crisis that led off the twenty-first century is just one more example of how actions promulgated far from the classroom nevertheless severely affect it.

Currently, SDCS principals and district staff members have been able to develop budgets for the new small schools that are viable within the district's existing financial boundaries (including the 7% budget cuts levied in 2004). Remaining financial challenges include finding building sites for the new small schools and redeveloping current facilities to accommodate redesigned schools. Keeping the cost of site acquisition and development within budget will be daunting.

The district has continued to capitalize on grant opportunities that have helped alleviate the budget crunch and move the new reforms forward. Funding from the Carnegie Corporation and the Gates Foundation led the high school change effort away from a content-driven reform to a structural reform. The district's new emphasis on organizational changes such as small schools, both within existing comprehensive facilities and as freestanding units, allows the high schools to take advantage of these and other funding opportunities. Large infusions of money from outside sources, including sources that attach significant strings to their awards, potentially is a very important factor shaping the direction and substance of the reform. Grant monies are an example of outside influences that significantly affect classroom learning. The relationship between grant money and the shape and goals of educational reform in this and other large urban school districts should be carefully scrutinized in future research.

A Differentiated Model of School Reform

Starting in 2003, the district's modified theory of action was more incremental in scope and differentiated by locale, decentralized in direction, and slower in pace. These changes made the reform less contentious because district leaders adapted reform ideas to local contexts.

The high school reform, especially, reflects district leaders' new approach. Not all comprehensive high schools, pilot schools, charter schools, and alternative high schools are on the same timetable or are enacting the same strategies for reform. High school leaders are responsible for devising local solutions to general educational problems, but they do so guided by a shared set of nonnegotiable principles that affirm the districtwide commitment to instructional quality. The high school plan is decentralized in that each high school, or affinity cluster of schools, is recognized as having different needs. For challenge schools, the need is to close the achievement gap between white and underrepresented minority students; for community engagement schools, the need is to return white, middle-class students to classrooms in their own neighborhoods; and for the big comprehensive schools, the need is to personalize students' educational experience by creating smaller schools within schools.

The changes in the district's practices we have described in this chapter continue to be institutionalized as new policy statements that are inscribed in organizational charts, job titles, and job descriptions. These new policies, of course, will not automatically wend their way through the instructional corridors of the system. Like the policies associated with the earlier, content-driven reform, they are subject to negotiation, interpretation, and revision. The district's new policies will be co-constructed by all the other actors in the system, shaped by their actions, and constrained by cultural meanings, technical resources (including fiscal conditions), political struggles, and structural limitations.

This co-construction can take at least two forms. One is an intentional, planned, integrated feature of a reform. This form of change occurs through deliberately created channels and structures that encourage or at least allow organizational members at multiple levels to *jointly* implement and thus *jointly* construct new knowledge. A second form of co-construction is *reactive.* This form of change occurs more haphazardly. It is shaped by the everyday actions of people and by external events and forces that impinge on the reform but are not integral parts of the planned organizational change. These reactive efforts may be aimed at placating a restive community, whether that community is internal (e.g., district employees) or external (e.g., parents, union, businesspeople). In more extreme cases, reactive changes may constitute survival tactics—measures designed to preserve the organization's existence, or at least the organization leaders' positions.

Understanding the district's new policies as co-constructed is an acknowledgment that reform does not occur in a vacuum. It is certainly true, as we have documented in this chapter, that being forced to confront external factors can result in fundamental, organic change to the plan of a reform and that such change may deliberately incorporate collaboration and co-construction. But, as we also have shown, the incorporation of collaboration as an integral aspect of reform is not *inevitable.* This district, like any other large organization, may opt for superficial changes undertaken simply to address a current crisis and then attempt to lumber on with its basic goals and assumptions, roles and responsibilities intact. Similarly, as an organization dependent on other organizations and institutions (such as state and federal governments and granting agencies) and involving real people undertaking daily practices and enacting procedures, the district's plans will necessarily continue to undergo *some* changes.

Prospects for the Future

The leading edge of the Alvarado-inspired reform was instruction sheathed in a technical rationality. Improved instruction leads to improved student learning, and improved learning, in turn, leads to a culture change within schools. This logical progression, Alvarado asserted, occurs because all concerned come to see the value of concentrating on instruction, thanks to the generation of supporting empirical evidence (e.g., rising test scores). By contrast, the Bersin-led redesign effort for high schools tries to weld structural change to instructional change. The imperative to improve schools by making them smaller or more personal or attractive to neighborhood parents has supplanted the instruction-first mantra.

It will be interesting and informative to see how this new reform initiative plays out, especially what relation between instruction and structure emerges. Bersin (2005: 325–336) insisted that he did not abandon the quest for improved classroom instruction; instead, he said, he came to realize that he had to build the conditions for instruction (by which he meant smaller, more personalized schools with strong leadership) before concentrating resources on instructional improvement. It is not clear, however, how placing structural change before instructional improvement squares with the urgent and absolute moral imperative that was the clarion call of the original reform; that is, the need to correct the injustice of allowing children to sit through even one more day of substandard instruction.

Another problem associated with putting structural change ahead of instructional change is that change agents can become so absorbed by the practical problems associated with organizing the structural features (such as designing a new course schedule, assigning teachers to new theme-based small schools, and deciding which small school gets the science labs or sports teams) that they fail to engage in the extremely hard work of improving instruction. If educators committed to redesigning large comprehensive high schools into smaller more responsive ones do not get past solving the practical problems, then the result will be not a paradigm shift in education but oases of excellence within a desert of mediocrity.

The choice of the leading edge of reform may be overtaken by political considerations, however. The bitterly divided school board of the Bersin–Alvarado years has disbanded. As of November 2004, three new members joined the board, replacing past-president Ron Ottinger and trustee Ed Lopez (strong supporters of Bersin's reforms), and trustee O'Neill Zimmerman (a strong opponent of the reforms). Bersin's term of office expired in June 2005, and new superintendent Carl Cohn, formerly superintendent in Long Beach, California, was hired (Cohn's term officially began in October 2005).

Superintendent Cohn must decide whether to pursue an instruction-first strategy, continue with Bersin's differentiated policies, or chart yet another course of action. Any of several different relationships between instruction and structure could come to define the San Diego reform in the future. For example, it is possible that the district has developed sufficient capacity to sustain a focus on instruction regardless of political changes. If so, SDCS teachers and principals could continue to concentrate on instruction, no matter what new reform strategies are adopted. Alternatively, Superintendent Cohn may opt to steer the district in a new direction. In that case, San Diego could emerge as another example of a district caught in the "reform mill" (Oakes, Quartz, Ryan, & Lipton, 1999). If this last scenario unfolds—if yet another reform model replaces the Bersin- and Alvarado-inspired ones—then it will be difficult to conclude what the SDCS organization as a whole has learned. Perhaps the new district leadership will change course based on past experience and changing circumstances, but if new policies do not propel the district toward its clearly stated goals of closing the achievement gap by improving instruction, then we cannot say what this organization has learned.

Perhaps the new superintendent and school board will not change course dramatically and precipitously. But to the extent that elements of the Bersin–Alvarado theory of action remain in place, and the initial goal of the improved achievement for all students remains unchanged, the dramatic alteration in how that goal is to be reached makes at least one fact exceedingly clear: the route to the goal of increased student achievement is not singular, is probably not direct, and does not require lockstep synchronization.

CHAPTER 10

Conclusion

Our account of events at the intersection encounters between instructional leaders (ILs), principals, and teachers intentionally takes no position on the overall merits of the San Diego City Schools (SDCS) reform or does it make any judgments about any group of individuals' willingness or capacity to carry it out. It is possible to view the teachers', the principals', and the ILs' experiences from any of several different perspectives. Some readers, for example, may consider the teachers a group of ill-informed, uncaring educators who willfully obstructed an inspired reform; others may focus on the role of the ILs and lament their lack of experience in transmitting the ideas of the reform to an audience of principals who initially had been eagerly enthusiastic. A third group of readers might conclude that a thoughtful reform had foundered on the shoals of political forces and cultural clashes beyond the control of all concerned. Each viewpoint carries its own truth; which interpretation ultimately is most satisfying will depend on readers' individual perspectives.

The theoretical framework we introduced in Chapter 1 shaped our understanding of the SDCS reforms and the lessons we draw from it. That framework depicted the SDCS as a set of nested learning communities and proposed that learning that spans the boundaries of the various layers of communities—learning that occurs within what we call "intersection encounters"—is the most fragile. Stepping back from our analysis, we can see how the intent of the reform was altered as it was handed over from district leaders to ILs, from ILs to principals, from principals to teachers, and, finally, from teachers to their students. A reform that began as conceptually driven was proceduralized; an approach to learning that began as student-centered became teacher-centered; and a framework with many openings for the application of professional judgment became understood as scripted. We think the explanation for these transformations lies in the overlapping and sometimes contradictory relationships among several factors: the challenging nature of the reform; the capacity, norms, values, and standard operating procedures of the district that Alan Bersin and Anthony Alvarado inherited; and the exceedingly rapid pace with which all principals, teachers, and students were brought into the reform. We explore key aspects of those interconnections in this final chapter.

The chapter is organized as follows. First, we describe the lessons we learned about school improvement from our study of the reforms as they unfolded in San Diego between 1998 and 2002. Then we use San Diego's experiences as a guide for making recommendations for implementing school reform in other districts. Finally, we consider the implications of the SDCS school reform efforts for knowledge in other contexts, specifically perspectives on learning and organizational theory.

Lessons Learned about School Improvement from the 1998–2002 Reform in the San Diego City Schools

What was dramatic, daring, and possibly unprecedented in the SDCS reform was its firm commitment to instruction as the driver of improved student achievement. What do we learn from the first four years of the implementation of this bold experiment in San Diego? The answers are to be found in the interrelationships among the technical, cultural, and political dimensions of the reform and the mismatch between the learning demands of the reform and the capacity of the district to deliver support quickly and comprehensively.

Technical, Political, and Cultural Dimensions of Reform Are Significant

The long tradition of research on policy implementation we reviewed in chapter 1 concludes that public policy is contingent, co-constructed, and mutually adaptive. Therefore, "implementation dominates outcome" (McLaughlin, 1998: 72); that is, local choices about whether or how to put a policy into practice are of greater importance than policy design features such as technology, funding, or governance. Oakes, Quartz, Ryan, and Lipton (1999: 19) were emphatic on this point:

> School improvement is [not] a technical problem that can be solved by such technical means as coherent policies that send a clear and consistent message; resources and technical assistance that help locals acquire new knowledge and skills; and monitoring mechanisms that provide information for fine tuning, holding educators accountable, and evaluating the reform's effectiveness. Such reform minded policy does not begin to capture how reform actually works. Reform is much less logical and technically rational. It is much more idiosyncratic—dependent upon the context of local relationships, histories, and opportunities.

In short, the success of policy implementation depends on how policy is interpreted and transformed at each point in the policy process (Hall & McGinty, 1997). "Policy can't mandate what matters," McLaughlin (1998: 72) concluded; local circumstances will.

These observations were vividly manifested in the San Diego context. The district leaders assumed that an enthusiastic concentration on improving instruction would improve all students' learning and close the achievement gap between low-income students and their more economically and socially advantaged contemporaries. To be sure, the district leadership was not ignorant of the literature that emphasizes the importance of the cultural and political dimensions of reform (see, for example, Bersin, 2005). Instead, they firmly believed that an excellent academic program that showed empirical results would not only improve students' learning but also win converts to the reform and silence its critics. Despite their familiarity with the literature on the cultural and political dimensions of reform, district leaders seem to have *miscalculated* the potency of the effects of students' background characteristics; local relationships; teacher buy-in; past histories; habits, beliefs, routines, and standard operating procedures; cultural norms; and politics. All influence the fate of a districtwide reform effort.

Insofar as Bersin and Alvarado attempted to "reculture schools" (Hargreaves, 1994) by focusing on improving instruction, developing a community of learners, and opening teaching to public scrutiny, they did not *ignore* the cultural and political aspects of education. Yet the process by which they attempted to achieve this cultural change seems to have had many of the drawbacks Oakes attributed to overly technical approaches to change. The district leadership miscalculated:

- The difficulties involved in raising students' scores on state-mandated standardized tests that were at best orthogonal to the district's instructional program.

- The importance of teacher buy-in, especially how calls for improved teacher quality and instruction would be perceived by teachers as disrespectful of their craft and thus would alienate them from the reform.
- The differences between elementary and secondary schools, especially for absorbing a literacy-based reform that requires significant changes in organizational features, such as the distribution of instructional time and the arrangement of the master calendar.
- The extent to which the size of the district and the speed of the reform influences the enactment of reform goals and strategies throughout the organization, and especially in classrooms.
- The importance of cultivating relationships with local educational experts and leaders, including the teachers' union, and, relatedly, how alienating the use of "imported experts" can be.
- How deeply some teachers, parents, and community members believe intelligence *is* stratified by race, ethnicity, and gender, and thus how strongly they believe that not all students *can* learn.
- How deeply some people believe that high schools *should be* comprehensive, with a stratified curriculum, including vocational education and an extensive sports program, and *should not* provide a rigorous academic program for all students.

Respect, relationships, and deep-seated cultural beliefs are all fundamentally important aspects of the culture of the school. Not adequately taking them into account thwarted much of the San Diego reform. This is not to say that the San Diego reform is dead. Many aspects of the Balanced Literacy framework are planted firmly enough in the soil of the district to thrive despite changes in upper management. Promising practices in reform modification are also underway, such as new mechanisms for communication, planned variation, and incremental reform (see chapter 9).

Unexamined Assumptions Have Serious Consequences

When describing the components of a theory of action, Argyris and Schön (1978) asserted that the assumptions underlying beliefs are sometimes more important than the beliefs themselves. The San Diego reform constitutes a cautionary tale of why it is important to consider one's assumptions along with beliefs about schools and reform ideas. In many if not most cases, people do not examine the assumptions underlying their beliefs, let alone state them formally. This is one reason why conflict can be both deep and unexpected. People assume that agreement on a principle such as "raising student achievement" as a bottom line also means a shared understanding of what constitutes student achievement, including what it is based on and how it is measured. But, as we discussed in Chapters 5 through 9, such agreement may be difficult to achieve because people diverge in terms of what they assume students are capable of, what they assume teachers are capable of, what they assume tests are capable of, and so forth.

The reformers and their critics appeared to have embraced very different (and very fundamental) assumptions about whether there was a problem in the SDCS that needed fixing and, if there was, how to go about fixing it. These assumptions, in turn, underpinned their beliefs and associated actions. San Diego reformers often perceived themselves as open and explicit about their beliefs; they were less open and explicit about their assumptions, however. They hoped to infuse the entire organization with a set of shared beliefs without first examining what assumptions those beliefs were built on and whether they were broadly shared by those in the education community and those in the wider San Diego community.

Competing Assumptions about Sources of Students'
Achievement Can Cause Confusion and Conflict

Some of San Diego leaders' assumptions produced considerable debate. Perhaps the most dramatic example concerns the influence of students' background characteristics on their academic achievement. Bersin and Alvarado asserted repeatedly that students' background characteristics (e.g., their poverty level, their home life, their language status) should not be used as an excuse for students not learning and for teachers not teaching. Too often, they argued, teachers "gave up" on such children when, instead, they should see it as their responsibility to reach out to these students and ensure that they learn. Critics heard Bersin and Alvarado as saying teachers should leave factors such as the conditions in students' homes, their primary language, and social services they might need outside the realm of instruction. That is, the critics interpreted Bersin and Alvarado's assertions as indicating that such factors did not matter. In doing so, they echoed Beane and Apple (1995: 11), who claimed that many school reforms have failed because "reformers fail to take into account the social [socio-economic] conditions surrounding the school. Only those reforms that recognize those conditions and actively engage them are likely to make a lasting difference on the lives of the children, educators, and communities served by the schools."

Unfortunately, in the area of education, empirical evidence often does not resolve conflict—especially conflict about student achievement—because even well-conducted studies are subject to multiple interpretations and most research does not address underlying and often competing assumptions about learning. As a result, studies that "prove" diametrically opposed positions are routinely marshaled by different sides in a debate. For example, we saw many instances of differing interpretations of student achievement data in the Bersin–Alvarado era. Most notable, the two evaluations of the *Blueprint for Student Success* conducted by the American Institutes for Research (AIR) (2002, 2003) were seen by reform supporters as evidence of growth in student achievement, whereas opponents of the reform used the same evaluations as evidence of too little growth to warrant the additional expense incurred.

Misunderstandings about the Meaning of a Key Concept Can Cause Confusion and Conflict

As we explained in Chapter 4, Superintendent Bersin pointed to the *Blueprint for Student Success* as encapsulating "our best thinking to date. It represents our belief system." We also discussed in that chapter an AIR (2002) survey that showed many teachers and principals did not feel included in the "our."

For these reasons, the *Blueprint for Student Success* sent a very mixed message about top leadership's commitment to shared leadership. Principals felt they had little or no say in the decisions that affected their schools, such as the elimination of classroom aides, and they were frustrated and sometimes resentful about being informed of major events only a heartbeat before they had to turn around and tell their teachers, parents, and community about how these latest developments would affect them. As the AIR (2002) report shows, even when the district did attempt to solicit teacher input, the efforts were seen as artificial and superficial gestures designed to pacify angry teachers.

Confusion about the meaning of the *Blueprint for Student Success* was also evident when Michael Fullan (2001b) addressed a principals' conference and commented that "this is a journey, not a blueprint." Principals in attendance felt that the interactive leadership process he referenced with his *journey* metaphor was decidedly absent from the SDCS, especially because the district leaders called the reform program the *Blueprint*. Blueprints are master plans and, in theory, they are meant to be followed exactly. In most situations, deviations from a blueprint require high-level approval, which in turn is issued only if a persuasive justification can be mustered. In the education setting, the expression *blueprint* carries an additionally charged meaning because of the long history of debate over the "right way" to teach, the "right way" to learn, and so forth. The expression the *Blueprint for Student Success* implies an end to debate, and the answer is in the blueprint—all that is needed now are willing workers to implement the plans. And the fact that these plans were drawn without consultation with the very people charged to implement them was viewed as implying a disregard for the expertise of those same people and the imposition of a "higher authority."

Assumptions often are hidden or are at least implicit. Some of the misunderstandings that plagued the SDCS could have been avoided if conscious efforts had been made to "unpack" underlying assumptions as carefully as possible, from the beginning. Even when the definition of a term such as *blueprint* is provided, people's unarticulated assumptions about its meaning may differ. And in those differences lie the seeds of many, many disagreements waiting to blossom into subversions.

Ambitious Reforms Lead to Unique Learning Challenges

Our analysis of the intersection encounters between ILs and principals (see Chapter 7), principals and teachers (see Chapter 6), and teachers and students (see Chapter 5) reveals that implementation of the San Diego reform required considerable learning on the part of adult professionals in the system. All were challenged to perform tasks for which they had had little or no prior experience, education, or training. Thus, during the early years of the reform, a major responsibility of "the system" was to support adult professionals' learning so they would be able to support the learning of others.

To enact the Balanced Literacy framework effectively, what teachers most needed was to understand the theory of how students learn to read and write and how to support that learning through the individualized and group processes recommended by the Balanced Literacy program. The good news from Chapter 5 is that the elementary school teachers appeared to be mastering the structural elements of Balanced Literacy quite well. Most elementary school classrooms in San Diego had the look and feel of a Balanced Literacy classroom. However, the enacted features, those that depend on deeper understandings of basic principles, were less consistently mastered. In particular, components that required teachers to base their instruction on *interactions* with children—guided reading and conferring—were the most difficult to enact well. The ongoing problems with these components were especially worrisome because the deeply interactive exchanges that occur between a teacher and student during an exemplary guided reading or conferring session also seem to present the most robust vehicle for deep learning. Done well, these sessions involve close listening, mutual respect and trust, and common space where each party understands the other and feels understood and where both work toward a common goal. All are essential elements for promoting the deep thinking that can advance individuals beyond their comfortable spheres of understanding.

Why were these kinds of interactions so difficult to do well? We argue that the San Diego teachers were unaccustomed to basing their instructional moves on an understanding of where students were in their learning and that they were uncomfortable with a form of teaching that involved guiding and scaffolding—as opposed to lecturing or directly imparting information. Among other things, interactive teaching involves knowing what you want students to accomplish, understanding the possible trajectories students can take to reach that end point, and then adjusting the type and level of the assistance you provide as students move along (or deviate from) those trajectories.

This is difficult work; it is work that most of today's teachers have not been trained to do. And it is work that cannot be guided by a script. We speculate that for teachers to successfully implement ambitious reforms like Balanced Literacy, they need support from more capable others who model the pedagogical approach they are expected to learn. We contend that teachers, like students, would benefit from a "gradual release of responsibility" approach. This approach would provide them with opportunities for closely examining the features of the framework and for practicing the tasks of gathering and analyzing data from students, designing instruction, and adjusting instruction as they implement the framework. In short, the San Diego teachers needed the assistance of knowledgeable experts as they grappled with this new form of instruction—and ideally that assistance would have been provided by school leaders who not only knew how to impart knowledge about the framework but also knew how to guide teachers in their halting attempts to apply that knowledge to their own practice.

We have shown that this was a tall order to fill. School leaders, too, needed to learn new roles. Moreover, the high demands associated with *teachers'* learning of the Balanced Literacy framework were recapitulated and intensified in *principals'* learning. Principals needed to fully understand the Balanced Literacy framework and be able to explain it to their teachers. They also needed to be ready and able to manage each teacher's application of newly learned knowledge about the framework to his or her classroom practice. This necessarily involved *interacting* with teachers one-on-one, figuring out what was working and not working, setting new goals that were tailored to teachers' individual needs, and providing appropriate assistance to help the teachers meet those goals. Like the interactive dimensions of guided reading and conferring, this kind of interaction draws on deep reserves of knowledge, occurs in the moment, and is not amenable to scripting.

Moving from plant managers to leaders of instruction constituted a severe break with standard operating procedures for the vast majority of principals. Although they learned to stand and deliver district messages and the main tenets of the Balanced Literacy framework, most principals had a more difficult time managing the application of knowledge and skills taught in faculty and grade-level meetings to teachers' practices. Guiding and shaping each teacher's uptake and translation of newly learned ideas into the classroom was challenging, in part, because standard operating procedures in most schools were devoid of even the expectation that professional development would change practice. As we noted in Chapter 7, teachers in most schools were accustomed to showing up at professional-development sessions, listening respectfully, taking part in the day's assigned activities, leaving, and then continuing to do what they had always done in their classrooms. Similarly, principals' frequent and unannounced observations of classroom practice constituted a major break with the routines of school life in most San Diego schools. The belief that professional development was supposed to change what teachers did in their classroom and the notion that principals should visit classrooms to see if teachers were indeed implementing the ideas learned in professional development went against the grain of established routines in most schools and violated most educators' traditional beliefs. As a result, it was exceedingly difficult to enact these new practices.

When the work of ILs is considered, the learning demands intensify to yet another level. ILs not only needed to learn the ins and outs of the Balanced Literacy framework and how to support teachers' enactment of it but also needed to become attuned to principals-as-learners, especially in their struggles to transition from plant managers to leaders of instruction. As we discussed in Chapter 7, ILs focused intensively on imparting knowledge (and passion) to their principals in their opening and closing addresses at the principals' conferences and on helping them apply their newly learned knowledge and skills at their school sites. Like the principals, ILs especially struggled with executing the latter responsibility. In particular, they had difficulty assisting school leaders as they tried to learn how to focus on more substantive aspects of instruction during walk-throughs and how to group teachers for what Alvarado referred to as the "guided reading of leadership." ILs were figuring out these and other aspects of their job as they went along, sometimes—but not always—with Elaine Fink by their side.

The case of IL Donna Burns and Principal Cynthia Oliver we discussed in Chapter 7 illustrates why, at this layer of the system, "figuring it out together" is a worthy alternative to knowing all the answers and simply telling principals what to do. Burns entered the relationship knowing more than Oliver about certain aspects of the district reform. However, she did not know Oliver's trajectory as a learner or did she have detailed knowledge of Oliver's school. Burns claims to have shifted within the first year of their relationship from modeling "the way to do it" to an approach based on questioning. Because she realized she did not have all the answers, and because she was confident regarding the knowledge she did have, Burns felt secure enough to embark on a joint learning enterprise with Oliver. Together, they figured out the best ways to approach the professional development of Oliver's teachers, including tailoring the timing of implementation of certain elements of the reform.

This dialogic approach to IL–principal intersection encounters contrasts sharply with the more didactic approaches we discussed in Chapters 6 and 7. This contrast demonstrates the greater potential for deep learning when interactions are composed of interpretation and meaning-making rather than being exercises in supplying the "right" answer to "known" questions. When didactic interaction dominated intersection encounters, the principals' learning was not generative but rather dependent on what ILs told principals to do. When dialogic interactions predominated, principals and ILs were continually solving problems together and inventing what the reform would look like in their schools in the process.

It is important to note, however, that the dialogic process was not left completely unconstrained. The Balanced Literacy framework was an important touchstone, as was the ILs' expertise. More specifically, the framework provided a set of boundaries within which meaning-making occurred. Using terms borrowed from sociocultural theories of learning, the Balanced Literacy framework provided guidelines for assessing teachers' "zones of proximal development" (Vygotsky, 1978), thereby helping the ILs to guide principals' learning in particular directions. At the same time, the Balanced Literacy framework never became a rigid script for pairs like Burns and Oliver, as it did for other ILs and principals. Their ability to work within it—but not become straitjacketed by it—suggests that the enactment of the reform was not always the one-size-fits-all approach that its critics accused it of being.

From the beginning, Alvarado and other top district leaders insisted that the reform was not about following a script. It was, instead, about learning to exercise professional judgment. Nevertheless, the reform appeared heavily scripted to most of the educators with whom we interacted. Why? We argue that the openings the Balanced Literacy framework afforded for authentic, interactive teaching and learning—openings that Burns and Oliver exploited—*were not visible* to most teachers or principals because these aspects of the framework represented an approach to instruction that was foreign to their standard ways of thinking about the teaching and learning process. Interpreted through the lens of "teaching what is in the book," these openings, and the opportunities they represented for professional decision making, were indiscernible. Hence, they could not be used productively. On the other hand, the more superficial, structural parts of the Balanced Literacy framework *were* readily discernible to all. It was these elements that were attended to and eventually resented.

What would it have taken for San Diego educators to learn how to productively use these openings for authentic, professionally grounded teaching and learning? Like other ambitious, theory-driven reforms, the Balanced Literacy program requires not only that users understand its undergirding theory but also that they be provided ongoing opportunities to learn the nuances of its enactment gradually, over time, and in interaction with more capable others. Communities of learners, not isolated learners, are ideal for fostering such development. Although top district leaders offered stirring rhetoric about establishing communities of learners, such cohesive groups cannot be created by decree. Encouraging the development of new communities that resist the pull of standard operating procedures and that have the capacity to assist the learning of their members is inordinately difficult. To complicate matters, the SDCS leaders were not building a new community from the ground up. They were trying to convert an already existing community, one that included many members who actively advocated and enacted resistance to the reform.

At the time we concluded our study, ILs were beginning to systematically guide principals' development and principals were beginning to better identify problems in teachers' practice and guide instructional improvement. However, the organization as a whole lacked the resources necessary for taking teachers and principals to the next level of development. In New York City's Community School District #2, a variety of levels of expertise and stages of development were in evidence and thus were available for use as models. San Diego had no such variation. As we noted many times throughout this book, everyone was learning to implement the reform at the same time. Thus, within communities of teachers, principals, and ILs—and even between communities at different layers of the system—there was often no asymmetry of expertise. Few educators anywhere in the system could learn from others because everyone was at the same or nearly the same stage of learning. Under such conditions, it was extremely difficulty to sustain deep interaction around a set of new and challenging ideas.

As a result, most educators did what learners have always done: they interpreted the new reforms within their existing frames of understanding. Those frames were, by and large, traditional in that they viewed teaching and learning from a knowledge-transmission perspective (Kohlberg & Mayer, 1972), in which teachers delivered information to learners rather than actively constructing and making sense of their environment with their students. Within this knowledge-transmission frame, the Balanced Literacy framework came across as a set of directives for *what teachers should do,* not as a theoretically grounded set of ideas about how to assist *the learning of students.*

Finally educators at all levels of the system seemed to be anxious about evaluation. ILs were anxious about how Fink and Alvarado would perceive their work. Principals were anxious about how the ILs would perceive their attempts to lead with an "edge." Teachers were anxious about how principals would perceive their attempts to implement the Balanced Literacy framework with their students. With evaluation dominating the picture, many educators became even more focused on "doing it right" rather than on the process of learning. As noted earlier, creating interactive and dialogic forms of teaching and learning between school leaders and teachers involves close listening, mutual respect and trust, common grounds on which to develop shared understanding, and mutually held goals. We saw over and over again how the establishment of such conditions was hampered by anxieties surrounding the evaluation of practice.

Incremental and Decentralized Initiatives Promise Both Possibilities and Limitations

The incremental and decentralized approach to reform currently being implemented in the SDCS has obvious political advantages. Encouraging school-site decision making and appealing to teacher autonomy neutralizes the complaints levied against Alvarado's more centralized approach (e.g., that it forced compliance, showed little respect for teacher knowledge, and stifled creativity).

Connecting site-specific and context-sensitive constructions with overarching guiding principles has proved to be a difficult endeavor in the history of educational reform, however, as shown by recent research on the lapse in attempts to detrack curriculum (Yonezawa, Wells, & Serna, 2002) and in attempts to establish democratic schools (Muncey & McQuillan, 1996). Guiding principles are often discarded or overtaken by practicalities at the school site, resulting in a superficial wash of rhetoric across the system, with few if any substantial changes in educational practice.

A particular challenge facing the SDCS is to stay true to its commitment to improve the quality of instruction while converting large comprehensive schools into small responsive ones. In their exuberance to exercise their newfound autonomy, educators in redesign schools may inadvertently allow themselves to become entangled in the trivialities of structural change—such as the length of class periods, the size of the science labs, and the organization of "houses"—and thus will fail to devote the attention necessary to improve instruction. Similarly, in rising to the superintendent's challenge to "close the achievement gap," educators in challenge schools may become so caught up in meeting such instrumental goals as improving SAT scores and *Academic Performance Index* rankings by teaching to the test (Amrein & Berliner, 2002; Kohn, 2002; McNeill, 2002) that they will fail to meet the broader goals of education, such as preparing students for college or the world of work—and most important of all—developing a well-educated citizenry.

Unevenness is the complaint levied against incremental change of the sort the district is now deploying in its high schools. Even with a set of nonnegotiable principles, such as a commitment to instructional quality, personalization, and leadership, guiding the effort to meet common goals and standards, the fear is that "pockets of excellence" will develop and "pockets of failure" will persist. The incremental and decentralized approach to high school reform faces the challenge of ensuring that the newly awarded autonomy in practice produces an even achievement of quality.

A second concern with decentralized reform efforts is that they exacerbate inequity, which takes the form of the have and have-not phenomenon. When large comprehensive schools are redesigned into small schools, the more sophisticated ones deliberately develop an organizing intellectual theme (Kluver & Rosenstock, 2002; Meier, 1995). Schools with attractive themes often seduce creative teachers and draw exceptional students to their campuses. But what happens to other high schools in a district if they have not also developed attractive themes? Do only uninterested or uninspired teachers remain behind? Are the remaining schools composed of discarded or uninformed students? If so, then we will have a system of tracking across schools, with attentive students, mostly from middle- and upper-income families, attracted to theme schools and uninformed students or those without the cultural capital to take advantage of new opportunities—often low-income and underrepresented minority students—left behind in all-purpose schools. The actualization of that fear has been driving reformers toward the very type of systemic reform that the SDCS is now revising.

The new decentralized initiative unfolding in the SDCS faces the challenge of ensuring an even distribution of high-quality schools across the district to increase educational equity. This requires the district to develop a plan to transport its redesign ideas from the original quartet to all schools. Otherwise, this initiative, although politically sensitive and attractive to the teaching corps, may unwittingly exacerbate inequity in the form of separate but unequal schools.

Recommendations for Reform in Other Districts

We want our research findings to be useful beyond the local San Diego context. To that end, we offer some recommendations to stakeholders in other communities that are now engaged in systemic (districtwide) reform or that may be considering such sweeping change.

Adapt the Reform to Local Circumstances

Understandably, educators are often enticed to adopt reforms that have been successful elsewhere. Doing so, however, overlooks the complicated process of negotiation and collaboration that is needed to adapt and develop reforms that local constituencies support. As Alvarado (1998) said when first arriving in San Diego, "I don't think this is an issue of emulation. Every reform has to be built in the soil of its city." Or, as Fullan (1999: 64) observed, the results of reform efforts often "fail to be replicated because the wrong thing is being replicated—the reform itself, instead of the conditions that spawned its success." Healey and DeStefano (quoted in Stein & Gewirtzman, 2003: 10–11) reinforced these sentiments:

> People's educational aspirations, needs, and contexts differ from place to place. Accordingly, what works in one location won't necessarily work in another. And even in those instances where an "outside" innovation addresses some of the specific needs and aspirations of a particular location, its fate is still precarious, for unless there is widespread ownership of the innovation (a factor largely engendered through the development of local solutions), chances are that it will not become a permanent part of that location's educational landscape. Instead of replication of the reform itself, we contend that it is the *conditions which give rise to the reform in the first place* that should be replicated. (emphasis in original)

Educators in New York's District #2 perfected the Balanced Literacy approach to reading and writing instruction over an eight- to ten-year period, during which they consulted with a wide range of local, national, and international experts; tried out different approaches; and made mistakes, adjustments, and corrections. It is not the briskly efficient adoption of tidy curriculum packages but rather this *messy process* of problem posing, field-testing, and collaborative decision making that makes reform elements successful.

Not only do reforms differ from place to place, they also differ from time period to time period. What is understood as constituting the best approach to teaching and learning changes over time, as does consensus over what the appropriate goal of K–12 education is or should be. So, in emphasizing the process over the product, it is important to be sensitive to both the temporal and the spatial dimensions of context. A lesson to be learned from the SDCS experience is to avoid the temptation of adopting and applying ready-made reform packages. Adopting any reform package just because it has been used successfully in some other district is a mistake. Of course, we recognize that following this recommendation is difficult for new district leaders, because they so often face considerable pressure to achieve results immediately. Nevertheless, engaging in the messy process of negotiation and collaboration is strongly preferable to installing a package of reforms that are not institutionalized. A negotiated, collaborative reform may take longer, but it stands a greater chance of being accepted and institutionalized by key constituents and thus is more likely to be sustained through time.

Attend to the Technical, Cultural, and Political Dimensions of School Reform

A second and closely related policy recommendation for districts considering systemic reform concerns the relationship between the technical, cultural, and political dimensions of reform. Strategies for districtwide reform must be sensitive to the complexity of the local cultural and political context and the complexity of what teachers and others must learn to carry off reforms successfully. No matter how powerful the theory of action guiding instruction and learning, unless such matters as local relationships; teachers' beliefs about students' capabilities; constituents' beliefs about the meaning and purpose of schools; and existing habits, norms, and standard operating procedures are taken fully into account, the reform will not reach fruition. There is a world of difference between compliance with the rules of a particular solution and genuine support for its principles (cf. Datnow & Castellano, 2001).

This proviso regarding contextual complexity is not merely a recommendation to improve lines of communication, clarify the message, or co-opt constituents (as recommended by Hill & Celio, 1998, and Ouchi, 2003). If reform leaders believe that a reform can be implemented by *telling* teachers, parents, and other constituents about it in ever more elegant ways, then they are implicitly engaged in a top-down reform process. The San Diego experience illustrates vividly the limitations of unidirectional implementation models, especially when quickly trained leaders have little choice but to adopt didactic instructional formats. San Diego's experience also underscores the need for models that are more collaborative and dialogic.

Build Trust among Key Constituents and Employ Local Knowledge to Maintain Trust

A powerful finding from the research on effective classroom practices concerns the use of students' local "funds of knowledge" (Au & Jordan, 1981; González, Moll, & Amanti, 2005; Rosebery, Warren, & Conant, 1992; Tharp & Gallimore, 1988). Instead of imposing a curriculum that is foreign to students' life experiences, teachers appropriate and use students' grounded knowledge. Some teachers have successfully employed in their classroom lessons the language practices and interactional styles common in students' homes; others have tapped into the social networks that connect families even in the poorest neighborhoods to glean suggestions that have invigorated curriculum content.

Educators, like their students, possess funds of knowledge. It makes sense, therefore, for reformers to become familiar with and take advantage of the knowledge that educators in the local context possess to advance the reform. Incorporating local funds of knowledge into design strategies can facilitate the building of trust among those initiating reform measures and those who are expected to carry them out. These relationships of trust, in turn, provide a shared foundation from which to launch improvements to the reform.

Trust seems to be an essential, constituent feature of successful reform efforts (Bryk & Schneider, 2003). Because all reforms are messy, roll out past schedule, face unexpected obstacles, are attacked by critics, and are undermined by the most mundane of practical circumstances, large reserves of goodwill, cooperation, and assent to participate among all concerned are essential. The building of trust can reduce the risk of hostility and the resistance it triggers—the withholding of assent to cooperate and participate in reform activities. But the absence of trust, or the failure to build and sustain it, can doom even the most thoughtful and carefully planned curricular reform.

Be Prepared: Build Capacity First

The leadership of the SDCS decided early on that it needed to implement the reform as quickly as possible. As we explained in Chapter 4 and have discussed elsewhere (Stein, Hubbard, & Mehan, 2003), one rationale provided for speed was moral: the fear that yet another generation of students would be left behind if reform strategies were implemented slowly or piecemeal. Another, and equally salient, rationale was political: the fear that the support of the business community that helped install the leadership would wither unless results, in the form of students' enhanced academic performance, were demonstrated quickly.

The push for a speedy implementation, coupled with the very large size of the district, strained the district's capacity to develop the leadership needed at all levels of the system. Leaders—including the building administrators, the former area superintendents, and the new peer coaches—had their roles redefined from operational to instructional in the earliest days of the reform. But the preparation for these new roles was not provided in advance; new leaders were not inducted into the theory supporting the reform or coached on recommended procedures for translating theory into practice in advance of accepting these new responsibilities. Instead, incumbents in these new positions had to learn their new responsibilities on the job, or, to use an expression that circulated in the district, leaders were "learning to fly the plane while building it."[1]

The district's efforts to build capacity, however, were hampered by the lack of capacity. ILs came with a variety of background experiences that prepared some more fully than others to accomplish their newly assigned tasks. ILs needed more training in the Balanced Literacy framework and in best-practice approaches to teaching adults, and they needed this training earlier on, before being expected to teach the principals in their learning communities. Similarly, principals came to their jobs with a variety of knowledge levels and backgrounds in leadership, a preexisting condition that demanded ILs be attentive to scaffolding knowledge in ways that would lead to independent leadership on the part of the principals.

In addition, rapid promotions drained leadership capacity at various levels within the system. Leaders who had demonstrated their expertise in one position often were promoted quickly to another. Examples include middle school principals who were promoted to high school principals one year and then promoted to ILs the next year, and classroom teachers who were promoted to peer coach positions soon after they had become effective in the classroom and then enrolled two years later in the Educational Leadership Development Academy principal apprenticeship program.

The absence of prior preparation, coupled with the rapid movement of personnel through the system as soon as they gained expertise in their current positions, created a capacity vacuum. This lack of prepared leadership was visible in many domains within the system. For example, peer coaches did not always know how to assist classroom teachers in solving instructional problems in the classroom, and principals and ILs tended to look at superficial artifacts of the reform during walk-throughs instead of focusing on the nuances of instruction.

We urge an incremental approach, because the costs of clumsy implementation and the ill-will that develops when underprepared coaches or allegedly "more capable peers" are unable to assist learners in need are not offset by the political benefits that accrue when leaders are able to proclaim, "We are reforming the entire district, and we are doing so now." Support for this recommendation comes from what might appear to be an unlikely source—Tony Alvarado. In his last interview with us, speaking with the benefit of knowledge gained in hindsight about the full extent of the political heat that his reforms generated within the system, Alvarado said that he would temper his enthusiasm for a comprehensive reform if he had the opportunity to begin again in San Diego. Instead of trying to improve all schools at the same time, he would start with the lowest performing schools because "there's a lot less power politics" there (Alvarado, 2003)—meaning that these schools lack the middle-class parents who frequently object both vocally and vigorously to changes in their schools and have in their place parents who welcome improvements to the often marginalized schools their children attend. Then, Alvarado continued, after successfully adapting his reforms to the local context and obtaining measurable results, he would expand his efforts to other schools.

Building capacity, whether systemically or incrementally, demands rigorous professional development for all concerned. Professional development cannot simply focus on teachers. It must be oriented to raise the skills, dispositions, and knowledge of school-site leaders and middle managers (whether they are called ILs or assistant superintendents) as well. Principals are primarily responsible for leading change because change ultimately occurs in schools and classrooms. Leading teachers to improve instruction requires that principals learn the reform strategies that support their work. Similarly, because the SDCS reform demanded that ILs teach, demonstrate, and model processes that supported the Balanced Literacy framework, these leaders needed to learn quickly but deeply if they were to be able to guide their learning communities toward achieving reform goals. Districts undergoing reform—whether organized systemically or incrementally—would be well advised to follow San Diego's lead and provide professional development not only for teachers but also for principals and middle managers, especially when they are asked to take on the role of leaders of instruction.

Finally, to institutionalize change it is critically important that all educators—but especially principals—develop a shared understanding, because this is what provides coherence and avoids fragmentation. Principals especially need to be supported in learning how to construct a community of learners and how to teach adult learners in a way that will support change. Reculturing a school or district requires that everyone share the same values and speak the same language. To achieve that shared cultural understanding, the district must foster the kind of dialogue that enables thinking in ways that might challenge the status quo. Otherwise, passive conformity can become a problem not only for the individuals involved but also for the reform. When individuals are not encouraged to think deeply and challenge principles and practices, they are unequipped to deal with the teaching and learning needs at their sites.

Challenges to a Learning Perspective Posed by the San Diego Reform

Our study of the San Diego reform presents significant opportunities to expand on the idea that policy implementation is a problem of learning. Most of the research that has focused on policy implementation as a problem of learning focused on *teacher* learning. The task of reform in San Diego, however, went significantly beyond increasing teacher learning. The goal was to *transform the entire system* so it could support teachers' learning of complex forms of instructional practice, such as Balanced Literacy.

Learning was required not only of teachers but also of *principals, ILs, peer coaches, and district leaders*. Principals needed to understand the new practices in a deep, theory-based way to provide support for teacher learning and hold teachers accountable for the intent of the reform, not superficial aspects of its enactment. ILs needed to understand the new practices deeply enough not only to judge the quality of enactment in classrooms but also to assist principals to lead the reform in their buildings. Peer coaches needed to understand how to provide the right amount and kind of assistance to help teachers learn how to support students in meaningful and effective ways in their classrooms. Finally, district leaders needed to learn to inspire their educators to activate the reform, persuade valued constituents to support the reform, secure supplemental funding, and listen to suggestions for improvement. Thus, the San Diego reforms challenge us to conceptualize implementation as a problem of learning for *all* of the educators in the system. *Everyone* was learning to do something new.

This inevitably raises questions about the range and depth of the knowledge base needed by those in leadership positions. Although Fink contended that what principals and ILs most needed to know was how to *lead,* she conceded that leading was difficult for those who lacked an understanding of good classroom practice in literacy. We agree. Moreover, we contend that leaders also need to possess an understanding of their learners—that is, what they do and do not know about the to-be-learned subject; how they learn, including typical pathways they might traverse as they learn various subjects; and what methods have proved useful in supporting learners' movement along those pathways. Understanding learners and the "learning to read" process is necessary for teachers to successfully enact the Balanced Literacy framework. Likewise, understanding teachers-as-learners and the "learning to teach" process is necessary for principals to successfully lead reform in their buildings. And understanding principals-as-learners and the "learning to lead" process is necessary for ILs to successfully lead reform in their learning communities.

With the exception of Spillane's (2000) work, research on learning in reform contexts has not attended to leaders' knowledge of teachers (or principals) as learners. Spillane showed that administrators typically hold behavioristic views of teacher learning; that is, they expect teachers will learn new ideas by first being told what to do and then receiving appropriate rewards and punishments (Spillane, 2000). We witnessed this behavioristic approach in San Diego. This suggests that future studies of district reform should attend to the type and kind of knowledge that leaders have about teacher (and principal) learning and how leaders use that knowledge when they design professional-learning opportunities.

The San Diego reforms challenge learning-oriented conceptions of reform implementation in additional ways. Implicit in many learning theories is the assumption that learning is primarily one way; that is, teachers teach students, principals teach teachers, ILs teach principals, and so on. Given what we know from co-constructed theories of reform, and from our study of the San Diego experience, where actors on the ground were just as apt to transform as to enact reform goals, we propose that learning perspectives on reform more consciously address the multidirectional nature of learning. How might those in leadership positions benefit from listening to and incorporating the ideas of teachers and others who enact the reform on a day-to-day basis with students? How might this "upward learning" be captured in our theories of learning?

The notion of multidirectional learning raises another issue. How much and what kind of modification to the intended reform by on-the-ground actors should be considered as an instance of learning, as opposed to subverting, reverting to standard operating procedures, or lacking capacity? Not all transformations represent progress in terms of creating more generative learning environments for students. It might be possible to measure progress toward an agreed-on end point of desired professional practice as an instance of learning. However, in the field of education, there is rarely an agreed-on vision of an end point that constitutes competent professional practice. (Our description in Chapter 7 of educators' doubts about the efficacy of the Balanced Literacy approach reveals some of the serious consequences of this lack of consensus in the field.) One way to address the dilemma posed by disparate understandings of ideal professional practice is to assess progress toward leaders' visions of desired end-states and movement beyond those visions toward more individualistic, yet competent, forms of instruction. Toward this end, Stein and D'Amico (2002a) proposed a developmental pathway of learning from mechanical to canonical enactments of an innovation, supplemented by more innovative, but still professionally grounded, forms of professional practice.

The San Diego reforms present one final challenge to theories of implementation-as-learning: for educators' learning to result in a unified approach to teaching and learning across the system, it had to be coordinated in some way across the various layers of the organization and across the types of educational professionals. Yet, given our conception of schools as social organizations and policy as being socially constructed, we know that educators cannot be expected to passively respond to district mandates. Command and control from the top cannot be expected to lead to coordinated action on the ground. Organizational theories contend that individuals interpret directives based on normal forms, routines, and standard operating procedures; sociocultural theories of learning suggest that the meanings of directives are negotiated in "communities of practice"—informal groups of individuals that mutually engage in locally defined, joint enterprises and that share a repertoire of practice (Wenger, 1998). Achieving districtwide synchrony in the implementation of reform thus entails orchestrating the learning of multiple communities of practice (Coburn & Stein, in press).

In our study of the San Diego reform, we examined the results of that attempted orchestration by focusing on the learning that occurred between layers of the system and on the conditions under which that learning unfolded. We found that the learning at these intersection encounters was often problematic. Generally, learners were neither enabled nor encouraged to participate in sense-making around the reform, suggesting that district leaders did not anticipate and design for mechanisms that would meaningfully connect communities in different layers of the system and manage their boundaries in ways that would create opportunities for deep learning. By focusing on intersection encounters, we took the risk of adopting a novel analytic unit—one straddles that two realms: organizational structure and individual agency. We chose to focus our investigation on these sites because we believe they are where meanings were negotiated and actions undertaken and interpreted. Exploring the connections and disconnections that occurred between different layers of the SDCS system provided insights that go beyond the particulars of the San Diego reform, however. Our approach also sheds light on challenges and opportunities for learning within the broader context of organizational change.

Organizational Learning

The idea that reform entails learning is powerful. The power of this perspective is enhanced when we explicitly consider learning in the context of social organizations. This, in turn, requires us to consider what it means to say "an organization learns." Developing and using a language of organizational learning requires us to consider what counts as an organization and what counts as learning. In doing so, we must be careful not to reify the notion of organization and to talk about an organization as "knowing something" or "learning something." It is important to specify where in the organization particular knowledge is stored, who has access to it, and who has learned it.

What Counts as an Organization

The conventional definitions of organizations can be arrayed on a continuum from individual to collective. Anchoring the individual end of that continuum is "a relatively common assumption in the research literature … that organizations learn like individuals—through a cognitive process" (Hanson, 2001: 640). That is, organizational learning is not distinct from individuals' learning. Organizations also have been defined as being composed of semiautonomous although somewhat interrelated entities, such as units or departments. The organization becomes the sum of the actions of these individuals or organizational units. At the collective end of the continuum, organizations have been defined as a reality *sui generis*. As an emergent phenomenon, an organization is not reducible to its individual parts—be they entities (such as departments or units within the organization) or all the individuals working within the organization. Expressing this idea in the language of cognitive science, organizations are distributed information processing systems (Hutchins, 1990, 1991). The basic idea is that knowledge in very large networks (organizations) resides in patterns of connections between individuals not in individual minds or actions.

These conceptions of organizations face daunting ontological problems. The definition of an organization as the sum of actions taken by a collection of individuals faces the problems associated with the flaws in comprehensive rationality. The facts of a *system* cannot be expressed as the sum of the actions of individuals because engaging in any particular action would require each actor to envision the possibility of the system in its entirety (Weick & Roberts, 1993). The collective definition of organization faces the problem of reification. The reification of social entities is avoided by saying they emerge from individual actions that construct interrelations. Hutchins (1991: 38), when describing how a group of sailors distributed across a damaged ship managed to bring it safely into harbor, captured this sentiment exactly: "While the participants may have represented and thus learned the solution after it came into being, the solution was clearly discovered by the organization itself before it was discovered by any of its participants."

What Counts as Learning in Organizations
Determinations of what counts as learning in organizations have paralleled determinations of what counts as an organization. The issue boils down to concluding that the results of organizational learning are either stored in the minds of individual organizational members or stored in the relations among organizational members.

Simon (1991) summarized the position that attributes learning to individuals: "All learning takes place inside individual human heads," he pronounced, although he conceded that "individual learning in organizations is very much a social not a solitary phenomenon" (Simon, 1991: 129). At the opposite end of the continuum, Weick and Roberts (1993) and Hutchins (1990, 1991) contended that organizational learning develops between people but is not located in any one individual's mind or memory. According to these theorists, organizational learning is not like individual learning. It is not a cognitive activity, because, at the very least, organizations do not possess what people possess and use in knowing and learning—that is, actual bodies, perceptive organs, and brains (Hanson, 2001). Moreover, schools and other organizations develop institutional cultures—which include a set of values, beliefs, and feelings; shared artifacts; and ways of talking and acting. Organizations learn through social and cultural processes. These entail the enactment of routines and the development of values, beliefs, understandings (such as myths, symbols, and metaphors), and rituals that are created, inherited, shared, and transmitted.

Staking out an intermediary position on organizational learning between the individual and the collective conceptions, Huber (1991) asserted that an entity learns if, through the processing of information, the range of its potential behaviors is changed. Huber's definition holds whether the "entity" is a human or other animal, a group, an organization, a unit within an organization, or even a society. With respect to organizational learning, he assumes that an organization learns if any of its units acquires knowledge that it recognizes as potentially useful to the organization. This implies three other components—the distribution of the new information throughout the organization, the interpretation of the information by other units within the organization (where interpretation is defined as the process by which information is given meaning), and the encoding or storing of the information in the organization's artifacts or memory (e.g., in regulations, rules, procedures, guidebooks, and instruction manuals).

Huber's specification of the components of organizational learning is indeed helpful. Nevertheless, questions remain. For example, how many units within an organization must be engaged before we can say an entire organization has learned? Do the interpretations of new information have to be similar? Or can they be different? Do *all* organizational units have to develop a common understanding? Or can different units develop different interpretations—thus increasing the range of new actions and practices? Within the SDCS organization, teachers, ILs, and principals seem to be equivalent to Huber's "units." So, when do we say the SDCS *system* has learned? When *all* of these units have adopted the new practices associated with the reform? Or is a subset of the total number of units all that is necessary to make a claim about organizational learning? And not all organizational units are uniform; that is, not all teachers within the district are similar in their enactment of the reform—a fact that makes it difficult to claim that an entire unit or a department has learned.

Then there is the issue of the role of intentionality in organizational learning. Must some entity within the organization start the process *on purpose*? In the case of the comprehensive school reform designs (Datnow, Hubbard, & Mehan, 2002) and special education laws (Mehan, Meihls, Hertweck, & Crowdes, 1986), we certainly had active, intentional agents initiating reform. But in other circumstances, organizational learning is accidental or unintentional. Perrow's (1999) analysis of nuclear power plant workers' response to an accident at Three Mile Island, Vaughan's (1996) account of the Challenger spacecraft failure, and Hutchins's (1991) rich description of sailors' response to a near-catastrophic breakdown of a shipboard electrical system are clear examples of unplanned organizational learning.

Implications of a Learning Perspective for Our Study

In our study, the relational sense of organization best represents the way in which a complex activity such as school reform plays out on the ground. An organization such as the SDCS district does not reside in individuals taken separately, even though each individual contributes to it, or does an organization such as the SDCS reside independently of the actions of individuals within it. Instead, an organization such as the SDCS is present in the interrelations between the activities of individuals.

We conclude learning in organizations is something that happens between people when they engage in common activities. An activity-based conception of organizational learning focuses attention simultaneously on individuals and the collective. Only individuals can contribute to an organization's learning; however, an organization's learning is distinct from an individual's learning because it inheres in the interrelated activities of many people, not in the heads of solitary people. Learning occurs when individuals bring varying perspectives and levels of expertise to the work before them. As individuals work toward shared goals, they together create new forms of meaning and understanding. These new meanings and understandings do not exist as abstract structures in individual participants' minds but derive from and create the situated practice in which individuals are coparticipants.

Adopting a sociocultural perspective on learning channels attention away from analysis of the cognitive attributes and practices of individuals and toward the interactions that occur among individuals as they attempt to develop and improve their practice. This realization led us to look for organizational learning in the intersection encounters between organizational units rather than in any one organizational unit or department in isolation. With intersection encounters as the unit of our analysis, we were able to look at how the ideas or plans espoused by the design team traversed the system. We define learning as ways in which communities of individuals gradually transform their practices over time as they engage with one another and respond to changing conditions in their environment. We say "the organization has learned" when new information has been instantiated in new practices, is made available within nested points in the system, and is encoded in organizational artifacts (such as instruction manuals, code books, or organizational charts) (cf. Huber, 1991).

Treating organizational learning in this way deemphasizes the attention given to choice in the rational models of action we discussed in chapter 1. Building on Mead (1934: 186), who said that mind is "the individual importation of social process," we propose that organizational learning begins with *actions*. Choice becomes one of many learned forms of organizational action, and rational choice becomes one learned form of choice (Cohen & Sproull, 1996).

The learning perspective also places organizational stability in a new light. In contrast to the rationalist assumption deeply embedded within traditional organizational theory that equilibrium is a natural, generally beneficial state that is sometimes temporarily disturbed, a learning perspective suggests that stability may be uncommon, hard won, and not always beneficial. Organizations may have entire ecologies of learning systems in which learning appears in many places and at many levels. In such systems, learning at one level or site may cause change that destabilizes others in the system who are also learning (Sarason, 1997).

Our Contribution to Organizational Theory and Research

Our study of the San Diego reform as a problem of learning also presents opportunities to reflect on organizational theory and research. Researchers' conceptions of organizations and how they work have shifted considerably from the time Weber (1947/1964) first called our attention to them. Organizations conceived as open systems interacting with their external and internal environments (Katz & Kahn, 1966) replaced rationalist conceptions of organizations composed of actors either making comprehensive calculations (Allison, 1971; Parsons, 1932) of means–ends relations or making bounded calculations (Simon, 1949) of means–ends relations. Open systems models portrayed organizations as receiving "inputs" and producing "outputs," often based on "feedback" from their surrounding environments. Applied to education, open systems models held that schools obtained inputs from the surrounding environment in the form of funding, teachers, and curriculum materials and produced outputs in the form of students prepared for higher education or the workplace. In studies based on open systems models, organizations such as schools were depicted as nimbly changing to establish efficient exchanges with other organizations.

New institutional theory radically altered that "loosely coupled" (Weick, 1976) conception of organizations. No longer were organizations viewed as changing to produce effective outcomes. Instead, new institutional theory focused on the constraints in the "field" of organizations that maintained their inertia (DiMaggio & Powell, 1991; Meyer & Rowan, 1977; Meyer & Scott, 1983). Constraints on schools and school districts emanated from such sources in the educational field as "the state," "the market," "the church," "the courts," and families (DiMaggio & Powell, 1991: 64–65).

The new institutionalism has contributed significantly to our understanding of organizations by accentuating the external forces that constrain the actions of organizational members. Unfortunately, though, the new institutional theorists' eagerness to establish the conditions constraining action in organizational environments leads them to downplay the importance of beliefs, values, and actions of people in the local context. This tendency can make organizations into reified abstractions detached from the social interaction that constitutes them (Barley & Tolbert, 1997: 95). To be sure, external macroforces *shape* organizations, but social organizations *are shaped by* social interaction within them (Datnow, Hubbard, & Mehan, 2002).

Institutional theory describes well the pressures and forces that reinforce stability and inertia but tends not to accent the fluidity of action or the contingent nature of struggles over organizational change (Aldrich, 2000). When new institutional theorists *do* emphasize the importance of human agency in shaping stability and change, it is the agency of the design team, not the agency of the educators "on the ground" or interactions between them, that they emphasize.

Organizations are not static, lifeless systems that respond only passively to external and constraining forces. Organizations are populated by people who collaborate with each other, argue with each other, console each other, even undercut each other. In contradistinction to new institutionalism's treatment of organizations as macroenvironments, we offer a more nuanced approach that trains attention on both the whole and its parts. Our rich field observations remind us that institutions such as schools and school districts are inhabited by vibrant people interacting across many venues (cf. Erickson, 2004; Erickson & Schultz, 1982; Hallet & Ventresca, in press; McDermott & Varenne, 1993; Mehan, 1992; Varenne & McDermott, 1998). Social organizations do not exist apart from the participants in them; it is people's interactions that compose the culture and structure of organizations.

To understand the organizational life of the SDCS, we shifted our theoretical lens to include actions on the ground, describing just how personnel distributed throughout the SDCS social system reacted to pressures exerted on them by actors in the educational field. Some of these actors resided inside the school system, such as teachers, principals, and ILs; others resided in the broader community, such as opinion leaders, business leaders, and granting agencies. Thus, we implore researchers to attend to the interactions within organizations that shape their culture and structure and to attend to the wider systems of meanings that shape those local interactions. Actions emanating from outside the immediate organizational context certainly *do* matter for people interacting within organizations. In San Diego, actions taken by the business leaders and opinion leaders who provided early support for the reform and actions initiated by members of the philanthropic organizations who provided grant opportunities to enhance the reform were highly influential.

Our study of school reform reinforces constructionist theorizing about social organizations. Educators—design team members, teachers, and principals—are not compliant actors, passively responding to directives mandated from higher levels of bureaucracies. Instead, they are active agents, making policy in their everyday actions. In concrete educational encounters, educators may act in a variety of ways in response to reform directives—conforming to them, initiating alternatives, resisting them, or actively subverting them. Most important, the agency of educators is part of a complex dynamic, *shaping* and *shaped by* the structural and cultural features of school and society.

To be more specific, educators on the ground helped to form the contours of the San Diego reforms. Educators located throughout the system modified the reform features designed by Bersin and Alvarado in various ways to fit their interpretation of sociopolitical and cultural factors, their local needs and practical circumstances, and their own ideologies. In some cases, reform features were enhanced. In other cases, reform features were constricted. And just as classrooms and schools changed during the period of this study, the design team also changed its plans—from a comprehensive, centralized, and fast-paced effort to a more differentiated, decentralized, and slower-paced effort.

We conclude that the SDCS has made significant organizational changes in response to powerful political forces, unplanned fiscal constraints, and organizational cultural conflict. That conclusion puts us at odds with the conclusions in Hess (2005). The contributors to that volume present the centralized, comprehensive, fast-paced reform as the first phase and the differentiated, decentralized, slower-paced reform as the second phase of an evolutionary process. That analysis makes it seem that district leaders had the shift from a centralized to a decentralized reform in mind from the outset. Privileging the agency of the district leaders over the agency of the social actors (such as teachers, principals, newspaper editorial writers) in other social contexts (such as the schools, government agencies, business boardrooms) trivializes the cultural clashes and political squabbles we have described throughout this book.

Our fine-grained observations, which complement the findings of other studies, lead us to formulate social policy as a conditional process unfolding in social organizations. That is, we conclude that public policy is generated in face-to-face interactions among real people, confronting real problems in concrete social contexts, such as classrooms, school board meetings, courts of law, and state legislatures. Because these contexts are inevitably connected to others (Sarason, 1997), contexts *throughout* the public policy system should be studied. It has been difficult for researchers to live up to this injunction, though. In most research on public policy, the interaction among social actors in one context is spotlighted and, of necessity, interaction in other contexts is relegated to the background. But a more complete analysis requires that we identify and describe the interconnections among contexts throughout the social system.

We also believe it is important to pay attention to the role of power and perspective when studying social organizations. To avoid the error of treating organizations as monolithic actors—and the attendant erroneous assumption that all participants share the same values, goals, and strategies—we detailed the point of view of actors located in different spaces within the organization. Doing so revealed that actors differently situated had different orientations to organizational goals and different understandings of the reform and the change process it entailed. That is, they experienced the reform differently. Indeed, our analysis reveals that many of the actors in the educational field that was San Diego at the start of the reform in 1998 did not share the same sense of urgency about the need for reform that drove the superintendent and chancellor of instruction to try to completely reculture and restructure the district. This lack of shared understanding at the outset persisted throughout the four years of our study.

Moreover, this lack of shared understanding was exacerbated by power dynamics. To put the issue of power simply, we say the educators in San Diego's schools *had* to respond to decisions made by actors who had the institutional power and authority to direct actions. Many educators resisted the reforms—even, ironically, when they thought the changes would be beneficial to student learning—because they viewed the new practices as rigidly imposed mandates. As a result of the institutional distribution and application of power, the meaning of the reform design was not commonly shared. The result was a lack of understanding, widespread disagreement, and many conflicts over the meaning of actions and events and practices prescribed by the *Blueprint*. On occasions when consensus was reached, it did not happen automatically. Consensus must always be achieved; it cannot be decreed. It is the result of negotiation and often of strife. Thus, consensus is always fragile, always subject to revision, and always vulnerable to disintegration.

To conclude, we maintain that bringing a rich set of data into the conversation on school reform produces a more complex and nuanced understanding of the school and school district as a social organization.

Furthermore, careful ethnography of reform on the ground makes clear that the interplay between organizational culture, social structural constraints, and human agency should replace the simplistic micro–macro dualism that so often dominates studies of social organizations, school reform, and student learning.

Notes

Chapter 1

1. One high school, one middle school, and one elementary school in the midcity section of San Diego were exempted from the dictates of the reform. See Chapter 8 for details.

2. This diagram is adapted from Teachers' Professional Development, a chapter of *Recommendations Regarding Research Priorities: An Advisory Report to the National Education Research Policy and Priorities Board* by Brown et al. (1999). The Professional Development Subcommittee that produced the original figure was chaired by M. Lampert.

Chapter 2

1. These and other professional development events are discussed in Chapters 4, 6, and 7.

2. The elementary school names are pseudonymes.

3. The high school names are pseudonymes.

4. URM refers to underrepresented minority students.

5. If information that emerged in those settings seemed to be privileged, we waited until official reports or documents were made public before using the information in our analysis.

6. IL = instructional leader.

Chapter 3

1. We have not looked deeply into the two system's methods for classifying students as proficient or nonproficient in English. Therefore, the reader is asked to interpret this comparison with caution.

2. Until 2003, New York City students left their K–8 community school districts to attend one of several comprehensive high schools. Although District #2 sponsored a few alternative high schools, the percentage of students who attended these small high schools was very small. District #2 buildings were organized primarily as pre-K or K–5 schools; there were a small number of K–8 schools, and approximately a dozen "intermediate" (grades six through eight) schools. Also a small number of "option" schools existed (director-managed schools with specific philosophical, thematic, and curricular commitments, often with a mandate for ethnically, socioeconomically, and gender-balanced populations).

3. Our research design did not permit us to make causal statements that the district's support led to consistent classroom implementation and that such implementation led to improved student learning, but both quantitative and qualitative studies (cited previously) suggest that to be the case. See also *High Performance Learning Communities Project: Final Report* (Stein, D'Amico, & Resnick, 2001).

4. The most common statistic cited for the District #2's improvement under Anthony Alvarado is the improvement of their rank among the thirty-two community school districts from eleventh to second during the time period of 1987 (the year Alvarado took over) to 1996 (when the High Performance Learning Communities [HPLC] project began). This measurement is for the average percentage of students scoring at or above grade level on the New York City version of the national standardized *Comprehensive Test of Basic Skills* achievement test in reading (grades three through eight). Although skeptics have pointed to the lower-than-average poverty rates enjoyed by District #2 compared to the other community school districts (only three other community school districts had fewer students eligible for free and reduced-priced lunch), this cannot explain the rise in scores over the time period of Alvarado's tenure (the poverty rate measured as such remained relatively constant during his tenure). Moreover, our analysis suggested that the rise in the number of students at or above grade levels was not due strictly to the district making just enough improvements to shift students near to that level up a notch. The proportion of students in the first (lowest) quartile also dropped. Finally, the HPLC project produced evidence suggesting that the Balanced Literacy program in conjunction with high-quality professional development may have been the factors that helped teachers to improve student learning and break down the barriers that impoverished students often face (see HPLC final report [Stein, D'Amico, & Resnick, 2001: 27–38] for details).

5. Because the vast majority of the district's teachers were female, we elected to use the feminine pronoun throughout.

6. The Educational Leadership Development Academy is a district collaborative project with a consortium of local universities and other agencies in San Diego that provides support and professional development for San Diego's leaders. See Chapter 6 for details.

Chapter 5

1. A Word Wall is an organized collection of words, usually displayed in large letters on a classroom wall. The list is a tool that supports reading and writing, in part by providing students with a visual reminder of certain words and general principles about words and their roles.

2. In elementary schools, the daily literacy block occupied a three-hour time slot. In secondary schools, students who scored in the third quartile of the state standardized test in reading attended daily two-hour literacy block classes and students who scored in the lowest quartile attended literacy core classes for three hours each day; both literacy block and literacy core classes originally were called genre studies classes and now are generally referred to collectively as workshop classes. In this chapter, we refer to daily literacy instruction for all grade levels as "workshop."

3. During our data collection period (1998–2002), guided reading was heavily implemented at the elementary school level but was only beginning to reach San Diego City School high schools. Instead, high school teachers offered a variety of instructional activities loosely known as "small-group instruction." Some of these activities, when implemented by teachers who were familiar with the model, resembled guided reading, but they were not officially identified as such.

4. Guided reading was not implemented at the high school level during our data collection period (1998–2002), so our discussion of guided reading activities is limited to elementary school examples.

5. Because guided reading was not formally implemented in the high schools, we limit our discussion of deviations in this area to patterns observed at the elementary level. Our high school observations did include teachers who used small-group instruction to provide a bridge in the gradual release of responsibility model, as district leaders expected them to do. The leaders' expectation was that teachers of the high school workshop classes would purposefully select student groups, thread small-group activities with the rest of the workshop sections, and closely monitor and influence students' progress. In practice, small-group instruction was idiosyncratic. The most common pattern was for students to be told simply to "work together" to complete a task. The majority of high school teachers in our study seemed to have continued their preform uses of group work, once again demonstrating the strength of prior routines and knowledge. They often allowed students to choose their own groups and to use the time to complete a wide variety of activities. Rarely did teachers sit with students as they worked, and often the students' activities were unrelated to the rest of the workshop. It may be that the deviations we observed were related to the widely held conception of guided reading as specifically directed at helping students improve their reading skills. Many high school teachers did not view themselves as teachers of reading, and they avoided activities that appeared designed for that purpose.

Chapter 6

1. The district appointed two expert teachers—one elementary school level and one high school level—to be "lab teachers." The two taught (separately) in a demonstration classroom designed to allow teachers and peer coaches to observe their practice for professional-development purposes.

Chapter 7

1. Before Elaine Fink's arrival in San Diego, Fellows of the Institute for Learning of the Learning Research and Development Center at the University of Pittsburgh provided professional development for the instructional leaders (ILs). As noted in chapter 3, the ILs also traveled to schools in New York City's Community School District #2 to see the results of Anthony Alvarado's work and to learn from successful principals and administrators there.
2. The University of Pittsburgh's Institute for Learning, which introduced the walk-through to the San Diego Community Schools, has recently reconceptualized this professional-development tool as a "learning walk" and has stripped it of its evaluative components (Resnick & Fink, 2001).

Chapter 8

1. The forum's full report can be found at http://www.sandiegodialogue.org.
2. The American Evaluation Association (2002: 1) asserted, "High-stakes testing leads to under-serving or mis-serving all students, especially the most needy and vulnerable, thereby violating the principle of 'do no harm.'" The American Educational Research Association (2000: 1) based its position on the 1999 *Standards for Educational and Psychological Testing*: "Decisions that affect individual students' life chances or educational opportunities should not be made on the basis of test scores alone."
3. A comprehensive analysis of student achievement in SDCS *did* become available but only after this was written. Using student-based data, Betts et al. (2005), compared students' performance on state-mandated achievement tests from 1999–2002. They reported that *Blueprint* interventions shifted more than 10% of participating elementary school students and 4% of middle school students out of the bottom tenth of reading achievement into higher levels. However, *Blueprint* interventions were not successful with participating high school students. Their data also indicate that the SDCS reforms reduced the Hispanic–white achievement gap in reading by about 15% and reduced the black-white achievement gap by 12% in elementary school. The achievement gaps also declined in middle school but not as much: 2% for the Hispanic–white gap and 3% for the black–white gap. However, *Blueprint* participation seemed to mildly aggregate existing achievement gaps among high school students.
4. The reasons for the gap between income and expenditures were debated by politicians of opposing parties and by policy analysts, but all agreed that the

following factors contributed significantly. The "dot-com" bubble burst—the high-tech firms concentrated in the Bay Area's Silicon Valley laid off personnel, cut back production, and curtailed growth, which meant that the state collected considerably less in corporate income tax. The decision to deregulate the control of energy led to wildly inflated energy costs starting in 2001, which required an unanticipated state expenditure of $10 million on energy.

5. For example, the business-oriented *San Diego Union-Tribune* (2000) praised the superintendent's efforts: "Bersin's rookie year. School superintendent gets an A for tenacity" and "Schools chief merits four more years" ("Schools Chief Merits Four More Years," 2001).

6. Two other reports provided a more somber assessment: American Institutes for Research (2002) and San Diego Achievement Forum (2002). Although applauding gains in elementary school students' assessment, they called attention to limited achievement gains in upper elementary, middle, and high schools.

7. "John and Frances get so outrageous that they upset the rest of the board members including me. ... The only idea I have is to shoot the both of them. I was thinking of a way to get them both with one bullet!" (Muñoz, 2001: 1).

8. Elements of the Latino community were particularly vocal about the removal of Tony Alfaro as principal of San Diego High School in May 2001—a few weeks before graduation (tenBerge, 2001).

Chapter 9

1. Not all high schools were involved in this process. La Jolla High (as a pilot school), Hoover High (as a midcity community school), the Preuss School on the University of California, San Diego campus, and High Tech High (as charter schools) all were exempt.

2. The API is designed to measure academic performance and school growth on a scale that ranges from 200 to 1000, with a state goal that all schools reach at least 800. To demonstrate that progress, schools with scores lower than 800 had a goal of improving at least 5 percent of the difference between one year's score and the next. For schools with an index between 781 and 799, the annual growth-rate target is 1 percent. A school with a score of 800 or more must maintain at least that level. Note that none of the high schools in the San Diego City Schools were in the 800–1000 point range.

3. "Mentor principal" was a new position; incumbents are assigned to coach newly appointed principals.

4. Not all members of the previous board supported charter schools, either. Before her last term ended in 2004, trustee Frances O'Neill Zimmerman accused charter school supporters of undermining the very foundation of public education, suggesting that the superintendent and the board were betraying public schools in a manner akin to Jews collaborating with Nazis to exterminate their own people (Gao, 2004).

5. The preservation of the teaching core was assisted by the bulk retirement of principals and assistant principals. The teaching core was also preserved

because several of the highest-paid managers left the district through retirements or elimination of their positions or because they took other positions.

Chapter 10

1. We recall the comments of a new instructional leader at the very first principals' conference, one conducted by Tony Alvarado and Lauren Resnick of the University of Pittsburgh's Institute for Learning, in September 1998. The new instructional leader was meeting with the principals in her learning community in a breakout session. When a principal asked, "What's an instructional leader?" she replied, "I don't know, but we'll find out together."

References

Aldrich, H. (2000). *Organizations evolving.* Thousand Oaks, CA: Sage.

Allison, G. T. (1971). *Essence of decision: Explaining the Cuban missile crisis.* Boston: Little, Brown.

Alvarado, A. (1998, September 5). Interview with KPBS.

Alvarado, A. (2001, January 14). Interview with Lea Hubbard, Hugh Mehan, and Mary Kay Stein.

Alvarado, A. (2002a, February 28). Address to principals' conference.

Alvarado, A. (2002b, April 15). Address to principals' conference.

Alvarado, A. (2003, January 29). Interview with Lea Hubbard, Hugh Mehan, and Mary Kay Stein.

Alvarado, A., & Fink, E. (2000, May 22). Interview with Mary Kay Stein, Lauren Resnick, Diane Burney, and Laura D'Amico.

American Educational Research Association. (2000). AERA position on high stakes testing. Retrieved from http://www.aera.net/about/policy/stakes.htm

American Educational Research Association, American Psychological Association, & National Council on Measurement in Education. (1999). *Standards for educational and psychological testing.* Washington, DC: American Educational Research Association.

American Evaluation Association. (2002). American Evaluation Association position statement on high stakes testing in prek-12 education. Retrieved from http://www.eval.org/hst3.htm

American Institutes for Research. (2002). Evaluation of the blueprint for student success in a standards-based system: Interim report. Palo Alto, CA: Author. (Submitted to the San Diego City School Board of Education, February 12.)

American Institutes for Research. (2003). Evaluation of the blueprint for student success in a standards-based system: Interim report. Palo Alto, CA: Author.

Amrein, A. L., & Berliner, D. C. (2002). High-stakes testing, uncertainty, and student learning. *Education Policy Analysis Archives, 10*(18). Retrieved [July 21, 2004] from http://epaa.asu.edu/epaa/v10n18/.

Andrews, R., & Grogan, M. (2002, February 7–9). *Defining preparation and professional development for the future.* Paper commissioned for the first meeting of the National Commission for the Educational Leadership Preparation. Racine: WI.

Argyris, C., & Schön, D. (1978). *Organizational learning: A theory of action perspective.* Reading, MA: Addison-Wesley.

Atwell, N. (1998). *In the middle: New understandings about writing, reading, and learning.* Portsmouth, NH: Boynton/Cook.

Au, K. (1980). Participation structures in a reading lesson with Hawaiian children. *Anthropology and Education Quarterly, 11*(2), 91–115.

Au, K., & Jordan, C. (1981). Teaching reading to Hawaiian children: Finding a culturally appropriate solution. In Trueba, Guthrie, & Au (Eds.), *Culture and the bilingual classroom* (pp. 139–152). Rowley, MA: Newberry House.

Ball, D. K., & Cohen, D. (in preparation). *Scaling up instructional improvement.* Ann Arbor: University of Michigan.

Barley, S. R., & Tolbert, P. S. (1997). Institutionalization and structuration: Studying the links between action and institution. *Organization Studies, 18,* 93–117.

Baxter, J. A. (in preparation). *The QUASAR Project: A case study of documentation research.* Eugene: University of Oregon.

Beane, J.A., & Apple, M. (1995). *Schooling for democracy.* New York: ASCD

Becker, H. J., & Riel, M. R. (2000). *Teacher professional engagement and constructivist-compatible computer use. Report #7.* Irvine: Center for Research on Information Technology and Organizations, University of California, Irvine.

Bereiter, K. (2002). *Education and mind in the knowledge age.* Mahwah, NJ: Lawrence Erlbaum.

Berends, M., & Bodilly, S. (1998). *New American schools' scale up phase: Lessons learned to date.* Santa Monica, CA: RAND.

Berliner, D., & Biddle, B. (1995). *The manufactured crisis.* Reading, MA: Addison-Wesley.

Berliner, U., & Magee, M. (1998, December 23). Chamber's political spending broke laws. S.D. group admits missteps in '96 school board election. *San Diego Union-Tribune,* p. B1.

Berman, P., & McLaughlin, M. W. (1978). *Federal programs supporting educational change. Vol. VIII.* Santa Monica, CA: RAND.

Bersin, A. (2000a, December 14). Interview with Larry Cuban.

Bersin, A. (2000b, October 10). Remarks at the dedication of the Preuss School.

Bersin, A. (2002a, February 28). Address to principals' conference.

Bersin, A. (2002b, March 21). Message to all SDCS employees.

Bersin, A. (2002c, April 5). Address to principals' conference.

Bersin, A. (2002d, September 12). *San Diego City Schools 2002 STAR Program Results*. Paper presented to the San Diego Chamber of Commerce, Business Roundtable for Education.

Bersin, A. (2002e, December 5). Electronic message to SDCS.

Bersin, A. (2002f, December 5). Address to principals' conference.

Bersin, A. (2003a, February 27). Address to principals' conference.

Bersin, A. (2003b, March 10). Proposed increase in Title I site discretionary fund allocations. Memorandum to the SDCS Board of Education.

Bersin, A. (2003c, October 9). Address to principals' conference.

Bersin, A. (2005). Reflections of an Urban Reformer. In Hess (Ed)., Urban School Reform: Lessons from San Diego. (pp. 325–336). Cambridge, MA: Harvard Education Press.

Bersin, A., & Alvarado, A. (1998, March). Comments to parents, teachers, and community. Lewis Middle School.

Bersin, A., & Alvarado, A. (2000a, March 6). Comments to parents, teachers, and community. Madison High School.

Bersin, A., & Alvarado, A. (2000b, March 9). Comments to parents, teachers, and community. Morse High School.

Bersin's rookie year. School superintendent gets an A for tenacity. (2000, August 6). *The San Diego Union-Tribune*, p. B2.

Betts, J. R., Zau, A. C., & King, K. 2005. From Blueprint to Reality: San Diego's Educational Reforms. San Francisco: Public Policy Institute of California.

Binder, A. J. (2002). *Contentious curricula: Afrocentrism and creationism in American public schools*. Princeton, NJ: Princeton University Press.

Blueprint for student success under fire. (2001, May 29). News 8 newscast.

Bowman, D. H. (2002, April 24). San Diego High School voted special status. *Education Week*. Retrieved from http://www.edweek.org/ew/newstory.cfm?slug=32sandiego.h21

Bransford, J. D., Brown, A. L., & Cocking, R. R. (Eds.). (1999). *How people learn: Brain, mind, experience, and school*. Washington, DC: National Academy Press.

Bridges, E., & Hallinger, P. (1995). *Implementing problem-based learning in leadership development*. Eugene: University of Oregon, ERIC Clearinghouse on Educational Management.

Brown, A. (1992). Design experiments: Theoretical and methodological challenges in creating complex interventions in classroom settings. *Journal of Learning Sciences, 2*(2), 141–178.

Brown, A. L., & Campione, J. C. (1990). The fostering communities of learners project: Communities of learning and thinking, or a context by any other name. *Human Development, 21*, 108–125.

Brown, A., Greeno, J. G., Resnick, L. B., Mehan, H., & Lampert, M. (1999). *Recommendations regarding research priorities: An advisory report to the National Educational Research Policy and Priorities Board*. New York: National Academy of Education.

Brown, J. S., & Duguid, P. (1996). Organizational learning and communities of practice: Toward a unified view of working, learning and innovation.

In Cohen & Sproull (Eds.), *Organizational learning* (pp. 58–82). Thousand Oaks, CA: Sage.

Bryk, A. S., & Schneider, B. (2003). *Trust in schools: A core resource for improvement.* New York: Russell Sage Foundation.

Bryk, A. S., Sebring, P. B., Kerbow, D., Rollow, S., & Easton, J. Q. (1998). *Charting Chicago school reform: Democratic localism as a lever for change.* Boulder, CO: Westview.

Burns, D. (2001, October 15). Transcript of walk-through, Scripps Elementary School.

Burns, D. (2002, September 11). Interview with Lea Hubbard.

Buroway, M. (2003). Public sociologies. *Social Problems, 51*(1), 103–105.

California Teachers Association. (2002). Isn't it time to treat teachers as professionals? [Electronic version]. *California Educator, 6*(6), 1–14. Retrieved from http:www.cta.org/cal_educator/v6i6/feature_teachers.html

Casey, C., Branvold, D., & Cargille, B. (1996). A model for peer review in instructional design. *Performance Improvement Quarterly, 9*(3), 32–51.

Cavanaugh, D. (2001, June 30). Interview with Lea Hubbard.

Cavanaugh, D. (2002, June 13). Interview with Lea Hubbard.

Chaiklin, S., & Lave, J. (Eds.). (1996). *Understanding practice.* Cambridge: Cambridge University Press.

Cicourel, A. V. (1973). *Cognitive sociology.* London: Macmillan.

Clay, M. M. (1987). Implementing educational reading recovery: Systematic adaptations to an educational innovation. *New Zealand Journal of Educational Studies, 22,* 351–358.

Clifford, J., & Marcus, G. E. (Eds.). (1986). *Writing culture: The poetics and politics of ethnography.* Berkeley: University of California Press.

Cline, J. (2002, March 13). Interview with Lea Hubbard.

Cobb, P., Confrey, J., DiSessa, A., & Schauble, L. (2003). Design experiments in educational research. *Educational Researcher, 32*(10), 9–13.

Cobb, P., McClain, K., Lamberg, T. D., & Dean, C. (2003b). Situating teachers' instructional practices in the institutional setting of the school and district. *Educational Researcher, 32*(6), 13–24.

Coburn, C. E. (2002). *The role of non-system actors in the relationship between policy and practice: The case of reading instruction in California.* Paper presented at the American Educational Research Association, New Orleans, LA.

Coburn, C. E., & Stein, M. K. (in press). Communities of practice theory and the role of teacher professional community in policy implementation. In M. I. Honig (Ed.), *New directions in education policy implementation: Confronting complexity.* Albany: State University of New York Press.

Cochran-Smith, M., & Lytle, S. L. (n.d.). *The teacher researcher movement: A decade later.* Unpublished manuscript.

Cohen, D. K., & Barnes, C. (1993). Pedagogy and policy. In Cohen, McLaughlin, & Talbert (Eds.), *Teaching for understanding: Challenges for policy and practice* (pp. 207–239). San Francisco: Jossey-Bass.

Cohen, D., & Hill, H. (2001). *Learning policy: When state education reform works.* New Haven, CT: Yale University Press.

Cohen, M. D., & Sproull, L. S. (Eds.). (1996). Introduction. *Organizational learning.* Thousand Oaks, CA: Sage.

Cole, M. (1996). *Cultural psychology: A once and future discipline.* Cambridge, MA: Belknap Press of Harvard University Press.

Coleman, J. S., Campbell, E. Q., Hobson, C. J., McPartland, J., Mood, A. M., Weinfeld, F. D., & York, R. L. (1966). *Equality of educational opportunity.* Washington, DC: U.S. Office of Education.

Comings, J., Garner, B., & Smith, C. (Eds.). (2000). *Annual review of adult learning and literacy, 1.* San Francisco: Jossey-Bass.

Cuban, L. (1992). What happens to reforms that last? The case of the junior high school. *American Educational Research Journal, 29*(2), 227–251.

Cuban, L. (1998). How schools change reforms: Redefining reform success and failure. *Teachers College Record, 99*(3), 153–177.

Cuban, L., & Usdan, M. (2003). Fast and top down: Systemic reform and student achievement in San Diego City Schools. In Cuban & Usdan (Eds.), *Powerful reforms with shallow roots* (pp. 77–95). New York: Teachers College Press.

Cunningham, W., & Cordeiro, P. (2001). *Educational leadership: A problem-based approach.* Boston: Pearson Education.

Dalton, M. (1958). *Men who manage: Fusions of feeling and theory in administration.* New York: John Wiley & Sons.

D'Amico, L., Harwell, M., Stein, M. K., & van den Heuvel, J. R. (2001, April 10–14). *Examining the implementation and effectiveness of a district-wide instructional improvement effort.* Paper presented at the annual meeting of the American Educational Research Association, Seattle, WA.

Dannin, E. (2000, February 4). Is this really the worst school in San Diego? *San Diego Union-Tribune,* p. B9.

Darling-Hammond, L., Hightower, A. M., Husbands, J. L., LaFors, J. R., Young, V. M., & Christopher, C. (2005). *Instructional leadership for systemic change: The story of San Diego's reform.* Lanham, MD: Scarecrow Press.

Datnow, A. (2000). Power and politics in the adoption of school reform models. *Educational Evaluation and Policy Analysis, 22*(4), 357–374.

Datnow, A., Borman, G., & Stringfield, S. (2000). School reform through a highly specified curriculum: A study of the implementation and effects of the core knowledge sequence. *Elementary School Journal, 101*(2), 167–191.

Datnow, A., & Castellano, M. (2001). Managing and guiding school reform: Leadership in success for all schools. *Educational Administration Quarterly, 37*(2), 219–249.

Datnow, A., Hubbard, L., & Mehan, H. (2002). *Extending school reform: From one school to many.* New York: RoutledgeFalmer.

Deal, T., & Peterson, K. (1999). Shaping school culture: The heart of leadership. San Francisco, CA: Jossey-Bass Publications.

DeBeck, J. (2002). Is San Diego beating the odds? San Diego: SDCS School Board. Unpublished press release.

Design-Based Research Collective. (2003). Design-based research: An emerging paradigm for educational inquiry. *Educational Researcher, 32*(1), 5–8.

Desimone, L., Porter, A., Garet, M., Suk Yoon, K., & Birman, B. (2002). Effect of professional development on teachers' instruction. *Educational Evaluation and Policy Analysis, 24*(2), 81–112.

DiMaggio, P., & Powell, W. W. (Eds.). (1991). *The new institutionalism in organizational analysis.* Chicago: University of Chicago Press.

Donovan, M. S., Wigdor, A. K., & Snow, C. E. (Eds.). (2003). *Strategic education research partnership.* Washington, DC: National Academy Press.

Elmore, R. (1996). Getting to scale with good educational practice. *Harvard Educational Review, 66*(1), 1–26.

Elmore, R. (1999). *Leadership of large-scale improvement in American education.* Cambridge, MA: Graduate School of Education, Harvard University.

Elmore, R. (2000). *Building a new structure for school leadership.* Washington, DC: Albert Shanker Institute.

Elmore, R. (2001, August 11). Presentation at principals' conference.

Elmore, R. F., & Burney, D. (1999). Investing in teacher learning: Staff development and instructional improvement. In Darling-Hammond & Sykes (Eds.), *Teaching as the learning profession* (pp. 263–291). San Francisco: Jossey-Bass.

End the sniping: City schools antagonists must meet half way. (2002, February 17). The *San Diego Union-Tribune*, p. G2.

Engeström, Y. (1987). *Learning by expanding: An activity-theoretical approach to developmental research.* Helsinki: Orienta-Konsultit.

Engeström, Y., & Middleton, D. (Eds.). (1994). *Cognition and communication at work.* Cambridge: Cambridge University Press.

Erickson, F. (1996). On the evolution of qualitative approaches to educational research: From Adam's task to Eve's. *Australian Educational Researcher, 23*(2), 1–15.

Erickson, F. (2004). *Talk and social theory.* London: Polity.

Erickson, F., & Schultz, J. (1982). *The counselor as gatekeeper.* New York: Academic Press.

Escmilla, Y. (2001, June 29). E-mail on KFMB Web site.

Farnsworth, M. C., & Kendricks, N. (2001, March). Diversity and division part II: Reading, writing and race. *San Diego Magazine*, 80–99.

Fink, E. (2001a, June 27). Walk-Through at Harvey Mudd Elementary School.

Fink, E. (2001b, November 8). Planning session.

Fink, E. (2002a, January 31). Interview with Lea Hubbard.

Fink, E. (2002b, July 25). Interview with Lea Hubbard.

Fink, E., & Resnick, L.B. (2001). Developing principals as instructional leaders. *Phi Delta Kappan*, April, 598–606.

Fletcher, R., & Portalupi, J. (2001). *Writing workshop: The essential guide.* Portsmouth, NH: Heinemann.

Fountas, I. C., & Pinnel, G. S. (1995). Guided reading. Good first teaching for all children. Portsmouth, NH: Heinemann.

Fountas, I. C., & Pinnell, G. S. (2001). *Guiding readers and writers (grades 3–6): Teaching comprehension, genre, and content literacy.* Portsmouth, NH: Heinemann.

Franke, M. L., & Kazemi, E. (2001). Teaching as learning within a community of practice: Characterizing generative growth. In Wood, Nelson, & Warfield (Eds.), *Beyond classical pedagogy in teaching elementary mathematics: The nature of facilitative teaching.* Mahwah, NJ: Lawrence Erlbaum.

Freedman, J. (2003). Shuttle diplomacy. *San Diego Magazine,* 4–10. Retrieved from http://www.sandiegomagazine.com/issues/february03/featurea40203.shtml

Freire, P. (1967). *Pedagogy of the oppressed.* Boston: Beacon.

Fullan, M. G. (1991). *The new meaning of educational change* (2nd ed.). New York: Teachers College Press.

Fullan, M. (1999). *Change forces: The sequel.* London: Falmer.

Fullan, M. (2001a). *Leading in a culture of change.* San Francisco: Jossey-Bass.

Fullan, M. (2001b, January 29). Presentation to principals' conference.

Gao, H. (2004, September 30). Jewish leaders want an apology for trustee's Nazi analogy. *The San Diego Union-Tribune,* p. B1.

Gao, H. (2005a, January 1). Parents and teachers walk door-to-door to fulfill a dream: Charter schools status is sought for Gompers, Keillor. *The San Diego Union-Tribune,* p. B1.

Gao, H. (2005b, January 8). New charter school requirement draws jeers. *The San Diego Union-Tribune,* pp. B1–B2.

Garet, M., Porter, A., Desimone, L., Birman, B. F., & Suk, Y. K. (2001). What makes professional development effective? *American Educational Research Journal, 38,* 915–945.

Geertz, C. (1973). *The interpretation of culture: Selected essays.* New York: Basic Books.

Gembrowski, S. (2000, March 12). Bersin's blueprint draws boos at rally. Speakers fear cuts in jobs, programs. *The San Diego Union-Tribune,* p. B8.

Glennan, T. G., Bodilly, S. J., Galegher, J. R., & Kerr, K. A. (2004). *Expanding the reach of education reforms: Perspectives from leaders in the scale-up of educational interventions.* Santa Monica, CA: RAND.

Goe, L. (2002). Legislating equity: The distribution of emergency permit teachers in California. *Education Policy Analysis Archives, 10*(42), 1–25.

González, N. (2004). Discipling the discipline: Anthropology and the pursuit of quality education. *Education Researcher, 33*(5), 17–25.

González, N., Moll, L. C., & Amanti, C. (Eds.). (2005). *Theorizing practices: Funds of knowledge in households and classrooms.* Cresskill, NJ: Hampton.

Goodnough, A. (2002, August 12). Schools' chief is soaking up advice in San Diego. *New York Times,* p. B7.

Greenfield, P. M. (2004). *Weaving generations together: Evolving creativity in the Maya of Chiapas.* Sante Fe, NM: School of American Research Press.

Greeno, J. G., & Goldman, S. V. (Eds.). (1998). *Thinking practices in mathematics and science learning.* Mahwah, NJ: Lawrence Erlbaum.

Gribble, J. (2001, September). Unbridled passion or New York pushiness? *San Diego Metropolitan,* pp. 36–42.

Guthrie, J. W. (Ed.) (1990). Special Issue. *Educational Evaluation and Policy Analysis, 12*(3).

Hall, P. M. (1995). The consequences of qualitative analysis for sociological theory: Beyond the microlevel. *Sociological Quarterly, 36*(2), 397–423.

Hall, P. M. (1997). Meta-power, social organization and the shaping of social action. *Symbolic Interaction, 20*(4), 397–418.

Hall, P. M., & McGinty, P. J. W. (1997). Policy as the transformation of intentions: Producing program from statutes. *Sociological Quarterly, 38*(3), 439–467.

Hall, P. M., & Placier, P. (2002). The Coalition of Essential Schools: Leadership for putting the common principles into practice. In Murphy & Datnow (Eds.), *Leadership lessons from comprehensive school reforms*. Thousand Oaks, CA: Corwin Press.

Hallet, T., & Ventresca, M. (in press). Looking back to see ahead: Institutions and interactions in Gouldner's *Patterns of Industrial Bureaucracy*.

Hanson, M. (2001). Institutional theory and educational change. *Educational Administrative Quarterly, 37*(5), 637–661.

Hargreaves, A. (1994). *Changing teachers, changing times*. New York: Teachers College Press.

Hartocollis, A. (2002, July 30). Hoping an outsider plus a bottom line approach equals reform. *New York Times*, p. B4.

Harvey, S., & Goudvis, A. (2000). *Strategies that work*. Portland, ME: Stenhouse.

Harwell, M., D'Amico, L., Stein, M. K., & Gatti, G. (2000, April 24–28). *The effect of teachers' professional development experiences on student achievement in Community School District #2*. Paper presented at the annual meeting of the American Educational Research Association, New Orleans, LA.

Hawley, W. D., & Valli, L. (1999). The essentials of effective professional development. In Darling-Hammond & Sykes (Eds.), *Teaching as the learning profession: Handbook of policy and practice*. San Francisco: Jossey-Bass.

Haycock, K., & Jerald, C. (2002, September). Report card on reform. *San Diego Union-Tribune*. Retrieved from www.SignOnSanDiego.com

Haycock, K., & Navarro, S. (1997). *The achievement gap in American education*. Washington, DC: Education Trust.

Healey, F., & DeStefano, J. (1997). *Education reform support: A framework for scaling up school reform*. Washington, DC: Abel2 Clearinghouse for Basic Education.

Heckman, P., & Peterman, F. (1997). Indigenous invention and school reform. *Teachers College Record, 98*(20), 307–327.

Heifetz, R. (1994). *Leadership without easy answers*. Cambridge, MA: Belknap Press of Harvard University Press.

Heifetz, R., & Linsky, M. (2000). *Leadership on the line: Staying alive through the dangers of leading*. Cambridge, MA: Harvard Business School Publishing.

Hess, F. M. (Ed.). (2005). *Urban school reform: Lessons from San Diego*. Cambridge, MA: Harvard Education Press.

Hightower, A. M. (2001). *San Diego's big boom: District bureaucracy meets culture of learning*. Unpublished doctoral dissertation, Stanford University.

Hightower, A. M. (2002). San Diego's big boom: Systemic instructional change in the central office and schools. In Hightower, Knapp, Marsh, & McLaughlin (Eds.), *School districts and urban renewal* (pp. 76–94). New York: Teachers College Press.

Hightower, A. M., Knapp, M. S., Marsh, J. A., & McLaughlin, M. (2002). *School districts and urban renewal.* New York: Teachers College Press.

Hill, P., and Celio, M. B. 1998. *Fixing urban schools.* Washington DC: The Brookings Institution.

Hjörne, E., & Säljö, R. (2004). "There is something about Julia": Symptoms, categories, and the process of invoking attention deficit hyperactivity disorder in the Swedish school; A case study. *Journal of Language, Identity and Education, 3*(1), 1–24.

Hopper, M. (2003a, March 10). Proposed use of Title I funding 2003–04. Memorandum to members of the District Advisory Committee, principals, and SSC chairpersons.

Hopper, M. (2003b, September 9). Status report on district high school reform. Minutes of the SDCS school board. Document E.b.y.

Hovenic, G. (2001, May 21). Time needed to reflect on Blueprint. *San Diego Daily Transcript.*

Hovenic, G. (2002, January 9). Feedback needed for the Blueprint's success. *San Diego Daily Transcript.*

Hubbard, L. (2004). *Evaluation of the Educational Leadership Development Academy: Final report.* Prepared for the Broad Foundation. San Diego: USD School of Education.

Hubbard, L., Beldock, D., & Osborne, C. (2003, April 21–25). *Struggles and challenges at the top: Principals must learn and researchers can help.* Paper presented at the annual American Educational Research Association meetings, Chicago.

Hubbard, L., & Datnow, A. (2002). Are single-sex schools sustainable in the public sector? In Datnow & Hubbard (Eds.), *Gender in policy and practice* (pp. 109–133). London: RoutledgeFalmer.

Hubbard, L., & Mehan, H. (1999). Race and reform: Educational niche picking in a hostile environment. *Journal of Negro Education, 12*(1), 115–130.

Huber, G. P. (1991). Organizational learning. *Organizational Science, 2*(1), 88–115.

Hutchins, E. (1990). The technology of team navigation. In Galegher, Kraut, & Egibo (Eds.), *Intellectual teamwork* (pp. 191–220). Hillsdale, NJ: Lawrence Erlbaum.

Hutchins, E. (1991). Organizing work by adaptation. *Organizational Science, 2*(1), 14–39.

Hymes, D. H. (Ed.). (1972). *Reinventing anthropology.* New York: Pantheon Books.

Jencks, Christopher S., & Meredith Phillips (Eds.). (1998). *The Black-White Test Score Gap.* Washington DC: Brookings Institution.

Jencks, C. et al. (1972). *Inequality.* New York: Basic Books.

Jencks, C. et al. (1978). *Who gets ahead?* New York: Basic Books.

Johnson, F. (2001, October 25). Address to principals' conference.

Johnson, F. (2002, March 14). Walk-through at Martin Luther King.

Johnstone, B. (1998, July 1). Interview with Mary Kay Stein and Laura D'Amico.

Jones, M., Yonezawa, S., Ballesteros, E., & Mehan, H. (2002). Shaping pathways to higher education. *Educational Researcher, 10,* 1–13.

Jones, M., Yonezawa, S., & Grimes, S. (2002). *Executive summary: SDCS community, teacher, parent, and student focus group data 2001–02.* San Diego: University of California, CREATE.

Katz, D., & Kahn, R. (1966). *The social psychology of organizations.* New York: John Wiley.

Keene, E., & Zimmerman, S. (1997). *Mosaic of thought: Teaching comprehension in a reader's workshop.* Portsmouth, NH: Heinemann.

Kennedy, M. M. (1998). *Form and substance in in-service teacher education* [Research monograph #13]. Arlington, VA: National Science Foundation.

Kluver, J., & Rosenstock, L. (2002). *Choice and diversity: Irreconcilable differences?* San Diego, CA: High Tech High.

Knapp, M. (n.d.). *Committed to partnerships for excellence.* San Diego, CA: San Diego Education Association.

Kohlberg, L., & Mayer, R. (1972). Development as the aim of education. *Harvard Educational Review, 42*(4), 449–496.

Kohn, Alfie. (2002). *Education Inc. Turning learning into a business.* Portsmouth NH: Heinemann.

Kotter, J. (1996). *Leading change.* Boston: Harvard Business School Press.

Kucher, K., & Washburn, D. (2003, May 18). Time to deliver. *The San Diego Union-Tribune.*

Labaree, D. F. (2003). The particular problems of preparing educational researchers. *Educational Researcher, 32*(4), 13–22.

Lagemann, E. (2000). *An elusive science: The troubling history of education.* Chicago: University of Chicago Press.

Lagemann, E. (2002). *Useful knowledge.* Chicago: Spencer Foundation.

Lareau, Annette. (1989). *Home advantage: Social class and parental intervention in elementary education.* London: Falmer Press.

Lareau, Annette. (2003). *Unequal childhoods: Class, race and family life.* Berkeley: UC Press.

Latino Coalition. (2001, October 9). Presentation to the SDCS Board of Education.

Latour, B., & Woolgar, S. (1979). *Laboratory life: The social construction of scientific facts.* Beverly Hills, CA: Sage.

Lave, J., & Wenger, E. (1991). *Situated learning: Legitimate peripheral participation.* New York: Cambridge University Press.

Levin, H. (1987). New schools for the disadvantaged. *Teachers Education Quarterly, 14*(4), 60–83.

Lewin, T. (2000, June 8). Leaders from other professions reshape America's schools, from top to bottom. *The New York Times,* p. A18.

Lewis, C. (2003). *Lesson study: A handbook of teacher-led instructional change.* Philadelphia: Research for Better Schools.

Lieberman, L., & Wood, D. R. (2003). *Inside the National Writing Project: Connecting network learning and classroom teaching.* New York: Teachers College Press.

Lipsky, M. (1982). *Street level bureaucracy.* Boston: Allyn & Bacon.

Livingston, T. (2004, April 20). Interview with Lea Hubbard.

Loucks-Horsley, H. P., Love, N., & Stiles, K. (1998). *Designing professional development for teachers of science and mathematics.* Thousand Oaks, CA: Corwin.

Magee, M. (1998, June 16). Bersin unveils school reorganization: Top New York educator to be head of new learning institute. *The San Diego Union-Tribune,* p. A1.

Magee, M. (1999, November 13). Chamber keeps up its support of Bersin. Group won't back all of its original trustees. *The San Diego Union-Tribune,* p. B1.

Magee, M. (2000a, January 8). Demoted administrators sue S.D. district, trustees. The *San Diego Union-Tribune,* p. B7.

Magee, M. (2000b, March 12). School board hopefuls get no vacation in their quest for backers. Bersin's reform plan is a hot button issue. *The San Diego Union-Tribune,* p. B1.

Magee, M. (2000d, March 16). Educators prepare for reform plan. Bersin plans meetings with parents, teachers. *The San Diego Union-Tribune.* Retrieved from www.SignOnSanDiego.com

Magee, M. (2001). State panel finds flaws in school reform funding. Bersin downplays error. Calls ruling string vindication. *The San Diego Union-Tribune,* p. A1.

Magee, M. (2000c, March 15). Sweeping School reforms approved 3-2. Decisions made despite thousands of protests. *The San Diego Union-Tribune,* p. A1.

Magee, M. (2000e, October 25). Zimmerman wins tight race with Dubick. *The San Diego Union-Tribune,* p. A1.

Magee, M. (2001b, November 6). School reform plan gets private boost, with a condition. *The San Diego Union-Tribune,* pp. A1, A7.

Magee, M. (2002a, April 10). Bersin's contract extended to 2006. *The San Diego Union-Tribune.* Retrieved from www.SignOnSanDiego.com

Magee, M. (2002b, December 6). Bersin says Alvarado's role to be curtailed. *The San Diego Union-Tribune.* Retrieved from www.SignOnSanDiego.com

Magee, M. (2004a, January 8). San Diego schools help decide what to cut. *The San Diego Union-Tribune.* Retrieved from www.SignOnSanDiego.com

Magee, M. (2004b, November 6). Former principals win case against district. *The San Diego Union-Tribune.* Retrieved from www.SignOnSanDiego.com

Magee, M., & Daniels, D. (2002, December 10). Fed-up parents stage walkout. *The San Diego Union-Tribune.* Retrieved from www.SignOnSanDiego.com

Magee, M., & Gao, H. (2004, November 4). Three new trustees for San Diego schools. *The San Diego Union-Tribune.* Retrieved from www.SignOnSanDiego.com

Magee, M., & Kucher, K. (2004, January 6). Schools' prop MM overseer quits post. *The San Diego Union-Tribune.* San Diego County Office of Education News Clips.

Malinowski, B. (1922). *Argonauts of the Western Pacific: An account of native enterprise and adventure in the archipelagoes of Melanesian New Guinea.* London: Routledge.

March, J. (2002). How districts relate to states, schools and communities: A review of emerging literature. In Hightower, Knapp, Marsh, & McLaughlin (Eds.), *School districts and instructional renewal: Opening the conversation* (pp. 30–57). New York: Teachers College Press.

Mathews, Jay. (2001, July 3). Recruiting a new class of leaders; Superintendents with military, business expertise are demanding new methods to enhance schools' performance. *The Washington Post,* p. A10.

McCarty, T. L., Stephen Wallace, S., Lynch, R. H., & Benally, A. (1991). Classroom inquiry and Navajo learning styles: A call for reassessment. *Anthropology and Education Quarterly, 22,* 42–59.

McDermott, R. P. (1980). Profile: Ray Birdwhistell. *Kinesis Reports, 2,* 1–4, 14–16.

McDermott, R. P., & Varenne, H. (1993). The acquisition of a child by a learning disability. In Lave (Ed.), *Understanding practice.* Cambridge: Cambridge University Press.

McLaughlin, M. W. (1998). Listening and learning from the field: Tales of policy implementation and situated practice. In Hargreaves et al. (Eds.), *International handbook of educational change* (pp. 70–84). London: Kluwer Academic.

McLaughlin, M., & Talbert, J. E. (1993). *Contexts that matter for teaching and learning.* Stanford, CA: Stanford University Center for Research on the Context of Secondary School Teaching.

McNeill, L. (2002). *Contradictions of school reform: Educational costs of educational testing.* New York: Routledge.

Mead, G. H. (1934). *Mind, self and society.* Chicago: University of Chicago Press.

Mehan, H. (1979). *Learning lessons: The social organization of classroom instruction.* Cambridge, MA: Harvard University Press.

Mehan, H. (1992). Understanding inequality: The contribution of ethnographic studies. *Sociology of Education, 65,* 1–20.

Mehan, H., & Grimes, S. (1999). *Closing the achievement gap in the SDCS.* La Jolla, CA: San Diego Dialogue.

Mehan, H., Hubbard, L., Villanueva, I., & Lintz, A. (1995). *Constructing school success: The consequences of untracking low achieving students.* Cambridge: Cambridge University Press.

Mehan, H., Meihls, J. L., Hertweck, A., & Crowdes, M. (1986). *Handicapping the handicapped: Decision making in students' educational careers.* Stanford, CA: Stanford University Press.

Mehan, H., Quartz, K. H., & Stein, M. K. (1997). Co-constructing San Diego's institute for learning: An analytic essay for the Spencer Foundation. La Jolla: University of California, San Diego, CREATE.

Meier, D. (1995). *The power of their ideas: Lessons for America from a small school in Harlem.* Boston: Beacon.

Meyer, J. W., & Rowan, B. (1977). Institutionalized organizations: Formal structure as myth and ceremony. *American Journal of Sociology, 83*(2), 340–363.

Meyer, J. W., & Scott, W. R. (Eds.). (1983). *Organizational environments: Ritual and rationality.* Beverly Hills, CA: Sage.

Milsap, M.A., Moss, M., & Gamse, B., (1993). The Chapter 1 implementation study: Final report on Chapter 1 in public school. Cambridge, MA: Abt Associates.

Mooney, M. (1990). *Reading to, with, and by children.* New York: Richard C. Owen.

Moran, C. (2003a, February 5). Chief S.D. school reformer to leave. *The San Diego Union-Tribune.* San Diego County Office of Education News Clips.

Moran, C. (2003b, March 6). Reassignments of principals in S.D. city schools district upheld. *The San Diego Union-Tribune.* San Diego County Office of Education News Clips.

Moran, C. (2003c, March 13). 325 more teachers in SD to get notices. *The San Diego Union-Tribune.* San Diego County Office of Education News Clips.

Moran, C. (2003d, May 14). SD city school retirement is three times normal. *The San Diego Union-Tribune.* San Diego County Office of Education News Clips.

Moran, C. (2003e, July 25). San Diego school budget approved. *The San Diego Union-Tribune.* San Diego County Office of Education News Clips.

Morgan, N. (2001, December 26). Good news for 2002: Some have made this city a world center. *The San Diego Union-Tribune.* San Diego County Office of Education News Clips.

Muncey, D., & McQuillan, P. (1996). *Reform and resistance in schools and classrooms.* New Haven, CT: Yale University Press.

Muñoz, D. L. (2001, October 5). San Diego unified school district trustees threatened with shooting. *La Prensa.* Retrieved from http://www. laprensa-sandiego.org/archieve/m

Murphy, A. (2002, May 20). Interview with Lea Hubbard.

Nathanson, C. E. (2002). It smelled like news to me, but the newspaper said it wasn't. *San Diego Dialogue,* Report 5 (4), 1, 3.

Newman, D., Griffin, P., & Cole, M. (1989). *The construction zone.* New York: Cambridge University Press.

New Zealand Ministry of Education. (1996). *Reading for life: The learner as a reader.* Wellington, New Zealand: Learning Media Limited.

No Child Left Behind Act of 2001. PL 107-110. 115 Stat. 1425.

Nolan, H. (2001, January 25). Walk-through at Martin Luther King High School.

Oakes, J. (1992). Can tracking research inform practice? Technical, normative, and political considerations. *Educational Researcher, 2,* 12–21.

Oakes, J., Quartz, K. H., Ryan, S., & Lipton, M. (1999). *Becoming good American schools: The struggle for civic virtue in educational reform.* San Francisco: Jossey-Bass.

Oakes, J., Wells, A. S., Jones, M., & Datnow, A. (1997). Detracking: The social construction of ability, cultural politics, and resistance to reform. *Teachers College Record, 98*(3), 482–510.

Oliver, R. (2001, October 15). Interview with Lea Hubbard.

Ottinger, R. (2002, July 9). Request for investigation of board member misconduct.

Ouchi, W. G. (2003). *Making schools work.* New York: Simon & Schuster.

Parker, C. (2001a, April 26). Interview with Lea Hubbard.

Parker, C. (2001b, June 27). Interview with Lea Hubbard.

Parker, C. (2002, March 21). Interview with Lea Hubbard.

Parsons, Talcott. (1932). *The social system*. New York: The Free Press.

Pea, R. D., Gomez, L. M., Edelson, D. C., Fishman, B. J., Gordin, D. N., & O'Neill, D. K. (1997). Science education as driver of cyberspace technology development. In Cohen (Ed.), *Internet links for science education* (pp. 189–220). New York: Plenum.

Perrow, C. (1999). *Normal accidents: Living with high-risk technologies*. Princeton, NJ: Princeton University Press.

Perry, S. (2001, May 8). Interview with Lea Hubbard.

Perry, T. (2000, October 17). Ads spark backlash in school race. *Los Angeles Times*. Retrieved from http://www.latimes.com/cgi/print.cgi

Pinnell, G. S. (1989). Reading Recovery: Helping at-risk children learn to read. *Elementary School Journal, 90,* 161–183.

Portin, B. S., Beck, L., Knapp, M., & Murphy, J. (2000). *Self-reflective renewal in schools: Local lessons from a national initiative*. Westport, CT: Greenwood.

Pressman, J. L., & Wildavsky, A. (1973). *Implementation*. Berkeley: University of California Press.

Ravitch, D. (2002). *Left back*. New York: Basic Books.

Resnick, L. (1995). From aptitude to effort: A new foundation for our schools. *Daedalus, 12*(4), 55–62.

Resnick, L., Elmore, R. F., & Alvarado, A. F. (1996). *Developing and implementing high-performance learning communities*. Proposal submitted to Office of Educational Research and Improvement.

Resnick, L. B., & Fink, E. (2001). Developing principals as instructional leaders. *Phil Delta Kappan, 82*(8), 598–606.

Rogoff, B. (1994). Developing understanding of the idea of community of learners. *Mind, Culture, and Activity, 1,* 209–229.

Rogoff, B., & Lave, J. (Eds.). (1984). *Everyday cognition: Its development in social context*. Cambridge, MA: Harvard University Press.

Rosebery, A. S., Warren, B., & Conant, F. R. (1992). Appropriating scientific discourse: Findings from language minority classrooms. *Journal of the Learning Sciences, 2*(10), 61–94.

Rosen, L., & Mehan, H. (2003). Reconstructing equality on new political ground: The politics of representation in the charter school debate at UCSD. *American Educational Research Journal, 40*(3), 655–682.

Rosenstock, L., & Steinberg, A. (1995). Beyond the shop: Reinventing vocational education. In Apple & Beane (Eds.), *Democratic schools* (pp. 41–57). Arlington, VA: ASCD.

Rowan, B. (1995, February). Research in learning and teaching in K-12 school: Implications for the field of educational administration. *Educational Administration Quarterly, 31*(1), 115-133.

Sanday, P. R. (1976). *Anthropology and the public interest*. New York: Academic Press.

Sandbrook, I. (1996). *Making sense of primary inspection.* Buckingham and Philadelphia, PA: Open University Press.

San Diego Achievement Forum. (2002). *Achievement in the San Diego City Schools: A progress report.* La Jolla: San Diego Dialogue.

San Diego charger: Think of Alan Bersin as Giuliani West. (2002, May 6). *Wall Street Journal.*

San Diego City Schools. (1998a). *Blueprint for student success.* San Diego, CA: SDCS Institute for Learning. (Passed by the SDCS school board, March 14, 1998.)

San Diego City Schools. (1998b). *Genre studies non-negotiables.* San Diego, CA: SDCS Institute for Learning.

San Diego City Schools. (1998–1999). *Principals' instructional conferences: Training materials.* San Diego, CA: SDCS Institute for Learning.

San Diego City Schools. (2001a). *San Diego high schools achieving rigorous performance: A proposal to the Carnegie Corporation's Schools for a New Society Initiative.* San Diego, CA: SDCS Institute for Learning.

San Diego City Schools. (2001b). *Student census 2000–2001.* San Diego, CA: Author.

San Diego City Schools. (2002). *2002 STAR program results, California Standards Tests, Stanford Achievement Test.* San Diego, CA: SDCS Standards, Assessment, and Accountability Department.

San Diego City Schools. (2002–2003, May 12). *Work plan, frame, literacy and math.* Paper presented to principals' conference.

Sarason, S. (1982). *The culture of the school and the problem of change* (2nd ed.). Boston: Allyn & Bacon.

Sarason, S. (1996). *Revisiting the culture of the school and the problem of change.* New York: Teachers College Press.

Sarason, S. (1997). Revisiting the creation of settings. *Mind, Culture, and Activity, 4*(3), 175–182.

Sawyer, K. (2004). Creative teaching: Collaborative discussion as disciplined improvisation. *Educational Researcher, 33*(2), 12–20.

Schoenbach, R., Greenleaf, C., Cziko, C., & Hurwitz, L. (1999). *Reading for understanding: A guide to improving reading in middle and high school classrooms.* San Francisco: Jossey-Bass.

Schön, D. A. (1983). *The reflective practitioner: How professionals think in action.* New York: Basic Books.

Schön, D. A. (1987). Teaching artistry through reflection-in-action. In *Educating the reflective practitioner* (pp. 22–40). San Francisco: Jossey-Bass.

Schools cease fire: Unions, administration to consult on budget. (2003, February 2). *The San Diego Union-Tribune.* San Diego County Office of Education News Clips.

Schools chief merits four more years. (2001, September 4). *The San Diego Union-Tribune,* p. B2.

Schutz, A. (1964). *Collected papers: The problem of social theory.* The Hague: Martinus Nijhoff.

Scribner, S., & Cole, M. (1981). *The psychology of literacy.* Cambridge, MA: Harvard University Press.

Sengupta, S. (1998, June 16). Ex-schools chancellor gets a new post. *New York Times*, p. B3.

Sergiovanni, T. J. (2000). *The lifeworld of leadership: Creating culture, community and personal meaning in our schools*. San Francisco: Jossey-Bass.

Silberman, C. (1970). *Crisis in the classroom: The remaking of American education*. New York: Random House.

Silver, E. A., & Stein, M. K. (1996). The QUASAR project: The "revolution of the possible" in mathematics instructional reform in urban middle schools. *Urban Education, 30*(4), 476–521.

Simmons, W., & Resnick, L. (1993). Assessment as the catalyst for school reform. *Educational Leadership, 50*(5), 11–15.

Simon, H. A. (1991). Bounded rationality and organizational learning. *Organizational Science, 2*(2), 125–134.

Simon, Herbert A. (1949). *Administrative behavior*. New York: The Free Press.

Simpson, A. (2001, August 22). Interview with Lea Hubbard.

Sizer, T. R. (1984). *Horace's compromise*. Boston: Houghton Mifflin.

Sjöström, S. (1997). *Party or patient? Discursive practices relating to coercion in psychiatric and legal settings*. Umea, Sweden: Borea Bokforlag.

Slavin, R. E., & Madden, N. A. (1999). *Disseminating Success for All: Lessons for policy and practice*. Report no. 30. Baltimore, MD: The Johns Hopkins University Press.

Slavin, R. E., Madden, N., Dolan, L., & Wasik, B. (1996). *Every child, every school: Success for All*. Thousand Oaks, CA: Corwin.

Smith, D. (1974). Women's perspective as a radical critique of sociology. *Sociological Inquiry, 44*, 7–13.

Smith, L., & Keith, P. (1971). *Anatomy of an educational innovation*. New York: Wiley.

Spielvogel, J., & Moran, C. (2002, August 30). SD school test scores up, but lag state goals. *The San Diego Union-Tribune*. San Diego County Office of Education News Clips.

Spillane, J. P. (2000). Cognition and policy implementation: District policymakers and the reform of mathematics education. *Cognition and Instruction, 18*(2), 141–179.

Spillane, J. P. (2002). The change theories of local change agents: The pedagogy of district policies and programs. *Teachers College Record, 104*(3), 377–420.

Spillane, J. P., & Jennings, N. E. (1997). Aligned instructional policy and ambitious pedagogy: Exploring instructional reform from the classroom perspective. *Teachers College Record, 98*(3), 439–481.

Spillane, J. P., Reiser, B. J., & Reimer, T. (2002). Policy implementation and cognition: Reframing and refocusing implementation research. *Review of Educational Research, 72*(3), 387–431.

Spillane, J. P., & Thompson, C. (1997). Reconstructing notions of local capacity: The local education agency's capacity for ambitious reform. *Education Evaluation and Policy Analysis, 19*(2), 185–203.

Spillane, J. P., & Zeuli, J. S. (1999). Reform and teaching: Exploring patterns of practice in the context of national and state mathematics reform. *Educational Evaluation and Policy Analysis, 21*, 1–27.

Star, S. L., & Bowker, G. C. (1997). Of lungs and lungers: The classified story of tuberculosis. *Mind, Culture, and Activity, 4*(1), 3–23.

Stein, M. K., & Brown, C. A. (1997). Teacher learning in a social context: Integrating collaborative and institutional processes with the study of social change. In Fenemma & Nelson (Eds.), *Mathematics teachers in transition* (pp. 155–191). Hillsdale, NJ: Lawrence Erlbaum.

Stein, M. K., & Coburn, C. E. (2003, August 26). *Toward producing usable knowledge for the improvement of educational practice: A conceptual framework.* Paper presented at the European Association for Research on Learning and Instruction, Padova, Italy.

Stein, M., & D'Amico, L. (2002a). District as professional educator: Teacher learning in District #2's literacy initiative. In Knapp & McLaughlin (Eds.), *Districts and instructional renewal: Opening the conversation.* New York: Teachers College Press.

Stein, M. K., & D'Amico, L. (2002b). Inquiry at the crossroads of policy and learning: A study of a district-wide literacy initiative. *Teachers College Record, 104*(7), 1313–1344.

Stein, M. K., D'Amico, L., & Israel, N. (1999, April 19–23). *Observations, conversations, and negotiations: Administrator support of literacy practices in New York City's Community School District #2.* Paper presented at the annual meeting of the American Educational Research Association, Montreal, Quebec, Canada.

Stein, M. K., D'Amico, L., & Resnick, L. (2001). *High performance learning communities project: Final report.* Submitted to Office of Educational Research and Improvement, Department of Education. Washington, DC.

Stein, M. K., Harwell, M., & D'Amico, L. (1999). *Toward closing the gap in literacy achievement.* Unpublished manuscript. Learning Research and Development Center, University of Pittsburgh.

Stein, M. K., Hubbard, L., & Mehan, H. (2003). Reform ideas that travel far afield: The two cultures of reform in New York City's District #2 and San Diego. *Journal of Educational Change, 5*(2), 161–197.

Stein, M. K., Silver, E., & Smith, M. S. (1998). Mathematics reform and teacher development: A community of practice perspective. In Greeno & Goldman (Eds.), *Thinking practices in mathematics and science learning* (pp. 17–51). Mahwah, NJ: Lawrence Erlbaum.

Stein, S. J., & Gewirtzman, L. (2003). *Principal training on the ground: Ensuring highly qualified leadership.* Portsmouth, NH: Heinemann.

Stigler, J., & Hiebert, J. (1997). *The teaching gap.* New York: Free Press.

Stipek, D. (2005, March 23). Scientifically based practice: It's about more than improving the quality of research. *Education Week* page.

Stokes, D. E. (1997). *Pasteur's quadrant: Basic science and technological innovation.* Washington, DC: Brookings Institution.

Stokes, L. (2005). *Taking on the real struggles of teaching: A study of the National Writing Project as an infrastructure for building practitioner knowledge.* Pittsburgh, PA: MacArthur/Spencer Meta Project.

Stringfield, S., Millsap, M., Herman, R., Yoder, N., Brigham, N., Nesselrodt, P., Shaffer, E., Karweit, N., Levin, M., & Stevens, R. (1997). *Special strategies, studies, final report.* Washington, DC: U.S. Department of Education.

Sweeping school reform is approved. 3–2 decision made despite thousands of protestors. (2000, March 15).

Teachers union honors Alvarado, Riley. (1999, July 17). *The San Diego Union-Tribune,* p. B2.

TenBerge, Y. (2001, May 18). San Diego High School still steaming over the loss of Alfaro. *La Prensa,* pp. 1–3. Retrieved from http://www.laprensa-sandiego.org/archieve/may18/alfaro.htm

Tharp, R., & Gallimore, R. (1988). *Rousing minds to life: Teaching, learning and schooling in social context.* Cambridge: Cambridge University Press.

Thompson, L. (2002, July 25). Interview with Lea Hubbard.

Tichy, N. (1997). *The leadership engine: How winning companies build leaders at every level.* New York: HarperCollins.

Turner, L. (2001, December 11) Walk-through at Emmanuel Jackson Elementary.

Turner, L. (2002, September 11). Interview with Lea Hubbard and Mary K. Stein.

Tyack, D. T., & Cuban, L. (1995). *Tinkering toward utopia: A century of public school reform.* Cambridge, MA: Harvard University Press.

Varenne, H., & McDermott, R. P. (1998). *Successful failure: The schools America builds.* Boulder, CO: Westview.

Vaughan, D. (1996). *The Challenger launch decision: Risky technology, culture and deviance at NASA.* Chicago: University of Chicago Press.

Vygotsky, L. S. (1978). *Mind in society: The development of higher psychological processes.* Cole, John-Steiner, Scribner, & Souberman (Eds.), Cambridge, MA: Harvard University Press.

Warren, J. (2001, November 8). What price for our children? *Voice and Viewpoint.*

Watson, N., Fullan, M., & Kilcher, A. (2002). *The role of the district: Professional learning and district reform.* Paper presented at American Educational Research Association annual conference in New Orleans, LA.

Weber, M. (1964). *The theory of social and economic organization* (A. M. Handerson & T. Parsons, Trans.). New York: Free Press. (Original work published 1947)

Weick, K. E. (1976). Educational organizations as loosely coupled systems. *Administrative Science Quarterly, 21,* 1–19.

Weick, K. E. (1995). *Sensemaking in organizations.* Thousand Oaks, CA: Sage.

Weick, K. E., & Roberts, K. H. (1993). Collective mind in organizations: Heedful interrelating on flight decks. *Administrative Science Quarterly, 38,* 357–381.

Weiss, C. (1995). The four "i's" of school reform: How interests, ideology, information, and institution affect teachers and principals. *Harvard Educational Review, 65*(4), 571–592.

Wenger, E. (1998). *Communities of practice: Learning, meaning and identity.* Cambridge: Cambridge University Press.

Wenger, E., McDermott, R., & Snyder, W. (2002). *Cultivating communities of practice: A guide to managing knowledge.* Cambridge, MA: Harvard Business School Press.

Whitaker, B. (2000, October 25). Business groups that back superintendent spend big in San Diego school board race. *New York Times,* p. A16.

Wideen, M. F. (1994). *The struggle for change.* London: Falmer.

Wilcox, B., & Gray, J. (1996). *Inspecting schools: Holding schools to account and helping schools to improve.* Berkshire, UK: Open University Press.

Williams, B., Wilson, S., & Berne, J. (1999). Teacher learning and the acquisition of professional knowledge: An examination of research on contemporary professional development. *Review of Research in Education, 24,* 173–209.

Wilson, S. M. & Berne, J. (1999). Teacher learning and the acquisition of professional knowledge: An examination of research on contemporary professional development. *Review of Research in Education, 24,* 173-209.

Yankelovich, D. (2001). *Other voices: Design for a feedback process among stakeholders on the* Blueprint for Student Success. La Jolla, CA: Viewpoint Learning.

Yonezawa, S., & Datnow, A. (1999). Supporting multiple reform designs in culturally and linguistically diverse school districts. *Journal of Education of Students Placed At Risk, 4*(1), 101–125.

Yonezawa, S., Jones, M., & Mehan, H. (2002). Partners for preparation: Constructing and distributing social and cultural capital to achieve diversity. In Tierney & Hagedorn (Eds.), *Extending outreach: Strategies for accessing college.* Albany: SUNY Press.

Yonezawa, S., Wells, A. S., & Serna, I. (2002). Choosing tracks: "Freedom of choice" in detracking schools. *American Educational Research Journal, 49*(1), 37–67.

Yourdon, E. (1989). *Structured walkthroughs.* Englewood Cliffs, NJ: Prentice Hall.

Ziegler, A. (1981). *The writing workshop.* New York: Teachers and Writers Collaborative.

Index